SELLING SCIENCE FICTION CINEMA

SELLING SCIENCE FICTION CINEMA

Making and Marketing a Genre

J. P. Telotte

University of Texas Press *Austin*

Copyright © 2023 by the University of Texas Press
All rights reserved
Printed in the United States of America
First edition, 2023

Requests for permission to reproduce material from this work should be sent to:
   Permissions
   University of Texas Press
   P.O. Box 7819
   Austin, TX 78713-7819
   utpress.utexas.edu/rp-form

♾ The paper used in this book meets the minimum requirements of ANSI/NISO Z39.48-1992 (R1997) (Permanence of Paper).

Library of Congress Cataloging-in-Publication Data

Names: Telotte, J. P., 1949– author.
Title: Selling science fiction cinema : making and marketing a genre / J. P. Telotte.
Description: First edition. | Austin : University of Texas Press, 2023. | Includes bibliographical references and index.
Identifiers:
   LCCN 2022045662
   ISBN 978-1-4773-2733-3 (cloth)
   ISBN 978-1-4773-2734-0 (PDF)
   ISBN 978-1-4773-2735-7 (ePub)
Subjects: LCSH: Science fiction films—Marketing—History. | Science fiction films—Marketing—History—Sources.
Classification: LCC PN1995.9.S26 T47 2023 | DDC 791.43/615—dc23
LC record available at https://lccn.loc.gov/2022045662

doi:10.7560/327333

CONTENTS

Acknowledgments vii

CHAPTER 1. Marketing and Making Science Fiction 1

CHAPTER 2. What Is This *Thing*?
Framing and Unframing a New Genre 27

CHAPTER 3. Pondering the "Pulp Paradox"
Pal, Paramount, and the SF Market 55

CHAPTER 4. Moppets and Robots
MGM Markets *Forbidden Planet* 79

CHAPTER 5. Another Form of Life
Audiences, Markets, and *The Blob* 103

CHAPTER 6. Selling Japan
Making, Remaking, and Marketing Japanese SF 127

Conclusion 157

Notes 173

Select Filmography 191

Select Bibliography 193

Index 198

ACKNOWLEDGMENTS

As ever, many people have encouraged and contributed in various ways to the completion of this book. My department head, Richard Utz, was consistently supportive and arranged for some release time at an important point in the project. Greg Waller, in his capacity as editor of *Film History*, both nurtured and published early versions of several chapters while also offering a number of useful insights. Also helping to shape this volume, sometimes without realizing it, were many others who know science fiction, especially in its literary form, far better than I do. Among them I especially thank one of my colleagues at Georgia Tech, Lisa Yaszek; close friends such as Susan George and Carrol Fry; the editors at *Science Fiction Studies*, especially Carol McGuirk, who provided invaluable input on some of the early material; and attendees at several iterations of the International Conference on the Fantastic in the Arts who heard and offered significant suggestions to several early presentations of this material. And contributing in a very material way by helping to sift through numerous volumes of pulp and trade publications in search of unexpectedly elusive publicity material was my research assistant, Lauren Moye. I am also especially grateful to the editorial group at University of Texas Press (UTP), particularly Jim Burr and Mia Uribe Kozlovsky, who responded so enthusiastically to my manuscript, shepherded it through the usual review process in a surprisingly expeditious manner, and were consistently available for any and all queries. Nancy Warrington provided sensible and sensitive copyediting that unfailingly resulted in a more readable book. And together, this team ensured that my latest UTP experience was a thoroughly professional, efficient, and pleasant one.

Finally, I would like to dedicate this volume to my wife, Leigh E. Telotte, who has endured many ramblings about science fiction in all its forms, while constantly—and with surprisingly little complaint—offering both technical and emotional support.

SELLING SCIENCE FICTION CINEMA

CHAPTER 1

MARKETING AND MAKING SCIENCE FICTION

> Sf is what is marketed as sf: that is a beginning, but no more.
>
> EDWARD JAMES, *Science Fiction in the Twentieth Century*

This book takes its inspiration and at least some of its direction from the above remark by the noted science fiction (sf) historian Edward James. Trying to address repeated calls for a simple definition of the form, he offered what some might see as a problematic or even dismissive comment, as he seemed to tie sf to the common tastes of the marketplace. But rather than sidestepping the question, James was simply and astutely condensing a point that has been made by many other commentators on the genre, which is that sf has always seemed to be a rather ambiguous and hard-to-define form and that the question of *what* it is should at least be coupled to the large market of genre fans/consumers who implicitly seem to know, as they make the sorts of choices that shape—and continually reshape—our sense of what constitutes sf. This way of thinking is clearly a pragmatic approach to the genre, insofar as it shifts the focus from the sorts of icons and plot elements that fans and scholars alike typically use to talk about the form (and that have changed over time) to something practical and perhaps even measurable, at least in box-office terms. However, it is also one that might eventually point us in the direction of that "more" to which, James implies, we need to proceed. Indeed, marketing is just a start and a slippery and imprecise activity, as it responds to constant shifts in taste, cultural needs, and even the changing shape of the industry; and market success may be little more reliable as a consistent measure of a form than are those icons and actions that we most like to discuss. As evidence, we might simply recall the initial box-office failures of films that, over time, have often been cited as common sf touchstones, even landmarks of the genre, works such as *Metropolis* (1927, Fritz Lang, dir.),[1] *Things to Come* (1936, William C. Menzies, dir.), and *Blade Runner* (1982, Ridley Scott, dir.). They remind us that a genre text is always more than just a commodified popularity contest. Even so, I want to take something of a commodity approach by considering the broad activity of marketing as a way of building on James's seemingly offhand suggestion that it might help us consider what sf is; why defining the form often seems a difficult, even frustrating proposition; and how the cinema has responded to this challenge.

Before proceeding to sf, though, I might offer some clarification for another slippery or ambiguous term, especially when it is used in a cinematic context: *marketing*. When asked to describe how the motion picture business worked, the film pioneer and founder of Universal Pictures Carl Laemmle offered his own rather ambiguous observation, noting that "there is probably no business in the world with as many curious angles as ours."[2] And among the many "angles" to the business that he proceeded to describe are "publicity, advertising, and exploitation," as well as the actual theatrical venue with its façade, lobby, and internal decor, all of which, he emphasized, form crucial components in the process of marketing any film.[3] This multiangled process represents, as Nathalie Dupont and Joël Augros have more recently put it, the point where "cultural demands meet industrial practices,"[4] as it typically involves how a film is aimed at or best directed toward a particular audience; how the film functions within a certain historical/cultural context (and thus displays how time dependent it is); and how the audience for the film differs from that for many other consumer products, especially since that audience has no special *need* to see or consume the cinematic product and so must be induced to *want* that experience. Because of these and other considerations, marketing, as distinct from a more self-evident term like "advertising," is not "a by-product or an afterthought of the movie industry; it is truly part and parcel of film production and the experience of movie going."[5] As such, we might think of it as comprising all of the intentional extensions of the primary text that are aimed at building both exhibitor and audience awareness and consumption. Moreover, it has increasingly become one of the costliest elements of the movie enterprise. As recent Motion Picture Association of America (MPAA) statistics indicate, the average marketing budget for a major US film production in 2019 was approximately a third of the overall expenditure for the entire film,[6] and as Jonathan Gray has observed, blockbuster productions, many of them benefiting from built-in audience recognition factors, often go far beyond this percentage, with some allocating as much as "two-thirds of their budget" to marketing.[7]

While I recognize that James's definitional remark was addressed to the broader genre of sf—and thus increased the difficulty of his task by trying to encompass a variety of media—I want to focus specifically on sf film, since the cinematic marketing process has typically seemed more immediately visible, more foregrounded, and even more obviously an extension of the product being marketed than is the case with any piece of sf literature. It also presents us with an interesting challenge, one described by Lisa Kernan in her analysis of movie trailers where she notes how "promotion and visual narrative have become increasingly difficult to disentangle," since marketing for sf cinema, as the percentages cited above already indicate, has become such a big part of "the show."[8] It seems that no sf film especially enters the movie marketplace without its share of television and online trailers, cast interviews, product tie-ins, publicity releases, Twitter comments, and other constellating communiqués, all of them composing the solar system—with the film providing the "sun" to these many orbital elements—of the anticipated film experience.

But a good bit of this productive entanglement, as I might term it, has long been the case, especially in sf film. As an initial example, I note the 1929 premiere of Fritz Lang's early space flight epic *Frau im Mond*. The German film historian Klaus Kreimeier describes how, for this initial showing, the Ufa-Palast am Zoo, the largest cinema in Germany at the time, had its façade almost covered in "a tapestry of lights," meant to suggest "an image of the cosmos," while above its three main entrances a mock-up rocket ship "was regularly shot out of a globe and then disappeared in

1.1. Souvenir coins given to the moon "tourists" viewing *Frau im Mond* (1929).

the artificial night sky."[9] As moviegoers approached this spectacle and then headed through one of the theater's portals, they were supposed to gain the impression that, much like the characters in the film they were about to see, they were themselves boarding a vehicle, a celluloid ship, that would launch them on a grand space adventure. Adding to this illusion, souvenir coins, denominated "10 luna," were distributed to attendees so that they might have spending money upon their arrival *im Mond*. Thus, the moviegoers were from the start meant to feel a part of a sf adventure that extended beyond the screen of the Ufa-Palast, as if the theater were just the highly visible vehicle, or rocket-like first stage, for some larger, far more ambitious undertaking, at least for something more than a movie.

By way of expanding my scope, though, I should note that such spectacular efforts at entangling moviegoers with the stuff of sf cinema have hardly been limited to the precincts of the theater or to the 1920s. *Things to Come*, arguably the most famous British sf film, came to America in 1936 surrounded by another and ultimately more complex sort of narrative extension that was equally integral to its marketing strategy. In this case, it was an aura of high seriousness and even polemic, connected both to H. G. Wells's reputation as a social critic—he had adapted the script from his earlier "future history" novel *The Shape of Things to Come* (1933)—and to the various and clearly concerning political uncertainties of the day that were echoed in the film. In fact,

James Chapman and Nicholas Cull have suggested that the film's "real historical significance" has always resided not so much in the epic narrative of dystopian and utopian developments scripted by Wells, but "in its relationship to various ideological currents in the 1930s," particularly the rise of Nazism and other authoritarian movements.[10] And this vein is precisely what the film's US distributor, United Artists, chose to mine as it situated the film, for both potential exhibitors and potential viewers, amid the public's growing anxieties over the lingering economic depression and the looming prospects of war. It did so by placing multipage photo-essays in the major news magazines of the day, including the respected *Time* and *News-Week*; providing two-page publicity inserts in such trade papers as *Film Daily* (April 6, 1936), *Motion Picture Daily* (April 7, 1936), and *Motion Picture Herald* (April 25, 1936); and producing two-page pictorials for the rotogravure sections of several major national newspapers. But these "news" announcements about a film that, as they said, "is big, important, and demands top consideration," only paved the way for a more significant effort: prior to the official US premiere in New York, United Artists staged a special preview showing in Washington, DC, that was carefully framed, as that setting itself suggested, as an important political event. Various reports noted that the showing was "reserved" for Supreme Court justices, congressmen, members of the president's cabinet, ambassadors, members of foreign legations, "and others comprising the elite of the nation's capital."[11] Adding to the significance of the event was a radio broadcast of comments by these attendees and a transatlantic telephone address by Wells himself, who sought to emphasize the links between his sf film and the current troubled state of the world—a point further underscored by news reports that the film was already being "debated in legislatures of [the] world," including the British Parliament and the French Chamber of Deputies.[12] *Things to Come* was thus presented not simply as an entertainment and certainly not as sf—a term that, it should be noted, was nowhere mentioned in its formal advertising—but rather as a significant extension of timely, extra-theatrical political discussions, and, as ads for the film would put it, a "Startling Forecast of the Future!"

With the coming of television, such elaborate profilmic experiences—or what has typically been termed "ballyhoo"—

would gain another tool for reaching even further into the public sphere and entangling potential audiences in other ways. For instance, as part of the 1953 premiere of its film *The War of the Worlds* (Byron Haskin, dir.), Paramount Pictures recruited as a sponsor the Federal Civil Defense Administration, which regularly provided public service announcements about Cold War readiness, and which thus sent a message linking the film's alien invasion subject with its era's international anxieties, particularly about civil defense preparedness against other types of foreign invasion. Underscoring that emphasis on civil defense, the showing was preceded by a citywide "parade of Army, Navy and Red Cross personnel and military bands," and various city and state officials appeared to further situate the event in the contemporary cultural context.[13] In addition to these by then almost conventional promotional activities, Paramount announced that those not attending the premiere could still be a part of this experience thanks to one of the period's new marketing developments: the studio's massive "radio-television saturation campaign," which was designed not just to reach out to local audiences but "to blanket the U.S."[14] As the studio proudly assured exhibitors, its "new techniques," particularly "the aggressive use of TV and radio," were "designed so that exhibitors all over America can cash in," since potential audiences throughout the country would hear about the film at almost the same time, as news of the alien invasion film—in a marketing echo of Orson Welles's famous 1938 radio broadcast of the same story—effectively *invaded* homes everywhere in the hope of building a broad "word-of-mouth" appeal.[15]

Representing several different eras, not only do the sf marketing efforts briefly recalled demonstrate an effort to craft a multiply extensive narrative, one that was designed to reach beyond the filmic experience and to entangle audiences within a broad filmic and cultural discourse, but they also remind us that the genre has generally tended to write itself large, that is, to market itself in highly elaborate ways and promote its posture as a spectacle of wonder, as selling images of what might be or at least how we might like things to be. As a further example, we might consider the first major sf film of the 1950s, the Eagle-Lion Films 1950 production *Destination Moon* (Irving Pichel, dir.), which was accompanied by what the company's publicity director, Leon Brandt, described as his studio's "biggest program of advertising

1.2. The Ralston Rocket attracts crowds of *Space Patrol* fans during its national publicity tour.

expenditure in its history,"[16] involving a wide variety of magazine and newspaper tie-ins, television advertising, and high-profile gimmicks, such as a partnership with the Hayden Planetarium in New York and the use of space-suited "astronauts" to welcome moviegoers to the theaters and walk around downtown areas to publicize the movie. But this film is especially noteworthy not because of the gimmicks and saturation advertising, but because its reported $475,000 publicity budget was nearly equal to its production cost, signaling a growing tendency to treat marketing as an equivalent and necessary extension of the production.[17] The profilmic experience had simply become part of the full sf film experience, and arguably more so than was the case for any of the more established film genres of the day.

In the 1950s, even sf television would prove open to such spectacular and text-expanding efforts at self-presentation. Consider, for example, one of the most elaborate bits of such genre marketing, which involved the popular CBS series *Space Patrol*

(1950–1955) and what was known as the "Ralston Rocket." While space operas of this sort were a highly popular and typically cheaply produced form of sf programming between 1949 and 1956, *Space Patrol* sought to differentiate itself from the competition,[18] not by increasing its production budget but by conducting a high-visibility, film-style marketing campaign. The life-sized rocket, a "specially commissioned $30,000, 35-foot replica of Commander Buzz Corry's *Terra IV* spaceship," served as the top award in a national contest created to publicize the Ralston Purina–sponsored space opera.[19] It was designed to serve as a children's space clubhouse, as well as a giant toy, allowing the winner to live out his or her own imagined outer space adventures. Before it was awarded and parked, on its forty-foot trailer, in the driveway of young Ricky Walker, the massive prize was paraded around the country, making stops "in supermarket parking lots and schoolyards all across the country,"[20] while inviting thousands of children and their parents to step momentarily into the world of *Space Patrol*, even sit at the "controls" of the *Terra IV*. So successful was this national promotional event that it was copied by the Silvercup Bread company, which created its own "Silvercup Rocket" to promote its sponsorship of a competing television space opera, the short-lived *Rocky Jones, Space Ranger* (1954). Like the Ralston Rocket, it, too, was trucked to various supermarkets and shopping centers and eventually became a fixture at the Michigan State Fair.[21] Even more so than most cinematic efforts, these elaborate bits of television marketing assured viewers of something that has always been fundamental to the lure of sf: the hope that its visions of what *might be* could conceivably *be materialized*, becoming a part of real human experience—or at least an eye-catching driveway ornament.

While I might point to many other examples of sf's spectacular marketing across the various screens of sf, as well as the tendency of that marketing to invite an imaginative participation or typical entanglement in those narratives—and thus something more—I want to especially emphasize these later instances from the 1950s, for they cluster at a most revealing time: when sf marketing was becoming increasingly elaborate and even, as noted, as costly as and sometimes costlier than the film production itself, and when it was reaching out to audiences in ever more complex ways, as in the case of 3-D films. In part it was, perhaps all too obviously, because in this period the film industry was in the midst of what Murray Pomerance describes as "hard times,"[22] as it was undergoing a painful period of contraction and desperately needed to encourage moviegoers. But it was also because audiences were beginning to sense how much their lives were already caught up in a world that was being fundamentally refashioned by science and technology, that is, by the very "stuff" that sf narratives were selling. Moreover, these and other marketing examples from the same period help usher us to a front-row seat at what was a special moment in the sf genre's history, and they better enable us to see to what extent cinematic sf's identity and development had become partnered with its effective marketing practices. They also remind us of another equivalence: that the story of sf's development as a significant cinematic genre and the story of its marketing in this period go hand in hand, creating some of that "more" that sf has always seemed to promise.

Of course, the sf film had been around since the earliest days of the cinema, as the initial efforts of such figures as Georges Méliès (*A Trip to the Moon* [1902]), Walter R. Booth (*The Airship Destroyer* [1909]), and Thomas Edison (*A Trip to Mars* [1910, Ashley Miller, dir.]) readily bear witness. And as the silent film period gave way to sound, there had even been a few international attempts at crafting almost epic-in-scope sf features, most notably the German *Metropolis* and *Frau im Mond*, the French *End of the World* (1931, Abel Gance, dir.), the British *Things to Come*, and the American *The Mysterious Island* (1929, Lucien Hubbard, dir.). However, despite extensive marketing efforts, none of these films proved to be a major box-office success in the United States. In fact, for many years the genre was typically encountered in a lesser livery that might have made it seem like something less. Those appearances were largely in the precincts of the cheaply made motion picture serials, such as *The Invisible Ray* (1920, Harry A. Pollard, dir.), *Flash Gordon* (1936, Frederick Stephani, dir.), *Buck Rogers* (1939, Ford Beebe, dir.), and *Brick Bradford* (1947, Spencer G. Bennet and Thomas Carr, dirs.). Fist fights and cliff-hanger conclusions dominated these narratives, while the story itself was commonly framed as a marketing device, the film industry's sly way of luring customers back to a particular theater each week to see what was always billed as "the next exciting chapter." Only much later did sf achieve the sort of marketplace embrace and secure identity that today is taken for granted. Heralding that point of change, Patrick Lucanio points to approximately five hundred feature films and shorts that appeared between 1948 and 1962—all of which, he suggests, might be "indexed under the broad heading of science fiction"—as he argues that "never in the history of motion pictures has any other genre developed and multiplied so rapidly in so brief a period."[23] It is indeed a signal event in film history, and one described in practically the same words by Joyce A. Evans as she notes the unprecedented nature of this "rapid proliferation" of a single genre.[24] Similarly, Bill Warren, author of the landmark sf encyclopedia *Keep Watching the Skies!*, has suggested that because of the great number of works produced, "the science fiction movie as we know it today" was effectively "born" in the period that extends from 1950 to 1962.[25] It is in this relatively brief era, its precise endpoints certainly arguable, that we can observe a genre burgeoning into a major form, being energetically marketed, and yet at the same time—as James's comment should remind us—still rather wanting for a widely accepted definition or even a common core of elements, as if there were always something more to be encountered and accounted for.

This notion that one could market a product with what might be termed an uncertain identity or product label must seem a strange proposition to some, and yet it is one that has hardly been questioned. What makes it especially curious is the commonly accepted sense of how the relationship between a genre film and its audience typically works. Thomas Schatz, who has extensively researched the inside workings of the film industry, explains how we tend to identify a genre film both by its use of certain "general filmic devices to create an imaginary world"—devices that are repeated from one text to another and thus help label it—and by the fact "that this world is predetermined and essentially intact."[26] That is, audiences are usually familiar with those generic elements and, in viewing a new work or simply weighing whether they *should* see it, measure the film against their prior experience with "the genre's preordained, value-laden narrative system."[27] Logically, film marketers rely on this familiarity as they try to tap into the audience's prior experiences with similar narratives and exploit the most memorable or pleasurable elements of past genre successes. But unlike many other popular genres, such as the western, horror story, detective tale, romantic comedy, and others, sf has had a long and difficult time establishing this sort of stable "system," of creating a kind of "objective," fully acceptable, and easily marketable identity, which might help explain why Schatz, although writing in the 1980s and after the onset of the *Star Wars* phenomenon, did not include sf in his study of the most popular Hollywood genres.

In an effort to explain this problematic situation, some commentators have pointed to how "different" sf is from many other genres. As Brooks Landon offers, "when considered as a formal genre," sf has typically demonstrated a certain indeterminacy, or what he insightfully terms "restlessness."[28] It is a point that Rob Latham seconds when he suggests that we might think of sf less as a traditionally "fixed and coherent genre" than as "a diverse and distributed ensemble of phenomena that resists totalization."[29] While there is a lengthy history of fiction that involves popular science—a history that much pre-dates the cinema—sf has always drawn from a variety of concerns and, despite its title, has never been strictly tied to that "science" focus, as evidenced by a number of films that are commonly described as sf, such as *Two Lost Worlds* (1951, Norman Dawn, dir.), *Untamed Women* (1952, W. Merle Connell, dir.), or even *Invasion of the Body Snatchers* (1956, Don Siegel, dir.). In an effort to account for this "restless" or shifty nature, John Cheng has offered one explanation for this difficult character, suggesting that sf, more so than other genres, is bound up in a pattern of historical and cultural "contingency," involving a variety of influences and contributions linked to "commerce, science, and the interests of participants," especially the fan culture, or genre consumers, of a specific time.[30] The result of such a contingent view, or what might be thought of as a pattern of constant cultural interchange, he offers, is that the genre has always seemed like one that has "emerged slowly, partially, and haphazardly"—all descriptions that might also be applied (as discussed later) to the historical efforts at marketing a sf cinema.[31]

That contingent character might also help explain the somewhat problematic efforts at naming the genre, efforts that continued even into the period Lucanio, Evans, and Warren see as a watershed for the form. Through the years, sf has gone by a variety of titles, many of them readily suggesting its links to or hybridization with other generic forms. One of the genre's founding fathers, Hugo Gernsback, writing in the first issue of his early pulp magazine *Amazing Stories*, took the lead in this sort of hybrid identification when he sought to market what he described as "a new kind of fiction," one composed of "charming romance intermingled with scientific fact and prophetic vision."[32] Unfortunately, he would tie that cumbersome combination of "romance," "fact," and "vision" to the equally awkward title of "scientifiction," a name that was nonetheless widely adopted and often abbreviated as "stf" by the readers of his and the other specialized pulp magazines of the 1920s and 1930s. Gernsback would later adopt the simpler "science fiction" as a more appropriate name when he sought to market the literature as an "educational" form, since, as he explained, sf represented the type of "stories that are discussed by inventors, by scientists, and in the classroom."[33] However, many other titles would continue to be employed, among them: scientific romance, scientific fiction, pseudo-scientific stories, invention stories, science fantasy, and speculative fiction, along with various non-English labels. Suggesting their own uncertainty about both the form and its fans, some of the film trade papers, including *Variety*, would continue to use a term like "scientifiction" into the mid-1950s,[34] and as Edward James points out, even a prestigious reference work such as *The Reader's Guide to Periodical Literature* employed the ambiguous identifier of "pseudo-scientific stories" up to 1961.[35]

Those varied terms also underscore another symptom of that generic "restlessness": the fact that both literary and cinematic forms of sf have had to work at differentiating themselves from other, nearly allied types, particularly horror, or, as was especially the case during the pulp era, what were commonly referred to as "weird stories." In fact, I might note that many later prominent sf writers, including Jack Williamson, Edmond Hamilton, Henry Kuttner, and Ray Bradbury, initially published many of their stories in such magazines as *Strange Tales* and *Weird Tales*, with the latter consistently publishing throughout its run from 1923 to 1954 sf stories along with supernatural horror and heroic fantasy. While there were some early efforts to segregate or, as Mark Bould and Sherryl Vint put it, separate sf "from the broader field of the fantastic and create it as a distinct genre or marketing category,"[36] the readership of the various pulps apparently found nothing incongruous about what some might view as generic crossovers. After all, the "weird" magazines often seemed to deal with the same sorts of fantastic materials as the sf pulps, including the latest scientific developments, even though they at times approached that matter in slightly different ways or might have framed it differently.

That linkage might be partly explained, as the sf writer and historian Adam Roberts argues, by an earlier cultural tendency that had "braided together the discourses of materialism and spiritualism," implying that the "supernatural," the "psychic," and the "scientific" were seen by many as closely allied, sometimes overlapping phenomena, all approaching—but from quite different angles—a similar desire for pursuing knowledge, for rendering the mysterious known through whatever means possible.[37] However, that rationale misses a key element of the form that the films and their marketing will repeatedly highlight: that sf has always been what might be termed multibranded, as evidenced by the editor of *Weird Stories* promising to give his readers "the cream of weird-scientific fiction"[38] and by Gernsback branching out in a variety of sf directions, as the title of his pulp *Scientific Detective Monthly* illustrates. But these sorts of linkages, as shall be seen, have also at times provided a useful tactic for marketing various sf films by appealing to different audiences and helping evoke what Schatz terms an established "value-laden narrative system."

We might also see the influence of this earlier pattern of combinatory or hybrid thinking haunting the most successful and widely accepted effort at defining sf, although it is one that has reified the genre's persistently elusive popular character while teasing the academic taste for something more definitive. Darko Suvin famously described sf as "the literature of cognitive estrangement,"[39] an appellation that aims to account for how the form, in whatever medium it is encountered, is fundamentally invested in its ability, by turns, to evoke a familiar world and then to render that world as "strange," as challenging to normal cognition and, by means of that challenge, prompting audiences to reexamine their own world. It is a laudably economical yet also sweeping effort at definition, focused on sf's altered attitude toward the real, that is, its strategy for compelling audiences to see and understand their world in a different manner. Moreover, it helps explain some of the pleasure bound up in the sf experience, a pleasure, as Freud would have suggested, that is fundamentally linked to the experience of the new. But while enabling a kind of comprehensive view of the genre, this definition also readily suggests the sort of "braiding" situation Roberts describes or the hybrid efforts of the weird magazines, and, since it could just as easily be applied to more traditional horror narratives, it is one that has often only furthered that sense of slipperiness with which genre commentators have so often wrestled.

As one might expect, these same problems of vague kinship and equally vague definition have carried over to the film industry's relationship to sf. In fact, before the period that Lucanio, Warren, and others specify as their birth, sf films were seldom labeled as such. In an effort to provide marketing direction for both exhibitors and audiences, industry trade papers historically included some generic indicators about upcoming releases, either through regular features, such as *Variety*'s "Film Booking Chart" and *Motion Picture Herald*'s "Release Chart," or in the papers' dedicated film reviews that were largely aimed not so much at potential viewers but at those involved in booking or marketing the films. In some cases into the 1950s, these papers still used the familiar "horror" or broad-stroke "fantasy" labels to describe forthcoming sf-type releases, as might well be expected in the case of films with a clearly mixed heritage, such as *Frankenstein* (1931, James Whale, dir.) and *Mad Love* (1935, Karl Freund, dir.), or hard-to-classify works like the H. G. Wells–scripted *The Man Who Could Work Miracles* (1937, Lothar Mendes, dir.). But in most cases, the labels provided were very broad and vague descriptors like "melodrama," "adventure," or "thriller," or they morphed into ambiguous hybrid designations. Thus *Film Daily*'s review of the H. G. Wells adaptation *The Invisible Man* (1933, James Whale, dir.) referred to it as a "novelty thriller"; the same paper listed *Non-Stop New York* (1937, Robert Stevenson, dir.), a film about futuristic air travel, as a "romantic melodrama"; while Roland Barton of *Film Bulletin* classified *Transatlantic Tunnel* (1935, Maurice Elvey, dir.), a narrative about the future underwater construction of a tunnel linking the United States and Britain, as a "dramatic spectacle."[40] The difficulty that might result from such hybrid generic labeling of sf, particularly its problematic effect on marketing such films, shows especially clearly in the

MARKETING AND MAKING SCIENCE FICTION — 15

1.3. *Just Imagine* (1930) blends elements of the comedy, musical, and science fiction film. Fox Film.

case of the feature film *The Invisible Ray* (1936, Lambert Hillyer, dir.), a work about a mysterious element brought to Earth by meteor and used to construct a ray machine that could, depending on how it is wielded, destroy matter or cure ills, including blindness. While *Motion Picture Herald* described it as "a type of horror melodramatic picture," *Film Daily*'s review consigned the movie to "the thrill trade," and *Motion Picture Daily* suggested that it "blended in romance, action, murder, but without mystery for the audience."[41] In any case, science—much less sf—was nowhere mentioned in this strange mélange of descriptors.

Given such often vague, even confusing or mysterious generic descriptions provided to exhibitors by the trade papers, it should hardly be surprising to find the audience-directed advertising also drawing on multiple generic connections in an effort to explain the films' identities and, hopefully, attract multiple audience segments. Thus, many of the posters for the comic utopian movie *Just Imagine* (1930, David Butler, dir.) show the featured comedian El Brendel's laughing face, juxtaposed with an image of an advanced monoplane with a smiling girl (Maureen O'Sullivan) incongruously astride it, as if she were riding some sort of technological horse. The majority of the ads for *Frankenstein* combine Boris Karloff's glowering, monstrous countenance with a printed legend telling of an unseen scientist and his apparently *scientific* endeavor: "The Man Who Made a Monster." The posters and lobby cards for *Six Hours to Live* (1932, William Dieterle, dir.), featuring a fantastic machine that can, for a brief time, bring the dead back to life, typically show the film's leads, Warner Baxter and Miriam Jordan, in a romantic embrace, usually against the backdrop of a giant clock face, emblematic of the film's miraculous machine that can restore life for a short period (the titular six hours). And a poster for *The Invisible Ray* shows two of the film's principal actors, the already-recognized horror stalwarts Boris Karloff and Bela Lugosi, in opposing corners of the image with a banner above promising "new, strange fields of mystery." Without mentioning sf, these advertised elements of comedy, horror, melodrama, and mystery effectively framed their respective narratives for varied audiences while trying to sidestep the ambiguities that might have attached even to a term like Gernsback's "scientifiction."

What I have tried to demonstrate in this section are some of the issues that typically confronted both the film industry and film consumers as sf was beginning to find a new level of prominence in popular culture and to be marketed for a mass audience. It was an audience that, throughout the twentieth century, was growing increasingly fascinated with issues involving science and technology, as might also be evidenced by the proliferation of sf-themed cartoons produced by the various film studios from the 1920s through the 1950s, works such as the Fleischer Studios' *Trip to Mars* (1924), Van Beuren Studios' *The Phantom Rocket* (1933), Disney's *The Plastics Inventor* (1944), or Warner Bros.' *Duck Dodgers in the 24½ Century* (1953).[42] Another cultural fingerprint of this influence can be found in the spate of science and technology–themed world's fairs of the prewar period, such as Chicago's Century of Progress International Exposition, San Francisco's Golden Gate International Exposition, or the "World of Tomorrow"–themed New York World's Fair. And in the postwar world—in an era when it seemed as if the genre was finally ready to be "born"—this mass audience could not escape being entangled with those issues, especially given the Cold War resonances of the new and highly publicized rockets, satellites, and atomic weaponry that would become some of the most commonplace icons and worrisome concerns of a developing sf cinema.

However, the film industry clearly had to grapple with a multifaceted problem that extended beyond the obvious question of how to approach such loaded subject matter without furthering audience anxieties. It also had to consider how to advertise and market a form that lacked the familiar "value-laden narrative system" of the sort common to most other genres, one that still did not have a widely embraced generic title, and one that was often difficult to distinguish from other, somewhat similar generic systems. The industry's conventional approach to marketing a genre that had an easily evoked objective identity and reaching an audience often conceived to be passive subjects would no longer prove very effective. Consequently, even as sf was coming into prominence and addressing those various pressing cultural concerns of the era, it would continue to be marketed in what almost seems a haphazard manner, as the film industry groped for a way to talk, in its customary generic fashion, about subjects that had rather forcefully come to the forefront of popular discourse. However, the various ways in which the film industry met these challenges, and how, as sf was finally coming of age, it found effective ways to market, advertise, and, in effect, speak the new language of the genre to new, and indeed changing audiences, does offer us some insight into the character of cinematic sf, at least in America, where ballyhoo, exploitation, advertising, or "what is marketed as sf" has, almost from the start, been an important if largely unexamined dimension of the larger film experience.

While sf cinema would remain a rather "restless" and often even a hybrid form in this period, its growing level of popularity required the film industry to explore a variety of ways to frame how audiences, as well as industry members, should see this still relatively unfamiliar genre. To address that variety here most effectively—and its slippery subject—we can also benefit from using multiple tools for examining it and for starting to untangle many of those entanglements that sf cinema inevitably seems to entail. In this section, I want to briefly detail several of the critical perspectives that will be employed to consider a number of these related concerns, including the nature of the sf genre, the broad and at this point evolving shape of the media environment that the genre inhabited, and the typical practices of film marketing as they inflected the presentation and audience reception of sf in this period of its emergence. It is a period, it should be noted, when marketing itself had to take on a double character. Government regulation of the movie industry following the Supreme Court's 1948 Paramount decision required the major studios to divest themselves of their theater holdings, thereby creating a situation in which film companies and distributors had to vie for the attention not just of audiences but of potential exhibitors as well. As a result, marketing, especially of an already difficult-to-market commodity like sf, now had to be directed both at those within the film industry, such as independent theater owners, and at traditional and even not-so-traditional moviegoers who were increasingly turning their attention to the new, free medium of television.

A useful starting point for such a multifaceted study is John Rieder's effort to situate sf historically within the functional system of popular genre narratives, or what he terms "the mass cultural genre system."[43] While he focuses primarily on sf's literary form as he tries to distinguish it from more traditional or what he terms "classical" genres, such as the epic, tragedy, comedy, and romance, he also provides a significant link for our film-focused discussion. For as part of his own effort at genre definition, he suggests that one might see "the commercial advertisement" as "the keystone" of this broadly popular "system," one in which sf today plays such a highly visible and powerful part.[44] Besides offering a more nuanced link to James's leading comment about marketing and the "more" that is sf, this focus on the commercial context and especially on advertising is especially pertinent to our thinking about sf because of what it suggests about the very nature of the genre. Rieder argues that advertising has at its core a "utopian anticipation of a world of fulfilled desires,"[45] as if advertising were itself a kind of disguised sf text, one that, in the best tradition of the genre, aims to offer its audience tantalizing glimpses of what might be, or at least what they might have or possess through a product, even if that product is just a film. Adding to this link's importance is the way it underscores the extent to which sf "takes shape within the milieu of mass culture," where it is molded—and constantly remolded—by the cumulative effects of changing "economic and ideological pressures,"[46] thereby suggesting that our appreciation of these effects, and thus of the work of marketing, might be crucial to understanding the genre's formation and function, as it, too, tries to sell us the future or at least a world different from our own.

Where Rieder's approach suffers a bit is in his emphasis on a specific part of this process, like *advertising* rather than *marketing*, which draws the boundaries of his investigation rather too narrowly, completely missing, for example, that double character of film marketing noted above. We might also recall the carefully constructed political context that was used to introduce *Things to Come* to the US market. Disseminating news about a film's being discussed in the House of Commons is not quite advertising, but it is an effective promotional ploy that illustrates the usefulness, even the necessity for thinking more broadly in terms of *marketing* activities, especially for how sf cinema frames and markets its ideas. In this same context, I might heed Thomas Doherty's argument that a movie is never simply a "passive" text, something *to be advertised*, but an active force; as Doherty explains, "as the subject doing the exploitation, the movie is active, an agent that caters to its target audience by serving up appetizing or exotic subject matter."[47] Thus I would also suggest caution about Rieder's basic assumption that all genre texts are "explicitly designed as commodities"—that is, that they are *just* products, objects "designed" by a different active agent—since that assumption ultimately brings us back to the vexed issue of auteurism, that is, of who the real author of a film is and thus who might be doing that "designing" and why. And yet, we should recognize that his underlying notion is a significant one. For Rieder argues that we need to view the entire mass-cultural genre system as, almost invisibly, involving a web of "commercial activity" surrounding the "production, distribution, and reception of storytelling."[48] That web, I would just emphasize, links together many of the elements that contribute to our sense of what constitutes a genre like sf: how it is marketed, to whom it is distributed, the sorts of pleasures or satisfactions it offers (which are ultimately distinct from its advertising), even the kinds of anxieties it addresses (and, I might hope, to some extent alleviates). Although focused largely on the nature of that "genre system" when viewed through a Marxist lens—which almost invariably seems to posit a passive rather than an active audience—Rieder's discussion valuably situates sf within a larger and constantly shifting context. And that context already points toward the "more" that has been noted, since it compels us to think about the genre's place within what I would term a complex media ecology.

Since Rieder's discussion tends to take the nature of that media ecology for granted or just assign it an economic dimension, I also want to draw from the work of Matthew Fuller to help evoke the dynamic context in which sf operates. While Fuller, like Rieder, ranges broadly as he surveys much of the contemporary media landscape, he does take genre narratives, including film, as one of his concerns. He emphasizes that something like sf is "always multiply connected" and thus always involves other sorts of ancillary texts and rhetorical processes through which it speaks to audiences—advertising, reviews, merchandise, even other films as they become parts within a series or franchise—and in which, as I have suggested, it *entangles* us.[49] These elements, as well as many others, work together to form what he terms a "complex medial system" in which many elements "cooperate to produce something more than the sum of their parts."[50] They might do so by extending the central text (as we saw in the advance publicity for *Things to Come*), by filtering how we see and experience that text (as in the case of those various hybrid namings that were employed to talk about a film like *The Invisible Ray*), or even by inspiring other, related texts, such as sequels and prequels (as is especially evident in the many *Star Wars*, *Transformers*, and Marvel Film Universe efforts). This ecological perspective, this sense of not just linked but interdependent, mutually supporting systems, can help remind us of how every sf text exists within a dynamic system and suggests that we think of it, as Fuller offers, as part of "a pattern rather than simply as an object,"[51] rather more a process than a thing.

Following his lead, as the subsequent chapters demonstrate, we need to consider not one element of sf marketing, such as a movie's advertising posters or online art, but rather a wide array of texts that help construct this pattern. In practice, this variety might involve a single film and a number of its extended representations, such as theatrical trailers, television advertisements, pressbooks, and publicity stories, or it might mean considering a

1.4. Building the "thick" relationship of science fiction for *Destination Moon* (1950)—space exploration, the movies, and magazines such as *Popular Mechanics*.

series of closely related and similarly marketed films appearing in rapid succession, as in the case of Japanese sf films like *Godzilla* (1954, 1956, Ishiro Honda, dir.), *Rodan* (1956, 1957, I. Honda, dir.), *The Mysterians* (1957, 1959, I. Honda, dir.), and *Mothra* (1961, 1962, I. Honda, dir.). All emerged from Japan's Toho Company and surged into US theaters in short succession during the 1950s and early 1960s, with each building on the impact of its predecessor while also establishing a kind of über-narrative or franchise-like framework for subsequent films. Using a particularly resonant image, Fuller suggests that through our experience with such textual groups, we manage to "enter into a thicker relationship with practice,"[52] that is, with a particular sf experience. This notion of a "thick" relationship, of our connection to various media inputs, adds an effective, almost sensory conceptualization of how sf and its marketing practices might actually produce the sense of "fulfilled desires" that Rieder sees as one of the *illusory* products of all advertising. But for Fuller, this effect is practically tangible, the satisfying result of our entry into the complex web of the sf media text—much as in moviegoers' entry through the elaborately decorated portals of the Ufa-Palast am Zoo that was earlier described—as those textual groups all participate in doing the work of the genre, perhaps even leaving a "luna" coin of sorts in our hand as a mark of our participation. That "thicker relationship" might also further explain the difficult issue of definition, that "more" James was talking about, which, even in the period of sf's burgeoning, marked the genre.

To lend a more precisely cinematic flavor to this consideration of sf and its marketing, and as an aid in measuring that "thickness," I also want to incorporate Jonathan Gray's foundational effort at addressing the specific character of film marketing. Like Rieder and Fuller, Gray employs a host of similarly evocative terms, such as "system," "web," and "connectivity," as he evokes the dynamic nature of the modern media experience while also giving that experience a pointedly filmic focus. He observes that one of the distinguishing marks of contemporary culture has been "the massive, extended presence of filmic and televisual texts across our lived environments,"[53] and he attempts to map at least a part of that presence by examining the proliferation of various film paratexts such as trailers, promotional giveaways, posters, games, and branded merchandise. But Gray also adds an important complication to this dynamic presence by reminding us that, just as the film industry depends on these proliferating marketing efforts to reach the widest audience, so, too, do viewers rely on these extensions of the film text, which help them determine "what to watch, what not to watch, and *how* to watch"—so much so, he argues, that even before we actually see a movie, "we have already begun to decode it and to preview its meanings and effects."[54] Thus the various "frames and filters" that the film industry creates to market its product also, synergistically, form a meaningful part of the overall film experience, as films, their merchandising activities, and even film-related products all share identities, vie for audience attention, and tell different parts or versions of a larger narrative.

Gray also cautions that there is a danger in trying to address these many paratexts: that we might well find ourselves lured away from thinking about the film itself, as we get too caught up in what he terms "off-screen studies."[55] Since my concern here is with a specific kind of text, even a certain body of texts—sf films especially from that period when the genre essentially came of age while the movie industry was in the midst of changing its own character—I will not be focusing solely "off-screen"; doing so is no more appropriate to this discussion than its opposite, a strictly "on-screen" emphasis or textual close reading. Rather, following the notion implicit in Fuller's more broadly focused discussion, that the text is a kind of "continuous productivity" and that this productivity generates the larger "storyworld as we know it,"[56] I will use those various "frames and filters" to look in both ways: into the sf text as it has been presented for our consumption/entertainment (especially, as shall be seen, in the case of *The Blob* [1958, Irvin S. Yeaworth Jr., dir.]) and into a variety of the marketing activities that attempt to construct or frame *us* as the desired audience for that text and its eager, even inevitable "decoders." This double perspective should help better account for the sort of entanglement that has typically marked the sf film experience.

Of course, today it is almost impossible for any film to go "unframed" and for potential audiences to avoid the many paratexts that similarly seek to frame them, insisting that the latest screen narratives are not just worthy of our attention but important to our lives. We simply cannot avoid saturation television

1.5. *Dark City* (1998) figures the constantly shifting landscape of science fiction. New Line Cinema.

spots; corporate sponsorships of programs and events; product tie-ins and placements; dedicated and often rather elaborate company/studio websites; tweets from filmmakers, cast members, and fashion influencers; social-media posts of every sort; pop-up ads on various streamed texts; and even streamed spin-offs any more than we can avoid sf itself. All these texts are not only multiple "parts" of a film but often its quite predictable, even enjoyable extensions. And sf can seem especially insistent and alluring in this regard. In part, this is because sf speaks the language of the moment, the language of science and technology in which contemporary culture is so steeped; in part, it is due to its characteristic fan culture, which eagerly embraces many of these framing effects and even contributes its own frames, as in the case of such activities as fan fiction, memorabilia collecting, cosplay, and filking, along with the many "Cons" that feature these and other activities.[57] But it is also in part because, thanks to the genre's typically large budgets and the veil of special effects it employs, sf film simply tends to look so enticing and seems to speak so authoritatively about both the present and the future. Of course, that same powerful framing activity should give us some pause. It might even compel us to give some thought to the nature of what the film industry has always termed "ballyhoo" and to the various ways in which that ballyhoo seeks not just to exploit the appeal of films but also to exploit the movie audience, to treat both film and fan *as if* they were passive, easily manipulable subjects. At least it might inspire us to consider what *more* is involved in this thing we call sf, the genre that has become arguably the most dominant contemporary film type.

Admittedly, much of this introductory commentary on marketing could also be extended to other film genres, since ballyhoo, advertising, and exploitation have consistently been parts of the film experience, and they continue even as that experience spreads across many new sorts of screens or media platforms and as we carry it, readily available, in our pockets via smart phones or on our digital tablets. However, I want to emphasize sf in this context for a variety of reasons. One is that it is, as I have suggested, the most popular of genres today and a kind of lingua franca for contemporary technological life, trafficking in a way that other genres do not in the images of technological culture. Sf thereby enables our understanding of how that culture and our individual lives are entangled or blended in a way that is not only useful but almost imperative. A second is that, as Paul Virilio has suggested, contemporary culture has itself come to seem rather science fictional, as it insists on how much of the world and the self is constructed rather than original or authentic, how much of the real often seems to be a reality illusion, as if modern life transpired inside of sf narratives like *Dark City* (1998, Alex Proyas, dir.), the *Matrix* films (1999, 2003, 2021, Wachowskis, dirs.), or the television series *Westworld* (2016, 2018, 2020, 2022), in all of which reality is constantly being reconstructed with or without its inhabitants' awareness. As Virilio puts it, very much like the characters in these works, we all—and all too often—feel as if we are "mediatized" or "cinematized," inhabitants of a technologically produced reality, a digital Potemkin village, and a predetermined world,[58] one that we vitally need to know more about. A third is that, as I began by noting, sf has struggled with its identity, which often seems a particularly contemporary malady, one afflicting much more than just a film genre; and it probably struggles more so in this regard than any other film form save for the allusively named yet similarly shifty film noir. By giving the genre a name like "scientifiction," the briefly used "scientifilm," or simply "science fiction," we would seem to have nailed down an identity and thereby gained some sense of control or at least understanding of it. And yet, perhaps because sf is so concerned with change and what might be, with prompting us to *wonder*, it ultimately seems more prone to asserting its "process" character than other genres and thus still proves a very "restless" form, always showing us, or suggesting that it will show us, something "more."

In the chapters that follow, I assume these more recent imperatives, as they look back at sf cinema in its most significant period of development, when it was already demonstrating some of that "more." They detail how the development of what came to be commonly recognized as sf has been bound up in a web of both deliberate and unconscious marketing/advertising practices and audience responses to those practices, all of them part of the constitution of the thick (and ever-thickening) sf text and important contributors to the genre's identity. We shall follow some of that web's strands into the following key areas: textual labeling, audience identification, cross-media marketing, industry responses to shifting audience patterns, and the (re)presentation of international productions. In these at times overlapping areas, we might better see and understand the complex series of relationships between the sf texts, their creators, their consumers, and their culture, all part of the developing *idea* of what constitutes a sf cinema. Those productive entanglements, all various components in not just the *economic* but also the *social* function of genre narrative, are always helping negotiate the nature of a genre such as sf, prompting the inclusion or exclusion of certain elements in its construction, and defining, at least for a particular but still restless cultural moment, what we assume it to be. They should not be expected to present us with an unwavering identity, foolproof definition, or some sort of certificate of authenticity; and indeed, in this volume I largely steer clear of such efforts at fixity. However, those entangling elements, particularly as they emphasize the very dynamic nature of the sf experience, should open onto some of that "more" that, as Edward James obliquely suggested, has both intrigued and bedeviled our efforts at understanding and defining sf, along with its place in the larger cinematic world.[59]

CHAPTER 2

WHAT IS THIS *THING*?
Framing and Unframing a New Genre

As a starting point for investigating the impact of marketing on science fiction (sf) cinema, I want to consider a particularly fitting film, *The Thing from Another World* (1951, Christian Nyby, dir.). Coming at the start of the decade and as the first sf film released in this period by a major studio, RKO, *The Thing* marked a different direction for the US film industry in the decade following the Supreme Court's Paramount decision, which had required the major studios to divest themselves of their theater holdings and thus to begin a new regime of exhibition practices. No longer able to rely on their own theater chains for an almost guaranteed placement and, usually, measure of profitability, the major studios began cutting back on many of their star contracts, striking deals with independent producers to provide films for studio distribution, and experimenting with new types of stories. Starring relatively unheralded actors such as Kenneth Tobey and Margaret Sheridan, being produced by the Hollywood veteran Howard Hawks through his independent Winchester Films company, and exploiting a current interest in flying saucers—stoked by the popular television space operas—*The Thing* was just the sort of picture that fit this new trajectory, and that fit was corroborated by its consistently good reviews, praise for the performances delivered by its "cast . . . of unknowns,"[1] and a projected gross of $1,950,000 on domestic rentals alone.[2] In sum, it predicted a profitable future for this developing genre.

The film also faced a relatively new marketing challenge for big studio releases. While most film ballyhoo had previously been aimed at luring customers into studio-owned or -affiliated theaters, the new Hollywood regime of the 1950s saw studios/ distributors also having to attract exhibitors to book their product while those theater owners were facing a host of their own challenges during this industry downturn period. A column in *Film Bulletin*'s "Exhibitors Forum" feature summed up their most common problems as owners talked about their "declining grosses," "increased costs of operation," and "greatly increased film rental" prices.[3] The result was a boosted effort on the part of major companies like RKO to "sell" exhibitors on their latest product while also enlisting them as partners in the marketing of their films to the moviegoing public. But as *The Thing* illustrates, this twofold marketing effort was complicated by the nature of the product, that is, by trying to sell a genre that, as was suggested in the first chapter, had never been particularly well defined, had seen only a handful of prior genre examples released in the immediate postwar period, and previously had seldom proved to be especially profitable. However, RKO's successful marketing of *The Thing* in this uncertain context begins to suggest the untapped—and, at this point, still little understood—appeal of a burgeoning sf cinema.

It is practically a truism to note, as David Lipton does, that all movie advertising "is tailored to audiences who seem most likely to be attracted to it."[4] Certainly, we should hardly be surprised to find publicity images for *The Hunger Games* (2012, Gary Ross, dir.) in *Seventeen Magazine*, a full-page ad for the crime drama *D.O.A.* (1950, Rudolph Maté, dir.) in *Popular Detective*, or a spot for the romantic mystery *Nocturne* (1946, Edwin L. Marin, dir.) in *Romance*. The releasing studios simply gauged the audiences for these films and were targeting those prospective viewers. But what may be more curious is the *absence* of advertising for sf films where we might most expect to find it—along with a ready audience for those genre narratives—that is, in the popular sf pulp magazines. Publications such as *Amazing Stories, Astounding Stories*, and *Thrilling Wonder Stories* are where the genre essentially came of age from the 1920s through the 1950s, and where there was, as the always popular letters columns found in those magazines attest, an audience hungry for stories, in whatever medium, about the workings of reason, science, and technology. This curious absence was the case until 1951, when advertisements began appearing for a film that, most appropriately, had its own origins in the pulps, *The Thing*. Based on the story "Who Goes There?" by the famed pulp editor John W. Campbell Jr. (writing as Don A. Stuart), *The Thing* was one of a number of independently produced films being distributed by financially troubled RKO as it sought to attract new viewers by reaching beyond its normal advertising venues.[5] However, these notices, as part of a larger national marketing campaign for the film and similar to those placed in industry newspapers, avoided directly addressing *The Thing*'s generic identity even for what was, we might assume, a highly interested sf audience. This ambiguous approach, I would suggest, was symptomatic of some of the problems sf faced as both a literary and cinematic genre as it began to gain prominence in the 1950s.

In his study of cinematic paratexts such as advertising (and including trailers, promotions, toys, and games), Jonathan Gray observes that one of the primary tasks of all advertising is to create "frames for many of the items that surround us,"[6] that is, vantages that will help guide how we approach and appreciate them. Serving as "filters through which we must pass on our way to the film,"[7] those paratexts encourage some perspectives or expectations while discouraging or eliminating others, all as part of our formative encounter with a particular film and convenient links to the audience's sense of the larger supertext—or body of similar generic texts—of which it might be a part. Gray particularly emphasizes the influence that this sense of genre can have on film advertising and viewing when he notes that while a genre is not itself a paratext, it will usually "work paratextually to frame a text," situating our reading of a specific film in the framework of other, previously encountered examples of the genre, and in the process hopefully enhancing our experience and understanding of the film.[8] His larger argument is that an audience's experience of and general knowledge not only about a single film but also about a genre such as sf are inevitably a part of the total film experience, and as a result something that skillful marketers will usually try to exploit in the process of locating prospective viewers, attracting them to the latest release, and enhancing their experience of the film.

However, as outlined in the previous chapter, sf generally, and cinematic sf in particular, has at times proved problematic for our efforts at categorizing its texts and harnessing, for purposes of exploitation, what Matthew Fuller terms their "memetic buzz," that is, the way in which the "always multiply connected"—or paratextually connected—works that make up the genre materialize their ideas and energy for their audiences.[9] Thus, even when talking about sf *literature*, Edward James feels it is necessary to remind his readers that there has always been a "bundle of perceptions about what constitutes sf," some of them seemingly contradictory; that the "contents" of that bundle "are constantly changing"; and that in the course of this change, our sense of what constitutes sf is also often challenged.[10] Such challenges have been especially obvious in sf cinema, with movies from modern sf's formative period of the 1920s and 1930s clearly displaying their "always multiply connected" nature. For example, for all of its futuristic and monumentalist urban vision, much of it modeled on that of the landmark German sf classic *Metropolis*, a work such as the American futuristic film *Just Imagine* has as much of the social comedy and musical about it as it has utopian or dystopian aspirations, while films such as *Frankenstein* and *Six Hours to Live*, despite their common concern with the production of artificial life, are just as closely linked to horror and romantic melodrama, respectively. At least in its early cinematic manifestations, the sf film was often every bit the same sort of loosely connected "bundle" that James observes in early sf literature, with that looseness making the marketing of the genre, whether to potential viewers or to exhibitors, all the more challenging.

John Rieder has extended that bundled notion in his own description of sf's "array of shifting identities" that, he suggests, derive in any particular period from "an evolving and interconnected system of generic choices."[11] Echoing Rick Altman's earlier work on narrative genre systems, which suggests that we might best think of narrative types not so much as "inert categories" or constant formulas, but rather as a series of "discursive claims" made "for particular purposes in specific situations,"[12] Rieder describes sf as a "historical and mutable" system, lacking a "single unifying characteristic" but marked by a gradual "accretion of repetitions, echoes, imitations, allusions, identifications, and distinctions that testifies to an emerging sense of a conventional web of resemblances."[13] And it is that "web of resemblances," he suggests, that characterizes the mass-cultural genre system as "a historically situated and . . . ever-changing set of practices"[14] engaged in by multiple communities, embracing in the case of film not just moviegoers but also filmmakers and the larger film industry, including exhibitors, all articulating—or in some cases, simply assuming—their own sorts of "claims" about what constitutes sf, especially as those claims shift over time.

Given that constantly changing "set of practices," we should expect that the marketing or framing for such films might often produce a rather ambiguous memetic buzz, as we can see by considering the artwork attached to some of Universal's "Invisible Man" films, particularly those of 1933, 1940, and 1942. Broadly based on the 1897 novel by H. G. Wells, one of the foundational figures in the history of sf, these films were part of a consistently successful series whose basic premise—that once given invisibility, an individual might set loose or materialize normally repressed human impulses—clearly straddled the borders of horror and sf. The primary design features found in posters for the first film in the series, *The Invisible Man*, particularly emphasize that boundary issue. At the top of the frame the most common poster typically features a bandage-wrapped face with dark glasses and what appear to be beams of light coming from the glasses. In the center of the frame is the film's title and below it is a trio of figures suggesting the principal dynamic of the story—a frightened woman (Gloria Stuart), a strong-jawed man (William Harrigan) with his arms reaching protectively for the woman, and a scientist figure (Henry Travers) mixing chemicals in a test tube. On the face of it, the poster seems to suggest that scientific activity produces horrific effects. But advertisements for a later film in the series, *The Invisible Woman* (1940, A. Edward Sutherland, dir.), suggest little connection to the original *The Invisible Man*, much less to those same generic boundaries. Posters and lobby cards commonly feature, on one side of the frame, a silhouetted female figure, apparently scantily dressed, and raising a cocktail glass, with the title separating that figure from the featured actors arrayed on the right side of the frame—Virginia Bruce, John Barrymore, John Howard, Charlie Ruggles, and Oskar Homolka— and with three of the men smiling as they gaze on the shadow figure, apparently their imaginations pleasurably filling in what is supposedly "invisible." Adapting the basic element of scientifically induced invisibility to a wartime context, the later *Invisible*

2.1. Straddling the borders of generic practice in marketing *The Invisible Man* (1933). Universal Pictures.

Agent (1942, Edwin L. Marin, dir.) further shifts its discursive claims. The main posters commonly show a large, shadowy figure with arms held up in the background of the frame, with British bombers, parachutists, and multiple searchlights playing across the sky and dominating the middle, while the key characters, Allied agents played by Ilona Massey and Jon Hall and Axis operatives Sir Cedric Hardwicke and Peter Lorre, occupy opposing sides at the frame's base. There is no hint of the scientific or even the horrific at work in this obviously war-themed artwork that situates the "invisible man"—and his sf origins—in a nightmarish tangle.

I selected these three films for brief consideration, omitting other entries in this Universal series—*The Invisible Man Returns* (1940, Joe May, dir.), *The Invisible Man's Revenge* (1944, Ford Beebe, dir.), and *Abbott and Costello Meet the Invisible Man* (1951, Charles Lamont, dir.)—in part because they clearly sketch the range to which films in a supposedly sf series were pushed in these developing years of sf cinema, but also because they demonstrate how "historically situated" and flexible the imagery associated with sf narratives can be. While the images connected to the first film present it as a combination of sf (mixing chemicals), horror (the bandaged face), and melodrama (the implicitly threatened romantic relationship), the second moves in a very different, in fact pointedly humorous, direction, with its imagery suggesting a mixture of mystery (the shadowy woman) and ribald comedy (the upraised glass and leering male faces). The third film's images are largely divorced from those in the other two, with the primary emphasis—and one quite in keeping with wartime anxieties—on military conflict (the bombers and parachutists), with the shadowy figure seeming less a threat or attraction than an icon of humanity tangled within the web (crisscrossing searchlights, hands raised as if in surrender) of war. In any case, apart from the respective "invisible" figures, the main sf-inflected images—the chemicals and test tubes—ironically become *invisible* in promotions for the following films in what still proved to be a moderately successful series for Universal. The concept of chemically induced invisibility, admittedly difficult to evoke, sufficed as the studio attached this premise, this remembered meme, to a variety of narrative trajectories, including comedy. But lacking the sort of powerful or sufficiently evocative set of established sf memes, such as those that would, as Rieder suggests, gradually accrete or become more commonplace by the 1950s, these works, like others of the period, effectively drew on their multiple generic connections, primed by the studio's desire to speak to different potential viewers, by way of *partially* explaining their identities, but also with the hope of attracting multiple audience groups.

By the time that *The Thing* appeared, in early 1951, sf was just beginning to stake out a place as one of the more popular cinematic and televisual forms, and in the process it was accumulating several readily recognizable generic memes, such as rockets, robots, flying saucers, and various sorts of fantastic inventions, some of them already intruding into everyday postwar life. Late in that same year, for example, an early industry ad in *Motion Picture Daily* promoted the release of the new Columbia serial *Captain Video: Master of the Stratosphere* (December 14, 1951, 8), adapted from the popular television series *Captain Video and His Video Rangers* (1949–1955). It used the evocative images of a rocket and a ray gun, but mainly as framing elements for the central advertising image, which was of a customary, even expected *serial* event—a fistfight scene—thereby establishing its primary narrative claim as another exciting and action-packed chapter play, not remarkably different from many other adventure serials. And as part of the preview ballyhoo for a much more ambitious effort later that year, *The Day the Earth Stood Still* (1951, Robert Wise, dir.), 20th Century-Fox announced that it would exhibit the famed Westinghouse attraction from the 1939–1940 New York World's Fair, Electro the Moto-Man (along with his mechanical dog, Sparko), to greet audiences attending the film's New York premiere.[15] As a historically sanctioned, nostalgia-laden, yet also highly scientific construction, Electro lent *The Day the Earth Stood Still*—and, by extension, its featured robotic character, Gort—a kind of cultural respectability, even as it also drew on the sense of wonder that, as James and others argue, has always been central to the sf experience. Throughout the decade, these and other such iconic elements would increasingly become a regular part of viewers' expectations, helping attract an audience and frame in various ways its encounter with the large wave of sf texts that was starting to surge onto movie screens.

Prior to these and a few other films, though, there was very little specifically sf-oriented advertising in the postwar period, apart from the publicity surrounding the documentary-like independent production *Destination Moon*, which will be discussed in the following chapter. Moreover, as I previously noted, practically no conventional advertising for sf films made its way to what would seem the most likely place for such paratextual material,[16] as well as the one where film studios would most logically find a ready-made, even eager audience—the sf pulp magazines. Adding to that curious absence is the fact that other types of films were already being advertised there, and that the pulp readers were very familiar with the sorts of generic signposts we have observed. As further evidence of a felt connection between sf readers and popular film, I might note that during the prewar period, the pulp audience, in testimony to perceived links to a literary sf that had commonly been termed "scientifiction," often employed a similar label for cinematic sf, referring to it as "scientifilm."[17] And in response to numerous letters about why there were so few sf films, one of the leading pulps, *Wonder Stories*, had conducted a six-month campaign (December 1931–May 1932) asking readers to fill out petitions demanding that Hollywood produce "a reasonable number of Science Fiction movies" (December 1931, 904). That enthusiasm would only be ramped up in the early postwar period, which would see a steady run of letters to the pulps, such as one to *Thrilling Wonder Stories* that stated the obvious: "We numerous science fiction fans should be able to get some science fiction in motion pictures" (February 1948, 100).

Perhaps it might be argued that readers of "serious" sf would not have been interested in the exaggerated Hollywood treatment of the sf genre as it was entering into the postwar period, particularly since it was largely embodied in those action-oriented space opera serials such as *Brick Bradford* (1947), *King of the Rocket Men* (1949), *Flying Disc Man from Mars* (1950), and *Zombies of the Stratosphere* (1952). That Hollywood treatment, which continued well into the 1960s, would eventually inspire Susan Sontag's famous and somewhat dismissive description of most postwar sf films as at best offering "an inadequate response" to the times through their sensationalistic mining of an imagery of disaster and destruction.[18] However, the pulp audience was certainly cognizant of Hollywood's non-sf product, advertising for which had begun to appear in their magazines during the war years and would proliferate with full-page ads in the postwar era. The wealth of such full-page advertisements seems indicative of the film industry's efforts in this period to reach out to other, previously neglected audiences, especially with action-oriented, visually rich, and established formulas such as were offered by the western and the crime film. But if we are to judge by the sensationalistic, at times lurid, and frequently discussed covers for most of these magazines, the general run of pulp readership was also familiar with and would probably have been little troubled by the exaggerated treatment of those science fictional memes. The pulp magazine covers, especially those for *Thrilling Wonder Stories*, *Startling Stories*, and *Amazing Stories*, deployed the same sorts of rockets, robots, and action scenes—including constantly imperiled young women—that would surface in the movies, using them to build their readers' expectations, and thus similarly framing, for better or for worse, their experience of the stories that were to be found just beyond those pulp covers, and indeed priming readers to make their own discursive "claims" on sf.

Yet even with the obvious reader interest in cinematic versions of the popular literature of sf and a deep familiarity with the genre's iconic representations, an element of film industry hesitance was clearly at work here: *not* simply to cross to another medium but to actively market feature-length sf films, even to a pulp audience that understood the conventional visual language of sf. An extensive survey of the major prewar pulps reveals just one notable marketing effort in this direction, which at least reminds us that the film industry was aware of this ready sf audience. In 1940, Paramount Pictures collaborated with the pulp *Thrilling Wonder Stories* to publish an adaptation of its just-released mad scientist film *Dr. Cyclops* (Ernest B. Schoedsack, dir.), written by the popular author Henry Kuttner and illustrated with stills provided by Paramount, punctuating that partnership with the headlined injunction "Read It Now—Then See It at Your Local Theatre."[19] During the war years, as film clearly assumed the mantle of the most popular mass entertainment form, numerous ads started to appear in the sf magazines, and in the immediate postwar period, such advertising began to proliferate, but, curiously, always for non-sf works. For example, postwar issues of *Thrilling Wonder Stories* were freely sprinkled with full-page

WHAT IS THIS *THING?* — 37

2.2. Paramount and *Thrilling Wonder Stories* combine to cross-market *Dr. Cyclops* (1940).

ads for various movies, including the Republic B-westerns *Plainsman and the Lady* (1946, Joseph Kane, dir.) and *Wyoming* (1947, Joseph Kane, dir.), Columbia's release *Renegades* (1946, George Sherman, dir.), the Warner Bros./Mickey Rooney racing drama

The Big Wheel (1950, Edward Ludwig, dir.), the Paramount westerns *El Paso* (1949, Lewis R. Foster, dir.) and *Whispering Smith* (1948, Leslie Fenton, dir.), RKO's *Blood on the Moon* (1948, Robert Wise, dir.), and dual ads for the novel and film versions of David O. Selznick's production of *Duel in the Sun* (1946, King Vidor, dir.). Comparable ads would crop up in many other pulps, demonstrating that the film industry knew about these specialized magazines and also knew that their readers were a movie-conscious lot. Of course, these samples might also suggest one reason for the absence of sf ads in that period, since throughout the war and immediate postwar years there was hardly an abundance of films that could easily claim sf status, save for such features as the remake of *Dr. Jekyll and Mr. Hyde* (1941, Victor Fleming, dir.); *Man-Made Monster* (1941, George Waggner, dir.); the various "Invisible Man" films already mentioned; *The Perfect Woman* (1949, Bernard Knowles, dir.); and serials such as *The Monster and the Ape* (1945), *The Purple Monster Strikes* (1945), and those cited above. However, the prewar years, which had seen such notable genre efforts as *Just Imagine*, *The Invisible Man*, *Things to Come*, and *The Invisible Ray*, also saw no industry attempts to "frame," that is, market, these films for a pulp audience that was already pressing Hollywood for more "scientifilms," as the readers' columns so often attested.

The early postwar period did witness the appearance of several sf efforts that seemed practically designed for that audience, particularly two rather similar narratives focused on space exploration, *Destination Moon* and *Rocketship X-M* (1950, Kurt Neumann, dir.). These films were widely discussed in readers' letters to the various pulps, with particular emphasis placed on their realistic—or, in the case of *Rocketship X-M*, not so realistic—depictions of space flight and their treatment of the conditions that astronauts might encounter on the moon and Mars, respectively. In response to several letters commenting on the films, John W. Campbell Jr., *Astounding*'s editor and the author of "Who Goes There?," said he thought *Destination Moon* in particular would herald the start of a "new series of seriously, carefully handled science-fiction pictures" of the sort that sf fans had long been advocating. In support of that notion, *Astounding* had in July 1950 published an article by the noted sf author Robert A. Heinlein, on whose novel *Destination Moon* was based and who had worked on the script, detailing the film's painstaking efforts to accurately depict the nature of space travel.[20] A still from the film, showing a rocket landed on the moon, even provided the cover art for that issue. But though both films would be reviewed in several pulps and *Destination Moon* would be widely publicized elsewhere, and with a particular emphasis on its factual or "science" elements, neither film would be formally advertised in any of the sf magazines. That absence begs a question about whether it was the result of an oversight on the part of these films' distributors or was symptomatic of a larger issue the US film industry had with its approach to sf, perhaps, as I would suggest, an uncertainty about how to represent or label such films for best effect.

As I began by noting, *The Thing from Another World* is noteworthy because it would finally break with this pattern and shed some light on the film industry's marketing of sf. Studio-sponsored advertising appeared in several of the sf pulps, just as it did in a wide variety of other national publications throughout the months preceding the film's release. In fact, attached to some of the movie's ads that were placed in film industry publications such as *Motion Picture Daily*, *Film Bulletin*, and *Variety* was a notice indicating that they were part of a saturation marketing campaign, and that similar ads were being placed "in 58 National Magazines and 93 Sunday Newspaper Supplements totaling 185,761,000 circulation."[21] Among those placements were such big-circulation "slick" magazines as *Collier's* and *Redbook*—the latter of which even named *The Thing* its "Picture of the Month"—as well as various pulps, including *Thrilling Wonder Stories* and *Startling Stories*. But just as significant as this first placement in a sf pulp is the thrust of these notices, for regardless of venue they were all similar in style, were obviously created without a specifically sf audience in mind, and their approach markedly differed from that usually employed in popular genres of the period such as westerns, film noirs, and adventure narratives, whose advertisements typically featured familiar memes, such as guns, cars, imperiled women, and so on—in short, exciting imagery and familiar genre iconography. In fact, what is especially interesting about *The Thing*'s pre-release ads is how little they do show, as the various placements, whether aimed at exhibitors or potential moviegoers, gave few clues as to the nature of the film. Offered

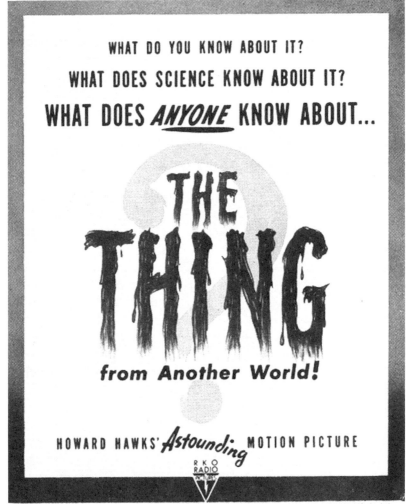

2.3. The mysterious ad type that fronted *The Thing*'s print media saturation campaign. RKO Pictures.

with only minimal graphics and billed in each typically quarter- or eighth-page spot as, for example, "Howard Hawks' *Amazing* Movie," "Howard Hawks' *Startling* Movie," or "Howard Hawks' *Astounding* Motion Picture," *The Thing* was presented as essentially an unknown subject, a mystery neatly bound up in its mysteriously allusive title.

But that sense of mystery, even a kind of generic evasiveness (underscored by the qualifier "*from Another World*" that always appeared in very small type) seems to have been a deliberate tactic on the part of the studio,[22] perhaps a way of coping with the not-yet-established status of sf as a high-profile genre or just an uncertainty about what sorts of discursive claims should or even *could* be made for the film or the genre. The approach was, in fact, part of a three-month marketing effort that *Film Bulletin*, in commenting on the campaign, described as a "terrific teaser build-up."[23] A contemporary article from the well-known gossip columnist Hedda Hopper further emphasizes this tactic. In a fan magazine piece offering her "predictions" for the top films of 1951, Hopper included a commentary noting that "the most hush-hush picture shooting in Hollywood right now is Howard Hawks' mysterious *The Thing*."[24] That sort of "gossip" notice is telling, not just for its omission of the tell-tale phrase "*from Another World*" but also for the way it carefully avoided revealing anything about either the film's plot or its generic identity, while also linking it primarily to its *producer's* (i.e., Hawks's) reputation for adventurous and exciting narratives.[25] At the same time, it situated the film within a larger context of *speculation*, as a *mystery* that even Hollywood insiders found intriguing and that Hopper might further investigate and comment on in future columns. Of course, her leading comment could well have been planted by RKO, with the studio using her popular column to further its unusual campaign, and doing so would hardly be a rare industry practice. In any case, other, more reliable film industry organs also followed this lead, similarly characterizing the production as cloaked in secrecy. Thus, under a headline about upcoming RKO releases—"RKO Will Have Mellers"—another *Film Bulletin* piece reported that "*The Thing* is being treated by RKO in an aura of deep mystery," while it provided little more background on the project other than describing it as "one of those pseudo-scientific melodramas."[26] After reading the piece, readers could be certain only that *The Thing*, whatever its subject, was one of a number of forthcoming RKO "mellers" (melodramas) and that the studio itself seemed to be taking a rather meller-dramatic approach to publicizing the film.

Another industry report represented the film in a slightly different way, in fact, in a trumpeting fashion that might have seemed almost at odds with Hopper's "hush-hush" comment. A *Motion Picture Daily* article reported that RKO had decided to include *The Thing*, along with two other independent productions, *Tokyo File 212* (1951, Dorrell and Stuart E. McGowan, dirs.) and *Jungle Headhunters* (1951, Julian Lesser, prod.), in a group of "exploitation special" releases for which the studio planned "extensive campaigns based on maximum use of publicity, advertising, and local showmanship."[27] Similarly, *Film Bulletin*, while giving away nothing of the plot, described the upcoming film as an "exploitation natural" for exhibitors.[28] While "exploitation" in this period was a general marketing term, with each of the major studios typically having its own exploitation department and a head of exploitation (for RKO at this time it was Terry Turner), the term did, for many, immediately suggest a rather loud, brassy, and high-profile treatment for the film, or what I have termed "ballyhoo." In fact, the famed exploitation filmmaker William Castle characterized this approach as follows: "Gimmicks, surprise, shock—that's what draws the crowds."[29] But perhaps more precisely, as Bradley Schauer describes the practice in this period, exploitation usually involved "playing up the more sensationalistic qualities of a genre,"[30] an approach that was rapidly becoming associated with low-budget films, provocative subjects, and the output of smaller studios, in effect forming almost a category in itself, although again usually relying on an *emphasis* on salient genre characteristics, thereby allowing the studio to make the sorts of deliberate, if often somewhat exaggerated, discursive claims that audiences would most readily recognize. Some Hollywood studios later in the decade, such as American International Pictures, would not only survive but prosper almost solely on the basis of these low-budget, heavily exploited films (bearing titles such as *Night of the Blood Beast* [1958, Bernard L. Kowalski, dir.] and *The Brain Eaters* [1958, Bruno VeSota, dir.]) that, as the executive Samuel Z. Arkoff admitted, heavily depended on "a sensational approach" to advertising "to lure customers to the box office."[31] But for a major studio like RKO, the exploitation approach was a bit less common, although it did speak to the need to address the financial problems that had resulted from Howard Hughes's mismanagement of the company.

I would suggest that the problem RKO faced correlates with that curious absence of advertising in the sf pulps that I began

2.4. The military and scientists prepare to extract the mysterious "thing" buried in ice and snow in *The Thing* (1951). RKO Pictures.

by noting. In the early postwar period, the larger and more prestigious Hollywood studios simply approached sf with some caution, in part because they had little experience with it, but also because of its excessive or sensationalistic associations in the industry and, as Schauer suggests, in the public consciousness as well.[32] To some, it seemed to evoke that realm of "gimmicks, surprise, shock" that Castle was describing and to suggest not an aura of prestige but one of simple sensationalism. That thinking helps explain why many of the independent producers and small studios of a fragmenting Hollywood might gravitate to this sort of material — a point only underscored by the surprising successes of those first two independent sf productions, *Destination Moon* and *Rocketship X-M*. But on initial consideration, running ads in the sf pulps, with their tradition of wildly colored and often sexually suggestive covers, might also have seemed a risky association, at least more chancy than placing notices in the usual slick magazines.

The route that RKO eventually charted for its marketing of *The Thing* proved to be an effective if rhetorically complicated one, although it is also one that we can still see later traces of when exploiteer Terry Turner left RKO and turned his talents to marketing sf pictures for other studios. That strategy avoided staking a specific claim for a genre, and it also resulted in what I have described as an effective "teaser" campaign. The promotion involved a consistent emphasis *not* on the usual genre memes of the sorts that were just beginning to make their way into some sf advertising—those soon-to-be ubiquitous rockets, ray guns, and robots—but precisely on a general sense of *ambiguity* surrounding the film's plot and type, an ambiguity that, as the industry comments cited here suggest, was being carefully cultivated by RKO. This emphasis was also abetted by various other marketing strategies: special midnight premieres in key large-market cities that drew on the aura of mystery or secrecy typically attached to such late-night showings; a studio-sponsored contest seeking new ideas from exhibitors and offering a $1,500 prize "for the best exploitation" effort they might devise;[33] and especially a series of similarly designed and visually low-key ads that, as already noted, were placed in a wide variety of national magazines and newspapers. All were designed to provoke both industry and audience interest while revealing as little as possible about the film, effectively "unframing" it, at least in any conventional sense.

It is an approach that seems perfectly consonant with *The Thing*'s own narrative about a mysterious crash near an Arctic research station. Unsure of who or what crashed in this frozen wasteland, the air force sends a plane with a detachment to investigate but also to keep things "hush-hush," particularly since, as we learn, Russians "have been nosing around" the area. When the group discovers what looks like a mysterious aircraft frozen in a lake of ice, they attempt to remove it but succeed only in destroying the vehicle, freeing its alien occupant, and prompting a confused buzz of communications, as both air force headquarters and the press demand to know more. Unsure what to make of their "find" and, thanks to a storm, losing all communications with the outside world, the military group tries to maintain secrecy until finally, after defeating the literally blood-thirsty alien, they send out a message of warning, alerting people everywhere to "watch the skies, keep watching." It is almost difficult not to see in this narrative the outlines of the film's marketing approach, from uncertainty about what to make of this "thing" (both movie and creature), to a general pattern of secrecy as plans are made for dealing with it or revealing its nature, to a sensationalistic release of information, accompanied by an injunction—to moviegoers everywhere—to "keep watching." For if RKO played this mystery properly, the hope was that viewers would look for similar vehicles, other movies in this same exciting, if generically still undefined brand.

But the nature of the studio promotions merits some special attention, particularly since it was precisely the mysterious ad type that had made its way to the sf pulps and their specialized readership. Drawing on a survey of various popular magazines, industry publications, and sf pulps, I have identified nine variations on a basic pattern in the ad campaign leading up to the April release of *The Thing*, all nine of which were subsequently repeated as background on the cover of the film's pressbook.[34] None of them follows the usual advertising practice of employing representative images from the film, depicting its stars in carefully posed shots, or even offering the sort of exaggerated or lurid imagery noted above, any one of which might well have been the feature of a conventional exploitation campaign or typical ballyhoo. Especially noteworthy is that none frames *The Thing* specifically as sf. Instead, the ads in this campaign, including those that appeared in *Thrilling Wonder Stories* and *Startling Stories*, other genre pulps such as *Exciting Western* and *New Love*, film industry papers such as *The Film Bulletin* and *Motion Picture Daily*, and various slick magazines (including unlikely venues such as the women's magazine *Redbook*), are all remarkably plain and, compared to most other US film advertising of the period, relatively understated. Each consists of a white box with a dark frame, inside of which most offer a variation on a simple query, one that RKO must have hoped would be on the minds of potential viewers and perhaps exhibitors as well: "What Is *The Thing*?" One ad, for example, simply poses a series of leading questions: "Where Did It Come From? How Did It Get Here? What Is It?" A second adds a darker tone to those questions about the ambiguous "It," asking "Is It Human or Inhuman? Natural or Supernatural? Will It Destroy Us All?" And a third more directly addresses the audience's relationship to this now vaguely named enigma, asking "What Do You Know about It? What Does Science Know about It? What Does *Anyone* Know about *The Thing*?" This group of ads with their teaser questions piques curiosity, hints of an element of danger, but otherwise does little to frame a specific sort of experience that the film is supposed to offer audiences or to suggest links to other films to which viewers might readily compare it.

Another set of variations on this box ad replaces the questions with images that help visualize the general aura of mystery surrounding the film. One of these shows a crowd of people all staring to one side, as if startled, at an off-frame spot where the "thing" is presumably located; a similar version offers a group of fur-clad Eskimos also gazing off-frame, as a caption identifies them as "the first people in the World to see *The Thing*"; a third depicts a child in a highchair looking off in wonder, while a legend ominously observes that, because of "the thing," "her life can be counted in seconds"; and a last version shows a map with an arrow vaguely pointing to the Arctic, indicating "the spot where *The Thing* was first seen." In each instance of this variation, the "thing" is simply a point of reference, an absence marked by directed looks or an arrow, but an absence that, as the child's image especially suggests, is freighted with menace. Apart from that hint of a threat, though, this group of notices provides no more identifying information, and once again employs no generic icons of any sort, as it strikes a note of the unusual and of possible jeopardy—a bit like the strange tail structure that is depicted rising ominously from a circular pool of ice in the film's discovery sequence, while suggesting something ominous hidden beneath.

Finally, a third ad variety, apparently the last in a chronological release of these promotions, emphasizes possible responses to this unseen figure. One ad depicts a lab-coated scientist type looking toward the reader and announcing, "We must destroy it or it will destroy us!" Another, more dynamic entry in this type shows a pistol firing through the film's title, accompanied by the message, "You Can't Kill *The Thing* with a Gun!" And like the other versions of the box ad, neither of these depicts a moment from the film, much less provides a clue as to its generic nature, although the word "science" and the lab-coated figure appearing in one of the pieces and the shooting gun in the other certainly serve as vague hints, perhaps recalling such earlier films as *Frankenstein*, *The Invisible Man*, or *The Man They Could Not Hang* (1939, Nick Grinde, dir.), all frequently linked as much to the horror genre as to sf.

WHAT IS THIS *THING*? — 47

2.5. *The Thing*'s ad campaign offers a vague clue to its generic associations: a lab-coated scientist.

However, none of these variations on the basic box ad provides any iconic identifiers to dispel the mystery posed by the limited and vaguely allusive wording. In fact, the only graphic in one of the ads is a large question mark. For the most part, these studio placements treat the film subject as a figure of absence: the *missing* image or visual complement to various off-screen glances. A group of people staring off, a child looking to the side, a few fur-clad indigenous people gazing into the distance are all explicitly visual mysteries, telling us almost nothing about either subject or genre, although one version includes a faint sketch of a thin figure looming in the deep background behind the title—a shadowy menace. The only more substantial clues to the film's nature might be inferred from the rest of the movie's title, "*from Another World*," which, as noted, was printed in small type, or perhaps from the ads' use throughout the series of what are often referred to as "fur" letters for the title, a graphic practice commonly associated with the horror genre. When, after the film's premiere, RKO offered a larger, two-page variation on these ads, it effectively amplified this element for exploitation purposes. These larger spreads appeared in several trade publications, including *Variety*, *Motion Picture Daily*, and *Box Office*, and were pointedly aimed at potential exhibitors. Once again omitting any tell-tale images, they maintained that vague mystery/horror nexus—and emphasized the exploitation angle—by printing "*The Thing*" in red letters dripping blood within an otherwise plain white rectangle, while announcing that "The Thing That's Doing the Business Is *The Thing*." In light of these efforts, it seems almost appropriate that *Motion Picture Daily* praised the effectiveness of the "horror-type campaigns" RKO was waging for its new exploitation efforts.[35]

With no major stars involved in the film (a point noted in several contemporary reviews), a neophyte director (Christian Nyby), and few precedents for effectively exploiting examples of sf, RKO had clearly decided to build its national campaign in an unusual yet telling way: not around a sf genre that was still only vaguely developed in audiences' minds and often associated with cheap serials, but around *absence*, the sense of mystery evoked by the film's title, and vague associations with something more familiar—thus those hints of horror. And possibly thanks to the film's early box-office success, that approach would linger. For weeks after its premiere, the Criterion Theatre in New York sustained that mysterious atmosphere by placing in various publications small box ads containing no graphics at all, just a repetition of the fundamental question "What Is *The Thing*?," along with a notation that the film was continuing its run at the theater. Ad models provided in the film's pressbook also promoted a continuation of this teaser strategy, most of them offering slightly more detailed visualizations of "*The Thing*" title, accompanied with variations of the original campaign's questions, such as "How Did It Get Here?" or "Natural or Supernatural?" Of course, after the film's initial aura of mystery had dissipated, and particularly as the film became widely reviewed, passed through its period of exhibition "clearance," and moved into smaller, neighborhood theaters,[36] many subsequent venues would turn to more detailed advertising, even though most of these notices made little additional effort to draw out the film's sf associations. These more conventional ads, now clearly aimed at moviegoers rather than theater owners, showed close-ups of the leading cast members, Margaret Sheridan and Kenneth Tobey, reacting to an out-of-frame menace—another point of absence; some added a background image of the head and hands of "the thing" as portrayed by James Arness; and others superimposed a question over a close-up of Margaret Sheridan's frightened face, asking, "Can She Escape the Thing?" But in these cases as well, the film is represented not in a sf vein, without even a hint of the alien invasion or flying saucer motifs central to its plot; rather, it is presented in older, more familiar contexts, as if it were a mystery or horror film (evidenced by the query "Supernatural?"), that is, using the same scant generic identifiers that would eventually surface in reports on the film in such publications as *Motion Picture Daily* and *Film Daily*, which, in keeping with the original campaign, often referred to it as a "mystery" picture or even, as one exhibitor struggled to describe it, a "suspense fantasy."[37]

Of course, by this time, sf was starting to become a more familiar part of the media and cultural landscape, building other associations besides those of the more lurid pulp or serial film variety. In addition to the various sf films cited earlier, numerous comic strips and comic books, radio dramas, and the suddenly popular television space operas of the early 1950s—*Captain Video, Space Patrol,* and *Tom Corbett, Space Cadet* especially—were all starting

2.6. Mixing mystery with suggestions of horror and the supernatural in a trade magazine notice for *The Thing from Another World*.

to demonstrate that there was an enthusiastic, if perhaps heavily juvenile, sf audience that was interested in such texts. Moreover, in its plot, *The Thing* effectively bound together a variety of the newly popular sf genre tropes: the flying saucer, the isolated scientific station and scientists, an alien invader, the rugged military protagonist, even a cool, strong woman, most of which would increasingly be imported into films throughout the decade. But using these tropes at the beginning of this decade, even to address the sf audience of *Thrilling Wonder Stories* and *Startling Stories*, must have seemed a difficult move for a big studio of the period, almost none of which had so far ventured into science fictional waters. And for RKO, a studio that, given its difficult financial situation, needed to cast its net more broadly without also alienating a traditional audience, relying on the new "buzz" of sf must have seemed especially chancy.

As this campaign might begin to suggest, then, even though sf was, by this time, beginning to outgrow its many early and confusing generic titles—as earlier noted, well into the 1940s it was variously referred to as scientifiction, scientific romance, pseudo-scientific stories, science fantasy, and other labels—it had apparently not yet found a secure place in the consciousness of the film industry, which would continue, at least for a period, to employ other tactics for representing it: folding sf into a variety of older, established categories, such as horror, mystery, or suspense; linking it, at least for exhibitors, to something new and effects oriented, such as the exploitation film; or simply keeping the generic associations indistinct, even intriguingly absent. On the one hand, this insistent blurring or shifting of categories reminds us that the film industry in general might have had only a vague sense of what sf was, echoing those shifting ways in which sf authors, editors, and fans also referred to the form, and affirming John W. Campbell's own opinion that "science-fiction is the freest, least formalized of any literary medium."[38] On the other hand, it underscores how, for the American film industry, genre often functioned as what Rick Altman terms "the temporary by-product of an ongoing process" of categorization, a process that allowed Hollywood films to attract "diverse demographic groups"[39] by deliberately mixing associations while that process was unfolding, as the genre, by means of increasing audience familiarity, recognition, and expectation, gradually built its frame from icons, events, and attitudes that were becoming more popular, even meaningful, within the larger culture. Certainly, the industry would capitalize on this process approach for other sf films in the decade, even after sf had become more identifiable and was producing big business—as is evidenced by a work like *Invasion of the Body Snatchers*, the mystery and noir elements of which were frequently played up. As in the case of *The Thing*, that intentional blurring offered a distinct advantage for a carefully managed publicity campaign, since it could be deployed across a wide range of venues, including, as noted, a high-class "slick" like *Collier's*, a fan magazine such as *Modern Screen*, and even a most unlikely pulp venue such as the romance magazine *New Love*.

The film's advertising simply took advantage of the generic ambiguity that was clustered around sf and that coincided with a general Hollywood practice of pointing effectively in a variety of directions during the "process" of genre building. Moreover, by framing—or unframing—the film with a series of interrogations, such as "Where Did It Come From?," "How Did It Get Here?," "What Is It?," the studio's marketing was able to respond to any curiosity about sf cinema by posing just the sorts of questions that the audience, as well as exhibitors, might have been asking about this as-yet-unproven player in the cinematic marketplace. "Where," after all, did this relatively new type of film "Come From," and what was it going to offer us? At the same time, those ads were also linking sf to the new industrial conditions of the movie industry, wherein exploitation was quickly forming another, equally ambiguous category through which all sorts of films might be "framed" and sold to an audience, one that, with a Cold War heating up, was dealing with a great many other uncertainties and fears felt about modern culture for which no one film formula might yet be able to offer an adequate or at least somewhat soothing response.

Reflecting on *The Thing*, the French director Jacques Rivette once offered a similarly reflexive suggestion, noting that one of the film's central thematic concerns is, in fact, this very issue of categorization on which I have focused. With this perspective in mind, he summed up the plot as being about how "some men of science are at grips with a creature worse than inhuman, a creature *from another world*; and their efforts are directed toward fitting it into the logical framework of human knowledge" so that they might better understand it.[40] While his description seems to address only the scientists in the film, not the military figures who play a central role in the narrative as they fight for their—and explicitly *our*—lives against this invader accidentally freed from the arctic ice, his point is a useful critical one as well. For if we take Rivette's vantage a step further, we might view the film's monster as symptomatic of a problem that at this time was confronting the film industry and even the general viewing public: that of whether sf constituted a distinct genre or was some monstrous hybrid that might prove challenging to develop or to market.

The Thing simply points to a general uncertainty in the industry about the sf genre: how it might appeal, what it might convey to audiences, and especially how it might be sold to them. Like the isolated humans at *The Thing*'s arctic research outpost, both the industry and the public were facing a challenge to the usual efforts to place this movie and its genre—along with its rather shifty "bundle" of elements—into a "logical framework." The prior absence of sf advertising aimed at the seemingly primed audience of the sf pulps, which I began by noting, only spotlights this issue. However, the still-new system of sf would soon overcome such uncertainty and even become ubiquitous, largely because, as the genre process further developed, it increasingly seemed to offer audiences help in coming to grips with the new challenging and threatening world of science and technology, a world that, as Sontag recognized early on, was repeatedly projecting a Cold War–inspired and science-supported round of "collective nightmares" about the very fragility of the human order.[41] But at this early point represented by *The Thing*, sf was still a type of narrative that resisted easy categorization; refused, just like the film's monstrous figure, to be frozen in form (or ice); and instead insisted for its part on an ongoing process of genre formation, one that would gradually earn sf a prominent role in postwar culture and eventually lead to its recognition as an almost indispensable player in contemporary cinema.

CHAPTER 3

PONDERING THE "PULP PARADOX"

Pal, Paramount, and the SF Market

While science fiction (sf) cinema was exploding in the 1950s, this development, as observed, posed several problems for the US film industry. With little in the way of a tradition of sf filmmaking and with many in the audience and the film industry often associating sf with the horror film, the serial, a sensationalistic pulp literature, or even the comics, the major movie studios had few models for effectively marketing the genre with their traditional paratexts. In fact, in the previous chapter I suggested that at least one reason the large Hollywood studios initially hesitated to produce sf, even as it was attracting viewers on television with space operas like *Captain Video* and *Space Patrol* and more adult-oriented anthology shows such as *Out There* (1951–1952) and *Tales of Tomorrow* (1951–1953), was this ongoing uncertainty about how to frame the genre for a wide audience. The big studios, already weakened by the Supreme Court's Paramount decision of 1948, faced what Bradley Schauer has described as a "pulp paradox," that is, the impression that although "playing up the more sensational qualities of a genre like SF" could attract new customers, it might also produce a "cultural fallout" and potential market loss if audiences linked the studio's product with the "less reputable variations of a genre," like the sort of material that was often, if also unfairly, associated with the sf pulp magazines.[1] The result was a fluctuating pattern throughout the 1950s as the major studios alternately "embraced, selectively adopted, or rejected outright" many of the generic elements that were just starting to make their way into the cinema.[2] While Schauer's account accurately describes the general attitude toward sf throughout the period, it omits the specific film industry strategies that developed for negotiating this situation, including the equally paradoxical possibility of both embracing *and* dodging some of those generic elements, even if doing so ironically meant revealing some of film's *own* pulpish potential.

John Rieder, as noted earlier, has speculated that we can glimpse traces of such strategies in one of the most visible of those paratextual elements, "the commercial advertisement," which constituted a kind of fingerprint for the "mass cultural genre system."[3] In this chapter, I examine a very specific effort to address that "pulp paradox" not simply in advertising but in the larger marketing approach employed by the industry. The producer George Pal, along with Paramount Pictures, sponsored a series of commissioned essays to help promote a string of sf releases in the early to mid-1950s, a period when the sf film would see its greatest success. Strategically placed in *Astounding Science Fiction*, ironically one of those very pulp magazines that supposedly prompted industry concerns about the genre's acceptability, these pieces were designed to attract an audience that was obviously already invested in sf narratives and, as many readers' letters underscored, even eager to see the promise of sf realized on the big screen. Yet while serving as targeted publicity, even as disguised ads for the Pal/Paramount films, these pieces highlight an element of irony that attached to the studio's efforts to counter that pulp-related "paradox."

Before examining this element of sf's framing, though, I need to clarify two components of the pulp-film relationship. The first is that the general reputation often cited for the sf pulp magazines was, even in the 1930s, largely unwarranted and probably due less to the nature of the pulp fiction than to the way *it* was framed, that is, literally within magazine covers that even regular readers of the pulps at times both resisted and embraced. Those covers by such artists as Frank R. Paul, Howard Brown, Hans Wesso, Earle K. Bergey, and Margaret Brundage were designed to attract eyes—and purchases—at newsstands, which they quite successfully did through their colorful, exaggerated, and frequently sexually suggestive elements: muscular heroes, rushing

3.1. A typical 1940s pulp cover from *Super Science Stories* depicts the "eternal triangle" of man, woman, and monster.

rockets, strangely figured aliens, partially clad and often imperiled women, and even, when contributed by women illustrators such as Brundage, "strong and sexy amazons."[4] While drawing many admiring fan letters, often asking for more of the same or even a chance to buy the original artwork, the covers also embarrassed some purchasers, leading to comments like that from one *Planet Stories* reader who lambasted the magazine for its "lurid and stereotyped covers"[5] or a purchaser of *Amazing Stories* who confessed that he "felt like hiding the lurid cover of the magazine while walking down the street."[6]

However, the fiction between those covers was usually of another character, especially as a clear division between a hard and soft sf began to emerge. Certainly, the purely fantastic space operas, or what Edward James simply describes as stories of "preposterous galaxy-spanning adventures,"[7] continued to be published, often containing the sort of sexual titillation that was also commonplace in many other sorts of war and postwar narratives, while working distinctive variations on what Paul A. Carter describes as "the Eternal Triangle" of early sf: "the man, the woman, and the monster."[8] However, it was also clear that the pulps were increasingly intent on pursuing the trajectories being laid out by current scientific advances and theories and were more often giving a technological thrust to sf's characteristic sense of wonder. In fact, many pulp readers sought out the more scientifically oriented stories, prided themselves on their own scientific interests (as their letters often attested), and would take both writers and artists to task for any technical gaffes, while many editors, most notably *Astounding*'s John W. Campbell Jr., famously insisted on scientific accuracy and plausibility in their magazines' stories. In short, pulp sf, particularly by the early 1950s, was hardly the sort of disreputable material Schauer's description, or possibly film industry attitudes, might suggest. The term "pulp"—both then and now, it seems—was simply a convenient, if also a bit outmoded, way of designating something as cheap or sensationalistic.

A second clarification is historical, as I should note that prior to its bankruptcy in 1933 and the imposition of the industry Production Code in 1934 with its cautions about "repellent subjects"[9] ("The Motion Picture Production Code"), Paramount had already made several forays into the genre with such hybrid sf-horror efforts as *Dr. Jekyll and Mr. Hyde* (1931, Rouben Mamoulian, dir.) and *Island of Lost Souls* (1932, Erle C. Kenton, dir.). As I observed in the previous chapter, when the studio again sought to try its hand at sf, Paramount partnered with those very pulps to help publicize its *Dr. Cyclops*. As *Variety* reported at the time, the studio was "dissatisfied with the publicity and exploitation results" for several other recent fantasy releases, most notably the animated *Gulliver's Travels* (1939, Max Fleischer, dir.), and so hired an outside group, the Tom Fizdale Agency, to develop new exploitation efforts.[10] These efforts would be particularly important for *Dr. Cyclops*, since it was the first sf feature to be shot in expensive three-strip Technicolor, a sure sign that it was both a prestige effort and one in which the studio was heavily invested. The resulting campaign did not bill the film specifically as sf; in fact, trade publicity commonly referred to it as an "exploitation" film, while reviewers variously described it as a "horror film," a "trick picture," a "thriller," and in one case a "pseudo-scientific study."[11] However, that campaign did add a new dimension to its marketing by placing a novelization of the film in *Thrilling Wonder Stories* and even furnishing publicity stills to illustrate the story and to provide a model for one of those "thrilling" covers for which the pulps were so well known. But to emphasize the serious or "hard science" elements of the story, adaptor Henry Kuttner, who had been invited to preview the film, offered a personal endorsement of *Dr. Cyclops* and its technical achievements, terming it a picture that "points the way to the movies of the future, in which the triumph of the technicians will be even more apparent."[12]

Paramount executives were apparently pleased with the general promotional campaign for *Dr. Cyclops*, since the film earned approximately $1.8 million, and, as *Variety* reported, following this "test publicity-exploitation job," the studio rewarded the Fizdale Agency with "a yearly pact to work on all of its films."[13] However, no similar joint efforts with the pulps followed in the 1940s, perhaps because sf itself—apart from the serials—was mostly absent from the screens in this period. And while the 1950s saw a rising audience interest in the genre, heralded in part by the upstart television medium's early investment in sf, the major studios were, as I have noted, initially reluctant to exploit that interest, at least until the independent producer

George Pal—previously best known for his critically acclaimed Puppetoon animation, which Paramount distributed—helped demonstrate a strategy for addressing sf's pulp associations with the campaign for his landmark feature *Destination Moon*, a picture often credited with jump-starting the sf film boom of the 1950s. That campaign, coordinated between the independent producer Pal and his distributor Eagle-Lion Films, was multi-pronged and had a distinctly scientific emphasis. It placed prerelease articles detailing the film's scientific concerns and technical effects in a variety of popular and well-respected publications, including *Life, Parade, Popular Science, Popular Mechanics*, and the *New York Times Magazine*. It did a mass mailing to a 23,000-name list, acquired from the prestigious Hayden Planetarium, of people who, after recently visiting the Planetarium, had expressed an interest in space exploration, with Eagle-Lion inviting them to see the film for free.[14] It had Pal do a variety of appearances and interviews both about the film and about generating what he predicted would be "hefty box office in the months to come."[15] And after the film's successful release, its marketing campaign would be discussed in the trade papers as an exemplary effort, with *Variety* observing how "every conceivable angle in the film—the unusual theme, the production values, the scientific approach, the entertainment inherent in probing the unknown—was trumpeted far and wide to a receptive film going public."[16]

But though it broadcast the scientific credentials of the film in a wide variety of regular venues, Pal's campaign also reached out to the sf pulps, this time in the form of a background article written by the noted sf author Robert Heinlein, illustrated with stills from the film, and featured in what was at the time the most respected—and certainly least lurid—of those magazines, *Astounding Science Fiction*. Accompanied by a cover illustration taken from the film, Heinlein's piece offered a behind-the-scenes account of the making of *Destination Moon*, as seen through the eyes of one of the film's coauthors. As letters to the editor indicated, it was well received by that audience, and it would provide the model for a new sort of sf ballyhoo. When Paramount once more returned to the genre and signed Pal to produce a group of films in the *Destination Moon* vein—*When Worlds Collide* (1951, Rudolph Maté, dir.), *The War of the Worlds*, and *Conquest of Space* (1955, Byron Haskin, dir.)—it accompanied them with a series

3.2. *Astounding Science Fiction* helps publicize *Destination Moon* (1950) with a special cover.

of similar "backstage" publicity/marketing efforts that trace the rapidly shifting attitudes toward sf in this period.

The first entry in this publicity series, "Shooting 'Destination Moon,'" is especially significant because Heinlein was already one of the most important and respected sf writers of the postwar years, while also being intimately tied to the creation of *Destination Moon*. As a cowriter and a technical adviser for the film, he was able to draw on his own experience—and authority—to describe to the pulp audience how the movie industry went about dealing with standard sf concerns, such as rocketry, space flight, and planetary exploration. Perhaps taking his lead from the many earlier letters written to the various pulps complaining about Hollywood's hesitance to take up sf as a major genre, he focused his comments not on the sorts of plots that the film industry might profitably draw from the literature but on what he saw as the major hurdles "to producing an accurate and convincing sf picture."[17] These included "finding someone willing to risk the money" on sf writers and their unusual "ideas"; overcoming "the *technical* difficulties of filming a spaceship picture," that is, of using the best available technology to present space science in an accurate way; and especially dealing with "the 'Hollywood' frame of mind," by which he meant the "people in authority who either don't know or don't care about scientific correctness and plausibility," much less the genre itself.[18] But Heinlein also lauded those involved in making *Destination Moon* who, he suggested, *did* care, especially the producer Pal, the director Irving Pichel, the well-known space artist Chesley Bonestell Jr., and, echoing Kuttner's comment of a decade before, the various "technicians" who had "triumphed" in creating "movie magic." Still, Heinlein identified two hurdles that he believed might block any major outpouring of sf features in the coming years, as he described the difficult and lengthy production schedule that this film involved and his own realization—one quickly shared by the Paramount executives—that "realism is confoundedly expensive."[19]

Those points about the production of sf films contribute to a two-pronged *educational* thrust that characterizes Heinlein's piece and most obviously differentiates it from traditional Hollywood ballyhoo. On the one hand, Heinlein emphasizes how much *he* had learned as someone new to the world of film, as he personally witnessed all "the planning and effort" that is required from everyone involved to produce a truly "realistic" space picture.[20] However, putting in that much effort—as he confesses, it "cost me eighteen months work, my peace of mind, and almost all of my remaining hair"—resulted in what he describes as a picture that "was as accurate as budget and ingenuity would permit."[21] In effect, Heinlein provides his own up-close experience of *Destination Moon*'s accomplishment as a "triumph of the technicians," while forecasting that this status should result in a strong possibility for "box office success"[22] and would open the door to the production of more sf films. On the other hand, and in keeping with the pulp readership's general skepticism about Hollywood and its frequent tendency toward exploitation and excess, he suggests that the movie industry was also in the midst of an education process, as its executives were just beginning to learn what was most important to fans of the genre—not "thrills," shocks, or lurid imagery, the supposed stock-in-trade of many pulps, but, he claimed, "scientific correctness and plausibility."[23] And the success of a sf film, he argued, should derive from the film's very distance from those pulpish expectations that many of the studios and some audiences of the period seemed automatically to link to the very idea of sf. It is a point that would echo in the *Variety* review of *Destination Moon*, which described the film as "a novelty," "a highly technical space travel subject that can be ballyhooed to stout grosses," and one that might even spawn "a new interplanetary film cycle."[24]

Given the success of *Destination Moon*—both financial and critical—as well as Pal's subsequent contracting with Paramount Pictures to produce those follow-up sf efforts, it is hardly surprising that the studio's first postwar foray into the genre would take a similar approach, largely following the marketing pattern described above, including a partnership with the pulps. While far more invested in "thrills" and visual spectacle than *Destination Moon*, Pal's 1951 production *When Worlds Collide* would largely adhere to the stricture of "scientific correctness and plausibility" that Heinlein had emphasized. Detailing the use of an Ark-like rocket to help a select group of Earth's population escape an impending world-destroying asteroid collision, the film would be the subject of an elaborate publicity campaign that again predominantly emphasized its scientific and technical dimensions. In fact, the campaign included a much-publicized mobile educational display that showcased the science of rocketry to high school students,[25] a piece on the upcoming release placed in slick magazines such as *Redbook* and *Popular Science*, a photo-essay in *Life* that contrasted serious or "philosophically pregnant" sf films—such as *When Worlds Collide*—with a new wave of "incredibly moronic" or pulpish efforts being prepared by other studios,[26] and a series of previews and special screenings for what the studio referred to as various "interested groups" in scientific and educational fields.[27] At the same time, it incorporated another outreach to hardcore sf fandom in the shape of a second article in *Astounding*. Just as telling about how the studio sought to frame the film and differentiate it from competing genre efforts, all of these moves were described in *Motion Picture Daily* as part of a new initiative that Paramount had announced for that year, "the placing of emphasis on quality pictures" rather than "exploitation" efforts.[28]

This second "making of" piece closely followed the tactics of the first, as it came from an equally solid, reassuringly scientific source, the noted astronomer R. S. Richardson, who was also a respected sf author (often writing under the pseudonym Philip Latham). His article "Making Worlds Collide" begins by echoing a point made in the Heinlein essay, that the film industry was not only becoming more receptive to sf but also showing an increased concern with technical accuracy in its genre pictures. As Richardson notes, "scarcely a week goes by without some studio calling up for information on the inner workings of an observatory or how long it takes to determine the orbit of a new asteroid or comet."[29] Like the *Destination Moon* piece, his essay was also illustrated with a number of production stills courtesy of Paramount Pictures, and it was even accompanied by an editorial endorsement from John W. Campbell Jr., in which he noted that the magazine would be "cooperating to the fullest with Paramount in promoting" the film (November 1951, 114). Although that cooperation went little further than allowing Paramount to place a full-page ad for the film in the December issue of *Astounding*, the ad would prove far less sensationalistic than those that Paramount typically placed in the popular press. Otherwise, Richardson's article struck many of the same notes as Heinlein's essay, recalling the impressive artwork and sets he observed while visiting the studio, detailing the complex

3.3. Paramount places one of its more "restrained" ads for *When Worlds Collide* in *Astounding* (December 1951).

and time-consuming technical elements involved in making this apocalyptic story, and also stressing the same budgetary imperatives that Heinlein had observed. Perhaps more significantly, as he emphasized those economic issues, Richardson would also sound a cautionary note. Based on his observations, he felt that because of the cost involved in an effects-heavy production such as *When Worlds Collide*, "if you insist upon strict scientific accuracy, then the picture could never have been made at all."[30]

Still, much of his essay managed a similarly educational tone as Heinlein's, and it, too, emphasized that the key to attracting the true sf fan was a commitment to scientific and technical correctness. Thus, early in the piece, Richardson explains his own criteria for judging a sf film, noting that for the film to be effective, "the science must be authentic, the characters and situations convincing, and the trick stuff done with careful attention to detail. There is no critic so hostile as the amateur scientist hot on the trail of a technical error."[31] That light-hearted jab at the over-zealous sf fan and the dismissive remark about "trick stuff" notwithstanding, Richardson, for much of the article, describes how these concerns were mostly shared and discussed by the main creative figures involved in the project. To that end, and again following Heinlein's lead, he gives special credit to the space artist Chesley Bonestell, the director Rudolph Maté, and the producer Pal, all of whom, he felt, played key roles in creating a film with solid sf appeal, mainly because all were dedicated to creating an accurate look and plausibly presenting how humans might escape a doomed Earth by rocket. Moreover, the last third of the essay has Richardson interviewing Pal, who recalls how his sons had prompted his interest in sf, emphasizes his own passion for getting the technical details right, and expresses his belief that such an effort will appeal not just to sf fans but to a wider, increasingly space-conscious popular audience that wants to know more about the subject. Such a response, he underscored, should also allow him to bring similar stories, which he was already preparing, to the public.[32]

The modest box-office success of this film,[33] along with *Destination Moon*, did indeed allow Pal to undertake another sf effort as part of his multipicture deal with Paramount, as he set about producing the legendary sf tale *The War of the Worlds*. Paramount had owned the film rights to the H. G. Wells story since 1925 and had even done some preproduction work for a version in the early 1930s,[34] but the studio finally decided to greenlight its production at this time because of the reception of Pal's previous genre efforts, along with the recent sf successes of various other studios, most notably *The Thing* and 20th Century-Fox's *The Day the Earth Stood Still* (both 1951). While many of these entries were of the B-film variety—and here I might note how this same time saw a truly pulpy sf cinema begin to flourish, as embodied in such films as *Abbott and Costello Go to Mars* (1953, Charles Lamont, dir.), *Cat-Women of the Moon* (1953, Arthur Hilton, dir.), *Phantom from Space* (1953, W. Lee Wilder, dir.), and *Robot Monster* (1953, Phil Tucker, dir.)—their appearance suggested that there was indeed a wider audience for such works. To ensure the success of *War of the Worlds*, Pal and Paramount would follow the broad marketing pattern used in the previous efforts. In advance of its release, various scientifically and technically oriented articles were placed in several slick magazines, typically emphasizing the science involved in the film, as in the case of a *Popular Science* piece on the "engineering" of Martian flying saucers,[35] and an article in the film industry newspaper *Variety* touted a specific scientific application of the film: its use, never fully described, within an investigative program by Dr. Mason Rose of the National Foundation for Psychological Research for "the testing of emotional and psychological responses of individuals" to film narratives.[36] In contrast to these relatively low-key and by-now-expected science-oriented notices, the studio, which at this point had become heavily invested in the television industry,[37] also added another dimension to its marketing approach, creating a television blitz that emphasized a different sort of technical "triumph," some of the movie's more sensational special effects scenes, especially those of the destruction caused by the depicted Martian invasion. But in a development that reveals much about the mixed tone this campaign would adopt, several television stations actually refused to run Paramount's trailers, claiming that the sensationalistic images used in the ads, including the representation of an atomic bomb explosion and scenes of humans being incinerated by a Martian heat ray, "would scare children" in the television audience.[38]

As part of its *War of the Worlds* campaign, Paramount again approached its previous pulp partner *Astounding* with another "making of" essay, but this one provided even more of an insider's view. It was authored by Pal himself (or perhaps "ghosted" by a Paramount writer) and offered a rather different take on Kuttner's "triumph of the technicians." The longest of these marketing pieces, it begins with Pal remarking proudly on the current "vogue for films of a science-fiction nature," a development that he took credit for helping to initiate and one, he offers, that explains why he was able to resurrect the Wells story after it had languished in the Paramount archives for so long.[39] But rather than emphasizing this project's scientific accuracy—admittedly a difficult task, given the story's sensational nature about a Martian invasion and the cultural baggage it carried thanks to Orson Welles's infamous 1938 Halloween radio broadcast—Pal took a different tack, describing the film as "the end result of technical feats that any laboratory man can appreciate,"[40] as he translated the notion of technical accuracy into something different, the special effects that were required to bring this tale to the screen, and heavily emphasized the cost that those effects added to this and to other sf projects. In an effort to link these "technical feats" to the earlier emphases on accuracy in scientific depictions, Pal reminded his readers that "realism is earned; it doesn't just happen,"[41] and he offered evidence to support that notion: comparing this film's much larger budget to that of his previous and far more modest sf productions; describing the long production schedule, particularly the eight months of special effects and optical work that followed just a month of regular cast shooting; and providing five production stills that show the building of elaborate models, set construction, and other behind-the-scenes film activities that, he says, attest to the "infinite pains with details" and attendant studio costs that were required to create the spectacular illusion of an alien invasion with all the destruction attending it, including that simulation of an atomic explosion.[42] At the close of this piece, though, Pal would pull back a bit from his emphasis on these exaggerated visual "feats" to credit a name that, at this point, had found special value within the sf community, the space artist and technical adviser Chesley Bonestell, who had worked on his previous films and did several matte and glass paintings for the opening scenes of *War of the Worlds* and, as Pal vaguely offered, "kept us on the right track" throughout the production.[43]

That "track," however, seemed somewhat less sure in this

PONDERING THE "PULP PARADOX" — 69

3.4. A lobby card plays up the sensationalistic aspects of Paramount's *War of the Worlds* (1953).

case, despite the highly favorable critical reception, a *Variety*-reported box office of approximately $2 million, and an Academy Award. While the review in the *New York Times* described the film as "an imaginatively conceived, professionally turned adventure,"[44] it clearly left many viewers less than satisfied, particularly in depicting both science and the atomic bomb as simply ineffectual against the attacking Martians—who were obviously Cold War stand-ins for the Soviets. One sign of that response is the reported gross, which, as Keith Williams notes, actually just covered the film's nearly $2 million production cost, with much of the budget attributed to its elaborate special effects.[45] And though *War of the Worlds* received an Academy Award for its special effects, I might note that it was the only nominee for that year. So, while nominally a success in the vein of both *Destination Moon* and *When Worlds Collide*, Pal's latest effort, even when accompanied by a great deal of traditional ballyhoo, including a two-page advertisement in *Motion Picture Herald* that touted Paramount's "nationwide" television campaign in support of the picture (August 22, 24–25), proved less successful than anticipated and sent very mixed signals to the studio.

However, at the end of his *Astounding* piece on the making of *War of the Worlds*, Pal announced that he was already preparing another sf production for Paramount, again one with a respected genre pedigree. This film would be an adaptation of the 1949 Willy Ley and Chesley Bonestell book speculating on the future of space travel, *Conquest of Space*. Prior to its premiere, the film would also receive much play in the popular press, especially when Pal announced that, due to its highly scientific focus, it was going to be featured at the Rotterdam International Exposition of 1955, which would take "the theme of the film"—space exploration—"as its motif."[46] However, such a plan never transpired; in fact, despite Pal's announcement, no such exposition occurred in 1955.[47] Still, in keeping with the approach demonstrated with *Destination Moon* and *When Worlds Collide*, a similarly serious, even scientific appeal was emphasized in much of the film's advance publicity. One of the advance articles in the film's pressbook emphasized that it might be presented to prospective viewers as a "science-fact film." Another was a series of comments by the noted rocket pioneer and technical adviser Wernher von Braun wherein he describes *Conquest of Space* as "an accurate preview of the adventures man will encounter" in space,[48] and a *Motion Picture Herald* piece advised exhibitors to market the film as a "visualization of science as it shapes up for the future" and to place some of the film's advertising "away from" regular film notices so as to attract "other readers than the usual."[49]

At the same time, though, and more in the fashion of *The War of the Worlds* and the flood of lower-budget sf movies that were starting to dominate the market by the mid-1950s, *Conquest of Space* would receive what another *Motion Picture Herald* notice described as "a saturation TV spot barrage."[50] This campaign extended beyond the typically sensationalistic and scientifically questionable trailers that appeared just prior to the film's debut. Rather, Pal himself, along with some cast members, made several national television appearances to promote the film. In at least one such appearance—and in a series of publicity releases—he was paired with the actress Joan Shawlee, who plays the minor character Rosie McCann in the film. In these TV spots, she was billed not as her film character, the unfaithful fiancée of an

PONDERING THE "PULP PARADOX" — 71

3.5. Joan Shawlee poses as "Space Girl" in an effort to promote the science-factual *Conquest of Space* (1955).

astronaut, but as "Space Girl," wearing a tiger-striped leotard with wire antennae perched atop her head, as she and Pal demonstrated a variety of what were referred to as "space gimmicks" that were featured in the film.[51] Pushing further in what might well be termed a "pulpish" direction, one publicity still even depicted Shawlee in this same "space" outfit seemingly flying across the New York City skyline like Superman. Such ballyhoo clearly ran afoul of the "science-fact" approach planned for some of the other publicity and reframed the film more pointedly in an exploitation vein, as did a multipage advertising insert, also in *Motion Picture Herald*, that described the film not as sf but as Pal's new "thriller." Moreover, due to what was termed an overly "suggestive sequence"—in fact, there are two such sequences in the film, one with Joan Shawlee—the Catholic Legion of Decency determined that the film was "morally objectionable" in character, thereby limiting its potential audience.[52] Of course, even including such a sequence in a film about space travel is itself a troubling sign, strangely akin to that earlier pattern of lurid covers on some of the pulps, and it suggested that both Pal and Paramount were probably uncertain how best to attract customers to *Conquest of Space*.

In this instance, too, though, the campaign was accompanied by another, if somewhat cursory, outreach to the pulps, with the May 1955 issue of *Astounding* featuring a cover image taken from the film and offering a brief production piece about *Conquest of Space* that might be read as part of an effort to balance the film's strangely disparate marketing efforts. But instead of another lengthy "making of" article or interview, this effort was just three pages of illustrations that might be viewed as symptomatic of the magazine's (and perhaps editor Campbell's) flagging interest in recent and increasingly over-the-top cinematic sf, as well as a hint of Paramount's own shifting interests. Slightly more than an elaborate announcement of the Pal film's forthcoming release, this unattributed photo-essay consisted of four Paramount-provided publicity stills, accompanied by brief descriptions of the content of each image. The first again suggests the concern with scientific accuracy that each of the previous articles had underscored in various ways, as it depicts Pal, director Byron Haskin, Bonestell, and Ley apparently in conference about the picture. A second is focused more on the film's "technical feats"—or, as Pal had increasingly come to characterize them, special effects—as it shows the three "principal props" or models used in *Conquest of Space*, a rocket, a circular space station or "wheel," and a Mars space plane—all versions of concepts that had originally been outlined in Bonestell and Ley's book. A third publicity still places viewers inside the narrative, as it depicts astronauts being transferred from the space station to the ship that will take them to Mars via a "space taxi." And the fourth provides the exciting payoff for a narrative that is, we are told, largely "speculation,"[53] as it illustrates a landing on Mars by the curious vehicle visualized for this expedition: a *winged* aircraft for landing on a planet with a minimal atmosphere. As the unnamed author of the captions offers, the hope is that these illustrations would demonstrate how Pal's latest sf effort is "as close to the facts-as-they-are-believed-to-be as possible, with a minimum of story-plot hokum."[54] However, it is also obviously a perfunctory piece, tantalizing with special effects images, hinting at the inevitable "story-plot hokum" of which there is plenty in this film—including a mission commander who suddenly decides that space exploration is an affront to the divine and tries to sabotage his own project—while again holding out hope that the movie will prove to be the sort of "financial success" that will encourage the production of yet more "carefully worked out presentations of science-futures."[55]

Unfortunately, *Conquest of Space* did not meet with the same success as any of the previous Pal productions, either critically or financially,[56] and it did not encourage Paramount to undertake additional sf films, at least in this period when sf, if cheaply done and ambitiously promoted, generally seemed to be attracting an audience. Rather, for the rest of the decade, Paramount largely pulled back from the genre, or at least from the sort of scientifically inclined films championed by Heinlein and Richardson, with the studio mainly serving as a distributor for low-budget independent productions that were more obviously in an exploitation vein, such as *The Colossus of New York* (1958, Eugène Lourié, dir.) and *The Space Children* (1958, Jack Arnold, dir.), both presented as part of double-feature bills.[57] The weak response to *Conquest of Space* was also partly responsible for the nonrenewal of Pal's studio contract. Part of the problem the film faced was obviously its "story-plot hokum"; as Bill Warren observes, it went through four quite different treatments, some of them stretching the bounds of believability, as various scriptwriters tried to wring an exciting narrative out of a largely factual book.[58] Still, it had the benefit of a big studio's resources, including its special effects expertise, and the guidance of many of the same people—Pal, Ley, Bonestell, and Haskin—who had proven to be a successful team on *War of the Worlds*. But Warren also points to the effects of "a bad advertising campaign," one that, he argues, might have overly stressed the film's "realism," leading audiences to expect "a documentary."[59] But as the previous description of the film's marketing, including that done through *Astounding*, should begin to suggest, the key issue was probably *not* its factual pretensions, which seemed to address at least a segment of the serious sf audience and which exhibitors were advised to address separately from their regular ads for the film, but rather the very *mixed* messages the overall marketing campaign sent out. Framing the film in a highly ambiguous way, as we can see even in the photo-essay intended for the pulp audience, the studio sought to sell simultaneously the film's technical credentials *and* its sensationalistic character, to describe, in effect, a film without a consistent identity, neither the sort of strict scientific account Heinlein had recommended nor a pure exploitation vehicle of the sort that would mark Paramount's few subsequent sf efforts in the decade.

Of course, the advertising features done especially for the pulp audience should have already hinted at this difficulty. Seeking to draw in the hard-core sf enthusiasts, along with the typical moviegoers who had begun to demonstrate an interest in the genre, both Pal and Paramount reached out to the pulp magazine that had the highest reputation; recruited writers who were trusted by that magazine audience (Heinlein, Richardson); and repeatedly invoked others who were respected within the sf community, such as Bonestell and Ley, the latter of whom was already writing a regular column on science for *Galaxy Science Fiction* magazine. The publicity pieces that resulted repeatedly lauded the "technicians" involved in crafting these films, as well as the time and money that had been lavished on their production. And, certainly, both Pal and Paramount occupied respected positions in the American film industry, the former as an award-winning animator and the latter as one of the powerful Big Five movie studios. Yet over the course of these pieces we see that emphasis on technology, technicians, and budgets being recharacterized, shifting into a marketing focus not so much on the films' scientific and technical accuracy but on how the movie industry was coming to interpret such technological work, that is, largely in terms of a film's exploitable character, especially its sensational special effects—building elaborate models, crafting aliens and alien worlds, producing exciting spectacles marked by explosions and destruction—all bound within the constraints of time and budget that were the hallmarks of a contracting Hollywood.

At the same time, and because of the rapidly changing nature of the American film industry and its advertising practices, such films increasingly tended to be framed within another "technical" context, that is, by using the new medium of television. Paramount at this time owned several television stations, as well as a share in the Dumont television network, and must have realized that television advertising worked in a very different way than any targeted magazine placements; it was simply more immediate, kinetic, and exciting. George Pal's sequential endeavors, on the one hand to write a thoughtful piece for the pulp audience and on the other to do sexy television spots with his "space girl" Joan Shawlee, only underscore the different, difficult, even contradictory propositions he faced in trying to sell the sf film in an era that was also, as Susan Sontag put it, quickly coming to embrace "the imagination of disaster," a sensibility readily on display in the many low-budget efforts that had begun to dominate the sf market and to be featured in the sensational television promotions for those films.

The efforts centered on the Pal and Paramount films, though, can help us gain a more nuanced sense of the difficult task of promoting sf in this period, as well as of what Bradley Schauer terms the "pulp paradox" confronting the film industry. Facing a rising popular interest in sf, when the movie industry was in the midst of a radical reshaping, large Hollywood studios like Paramount cautiously weighed and sought to address that new interest, even to the point of drawing in and on the established, if still somewhat suspect, sf pulp magazines whose readership might at least provide an easily targeted, specialized audience. While their initial efforts in this vein took something of a high road (or the "hard sf" road), emphasizing science, technical expertise, and the big budgets wielded by the studios, those promotions were gradually overshadowed by an emphasis on another side of technology, on the spectacle that could be produced by Hollywood special effects, accompanied by the usual ballyhoo of film exploitation, especially as television came into play, providing not just competition in the area of sf, with its cheaply done yet highly popular space operas of the era, but other avenues for exploitation, and

3.6. Paramount's late version of the "eternal triangle" of man, woman, and monster in *I Married a Monster from Outer Space* (1958). Paramount Pictures.

certainly avenues that were being explored and exploited by various small studios and independent filmmakers.

What the promotion pieces in *Astounding* might point to, then, is *another* sort of "pulp paradox" at work in Hollywood during the burgeoning of a popular sf cinema, one in which film studios like Paramount, as well as the various independents through which they would increasingly come to work, paradoxically became the real purveyors of sensationalism, exaggeration, and even lurid suggestion, that is, of some of those very characteristics that had previously been negatively associated with the sf pulps and that the studios were supposedly trying to avoid. In fact, I might note that the only other (indeed, the last) Paramount-produced sf film of the decade was another low-budget effort with the obviously exploitative—and often mocked—title *I Married a Monster from Outer Space* (1958, Gene Fowler Jr., dir.). So while the sf pulps, popular opinion notwithstanding, provided Pal and Paramount's sf entries with a rather sober and respectfully scientific stage for their promotion, these pieces for *Astounding* also point out how the film industry increasingly—and ironically—took what might well be described as a pulp turn, as American sf filmmakers progressively bent their technical prowess to tales of monstrous mutations, predatory aliens, and an aesthetics of destruction, that is, as our sf movies, at least for a time, *became* the very pulps from which they were supposedly trying to distance themselves.

CHAPTER 4

MOPPETS AND ROBOTS
MGM Markets Forbidden Planet

In the middle of the 1950s, *Variety* took stock of the market for sf films and announced that despite the "heavy rush of product of this type" during the first half of the decade, "the trend" for sf had finally "died down."[1] The Pal-Paramount films notwithstanding, the majority of that early "rush" comprised films that had been low cost, aimed at what seemed to be an emerging sf fandom, and had often proved to be profitable. It had been a generally effective industry formula, but as Bradley Schauer observes, though these early sf films were typically "quite successful in their initial weeks of release, their box office numbers quickly trailed off" as they played out to what seemed a "relatively small but fervent audience."[2] Despite the *Variety* forecast and this growing sense that the sf audience was fairly limited, a "new round" of sf productions soon followed, with mid-major studios Universal, United Artists, and Columbia publicizing ambitious genre plans for 1956, all of them including sf projects. Not to be left behind, the most prestigious of Hollywood filmmakers, MGM, announced its own first foray into the genre since 1941's *Dr. Jekyll and Mr. Hyde*, indicating that its slate of 1956 releases would include a sf "high-budgeter," *Forbidden Planet*.[3] It was an announcement that might have seemed somewhat out of character for the Dore Schary regime at MGM. He had assumed the role of vice president of production with a plan to produce "more timely and less costly films"—a plan that, the studio explained, would emphasize current cultural concerns and "more economical genres like the crime thriller and romantic comedy."[4] However, Schary was also known for following his "instincts" and taking a chance on projects that were "different," not necessarily in line with the studio's past production history,[5] such as the feminist western *Westward the Women* (1951, William A. Wellman, dir.) and the juvenile delinquency drama *Blackboard Jungle* (1955, Richard Brooks, dir.). We might see *Forbidden Planet* (1956, Fred M. Wilcox, dir.) as another one of those chancy efforts.

Taking that gamble would lead MGM not only to tackle a very different sort of narrative than the studio was accustomed to but also to try identifying and appealing to a diverse and, hopefully, more than a small audience. Although the studio had never before dealt with narratives about space travel and discovery, it did have some of the most extensive resources to draw on to tell this story about a rescue mission to the planet Altair IV, searching for survivors of an earlier colonizing expedition. Creating the sets and massive matte paintings to depict that distant planet would take up more than 98,000 square feet of the largest sound stages at MGM.[6] On Altair IV, the rescuers would encounter the complex character of Robby the Robot, servant to the expedition's survivors. Built by the studio's design and electrical experts, Robby was described in the film's pressbook as "the most amazing mechanical genius ever created for films."[7] And the rescue party would have to battle an invisible and seemingly invulnerable monster, created through the technology of a long-dead but highly advanced civilization and evoked with the aid of animation from the Walt Disney Studio. Not just a different sort of narrative, *Forbidden Planet* was obviously a complex, ambitious, and potentially costly effort that seemed to reach beyond the realms of most other media sf of the day.

Of course, MGM was well known not for the sorts of lower-cost films or programmers that typified much sf production of the period but for elaborate and sophisticated efforts such as this one promised to be. Typical of the studio's elaborate films were its extravagant and highly successful musicals, which it knew well how to market and which had largely been quite successful. However, MGM had almost no experience with sf, and its move into this segment of the market coincided with a difficult moment for the entire film industry: with overall attendance down; with the largest studios finally complying with the Supreme Court's Paramount decision (necessitating that they sell off their theater holdings); with television an increasingly powerful competitor; and with sf, as the *Variety* notice indicated, becoming a more unpredictable type to market. To counter these difficulties, MGM would approach *Forbidden Planet*—a film that Schary described as very "different" from others of its type, because "it had a different slant and a different villain"[8]—with a vigorous effort at both audience identification and cross-media marketing strategies. However, the result would prove to be a confusing array of what Jonathan Gray has described as the "frames and filters" of promotion that at times seemed to work at cross purposes, addressing multiple, distinct audiences, suggesting different sorts of story appeals, and ultimately reminding us that such "paratexts create texts"—in this case, that they effectively shape how audiences view sf.[9] In the case of *Forbidden Planet*, as will be seen, MGM's efforts conspired to produce a text about its own confusion, in part about the nature of the sf genre, but also about the audience for that genre and how best to reach it.

While the industry, as noted, often saw sf as a lower-budget or "B" type of film, MGM, one of the oldest and most prestigious studios, was challenging that perception much as Paramount seemed to do with the Pal productions. However, its initial approach was not just to allocate a bigger budget, despite the obviously higher costs associated with the genre's inevitable special effects work. In fact, the initial budget for *Forbidden Planet* was relatively modest, with Frederick Clarke and Steve Rubin reporting that it "was well under a million dollars, the dividing line which separated it from the first class A productions at the studio."[10] However, that budgetary line was quickly crossed, in part precisely because, as the art director Arthur Lonergan suggests, *Forbidden Planet* represented "a new kind of picture" for the studio, and "they didn't have any precedent as to how much it would cost" to do properly.[11] Consequently, the budget quickly grew, with the art department head Cedric Gibbons and the special effects chief Arnold Gillespie committing, according to Lonergan, to "design the picture the way it *should* be done, regardless of the damn budget."[12] Another issue Lonergan notes was that MGM's construction department "exceeded their budget on every set" as they tried to craft a realistic look for the futuristic story and its alien planet.[13] But perhaps most significant is the fact that Schary himself took an increasing interest in this unusual and progressively costly production. Curious about why the production was moving slowly and how the budget was being spent, he began visiting the sets during shooting, grew more "fascinated with what they were doing," and eventually okayed more spending for the project. Thus Schary recalls telling the production executive Joseph Cohn, "We've got something very good, just give them the money, transfer the funds."[14] Whatever the reason (or reasons), these efforts resulted in the higher-than-expected cost of more than $1.9 million (nearly double the original estimate), thereby prompting MGM's prerelease recharacterization of it as a "high-budgeter,"[15] which would also require increased attention on how to market the film most effectively.

More than just an unexpectedly flexible budget (or unfamiliarity with the needs of sf), the film also benefited from all the other resources that marked MGM as one of the largest and most powerful film companies. Thus, even though *Forbidden Planet*'s adventurous plot offered some echoes of television's early space operas with their predominantly juvenile appeal, there was little visual resemblance to those small-screen relatives, and that difference would certainly be an asset in marketing the picture. In place of television's cheaply done and rushed productions, often using cardboard sets and crudely fashioned backdrops, the MGM film included the extensive sets previously noted and one of the most expensive props in film history, Robby the Robot. Additionally, the film was shot in CinemaScope and Eastmancolor, providing audiences with the sorts of spectacular images unavailable on their small black-and-white television sets; it starred one of the studio's prestige actors, Walter Pidgeon; it offered the first entirely electronic soundtrack, created by Louis and Bebe Barron; it imported, at much expense, a top Disney animator, Josh Meador,[16] to supplement the studio's special effects department in designing and animating the film's menace, dubbed the "monster from the Id"; and it claimed a high literary pedigree, as it drew on Shakespeare's *The Tempest* for the broad outline of its plot. Fittingly, an MGM press release, cited in *Film Bulletin*, heralded the upcoming film as "the biggest outer-space picture ever made."[17] In short, *Forbidden Planet* represented the sort of product that readily distinguished itself from both television's numerous efforts in this vein and the many "B" sf films being offered by other film companies, while also living up to

4.1. The expensive "look" of *Forbidden Planet* (1956) seen in the underground remains of the Krell civilization. MGM Studios.

the studio's reputation for quality, emphasized in its motto: "Ars Gratia Artis" ("Art for Art's Sake").

However, by the middle of the 1950s, several of the other big-studio, big-budget efforts of this sort were already suggesting the accuracy of *Variety*'s warning about the waning sf "trend." As noted previously, Paramount's *War of the Worlds* and *Conquest of Space*, along with 20th Century-Fox's *On the Threshold of Space* (1956, Robert D. Webb, dir.), had all either just broken even or proved to be box-office duds. The other major studios—which were practically the only sources for those larger budgets—were beginning to suspect that regardless of the genre's early success on television, sf films were not only a different but a more difficult proposition and that, as Thomas Doherty argues, high-cost, adult oriented sf films were simply "not cost-efficient investments."[18] As Schauer observes, despite their appeal to a faithful fan base and "despite the studios' best efforts," such films most often "failed to cross over to a more general adult audience," and that pattern, he adds, was largely because of a "dominant SF paradigm, rooted in the juvenile fantasy of pulp SF"—the sort of fantasy that the television space operas had so easily and successfully tapped in marketing primarily to children.[19] And yet, there had also been a number of box-office winners, with even some of the larger studios managing to turn a strong profit from very modestly budgeted—if also a bit pulpish—sf productions, as in the cases of Warner Brothers' *Beast from 20,000 Fathoms* (1953, Eugène Lourié, dir.) and *Them!* (1954, Gordon Douglas, dir.), Columbia's *It Came from Beneath the Sea* (1955, Robert Gordon, dir.), and Universal's *This Island Earth* (1955, Joseph M. Newman, dir.). Moreover, Disney's first and far more expensive entry into the sf market, *20,000 Leagues Under the Sea* (1954, Richard Fleischer, dir.), had been the second-highest-grossing film the year it premiered. But that "juvenile" perception of the sf audience, evidenced even in the Disney effort, would have a significant impact on the marketing of sf in this period, particularly that of *Forbidden Planet*.

With *Forbidden Planet*, that imagined audience would converge with the film's marketing program in one of the most discussed marketing campaigns of the period, as MGM sales head Charles Reagan and vice president Howard Dietz took an initial approach that seemed, at least on its surface, to reach out to both adults and children. This key part of the ballyhoo surrounding the film's release was an ad campaign that involved a partnership between MGM and one of America's most established brands, the Quaker Oats Company. In fact, Quaker Oats had long been a leader in product marketing, even developing the sort of ballyhoo that would come to be largely identified with the movie industry. As Arthur F. Marquette chronicles, the company "pioneered scientific endorsements, customer testimonials, cash-prize contests, sampling, market testing, giveaways, and boxtop premiums."[20] It had even offered certificates for land in the Yukon as part of its sponsorship of the television series *Sergeant Preston of the Yukon* (1955–1958)—a particularly extreme bit of ballyhoo that MGM would eventually mimic for *Forbidden Planet*.[21] Among Quaker's many other coupon giveaways were tableware, model planes, and crystal radios, and its promotional department had built a long-standing relationship with the movie industry, as demonstrated by its frequent paid endorsements from film celebrities, including Ralph Bellamy, George Brent, Bing Crosby, Anita Louise, Ida Lupino, and Shirley Temple,[22] all part of the company's efforts to draw both children and their parents to the breakfast table to enjoy the company's cereals.

The film-marketing campaign that resulted was itself much ballyhooed, with *Motion Picture Herald* describing it as "one of the most unique and elaborate proposals ever presented in a nationwide program to encourage people to 'go out to the movies.'"[23] With this program, Quaker Oats and MGM teamed up to offer free passes to two of the movie studio's forthcoming releases, one, the fantasy-comedy starring Lucille Ball and Desi Arnaz, *Forever, Darling* (1956, Alexander Hall, dir.), and the other, *Forbidden Planet*. Hoping to use "the pressure of children . . . to bring their parents" to the theaters, as the *Herald* article explained, the campaign provided a free pass to children under twelve, when they were accompanied by an adult patron, to see either of these two studio offerings.[24] Placed in 80 million Quaker Oats cereal boxes, the free ticket offer did come with a few provisions. In addition to the requirement of an accompanying paid adult admission and a limit of one child per coupon, the advertisement noted that some theaters might not honor this offer on their peak attendance days: Saturdays, Sundays, and holidays. However, MGM also publicized in the trade papers the fact that, several months prior to the two films' premieres, it had already forged agreements with fifty-seven "leading theatre circuits" to participate in this potentially massive promotional effort.[25]

Moreover, the promises MGM made to the film's potential exhibitors—both those chains that had agreed to participate and others, especially independent theater owners—were impressive. A two-page advertising spread that ran in *Motion Picture Daily* (January 4, 1956) and other trade papers described the campaign as a "sensational and unprecedented national tie-in" that would supplement the studio's usual promotional work with an estimated $400,000 effort by the cereal company, mobilizing Quaker Oats' "staff of 75 merchandising men and 485 salesmen" to generate publicity and place promotional materials in 7,500 grocery stores nationwide, including "spectacular" cardboard versions of the movie's central sf attraction, Robby the Robot. Among the many other promises linked to the forthcoming "national saturation" campaign, MGM announced that full-page national ads would be placed in *Look* magazine, where they might reach as many as 19.5 million readers; a four-color ad would appear in 124 Sunday newspapers with an estimated 100 million readers; Sunday supplement pieces would go out to 101 newspapers with 7.5 million readers; 10 weeks of plugs would appear on the Quaker Oats-sponsored *Sergeant Preston of the Yukon* series, reaching a

86 — SELLING SCIENCE FICTION CINEMA

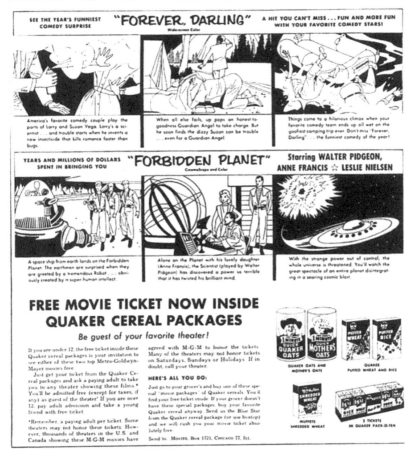

4.2. Poster for the Quaker Oats–MGM promotional campaign.

projected 15 million viewers; 500 Mutual radio stations would include spots on their program *Here's Hollywood* that could be heard by an estimated 962,000 listeners; and 88 national newspapers would run a second round of ads in Sunday comics sections that would be seen by as many as 85 million readers. In addition, the MGM saturation campaign announced placements in a host of other major magazines with varied readerships, including *Good Housekeeping*, *True Story*, *McCall's*, *Woman's Home Companion*, *Parents' Magazine*, *Redbook*, *Seventeen*, and *TV Guide*, as well as smaller-circulation publications aimed at a specialized audience, such as *Boys' Life*, the official magazine of the Boy Scouts of America, the February 1956 issue of which included a feature write-up on *Forbidden Planet* as a "Movie of the Month." This wide array of efforts seemed a sure bet to draw both children and parents not only to the table but to all theaters screening the MGM film.

In his study of Hollywood ballyhoo, Mark Thomas McGee claims that motion picture "exhibitors loved this sort of co-op advertising," arguing that "a few inexpensive children's tickets were a small price to pay for the kind of exposure their attraction received."[26] And indeed several industry papers spotlighted the campaign as an imaginative and effective gimmick that could prove beneficial to the entire film industry by demonstrating the value of such product tie-ins. *Film Bulletin*, for example, predicted that, at a time when the family trade was down, the "co-op promotion" would prove an effective device for "bringing the kids and, resultantly, the family into the theatres," with "moviegoing stimulation being the big payoff" of the campaign.[27] And *Motion Picture Herald*'s "On the Horizon" column described the promotion in similar fashion, as a "better-than-common measuring stick for computing the attendance potential of a straight family appeal" picture, predicting that "if it works out only fractionally as well as expected, the fiscal horizon shall have been brightened for exhibitors of all kinds and sizes."[28] Amid a tightening market for film exhibition and with fewer films in release, a campaign involving, as *Film Bulletin* observed, "no payment to any of the parties"—MGM, Quaker Oats, or the theater owners—seemed like it might be a popular and praiseworthy bit of marketing strategy.

But despite all of this promise, the trade papers tell a different story about exhibitor reactions to this highly touted part of *Forbidden Planet*'s marketing. In fact, there is evidence of considerable pushback from the film exhibitors, with several associations complaining loudly about MGM forcing this promotion on them. Exhibitor groups from Indiana, New Jersey, and Ohio were especially voluble in their protests against the arrangement.

4.3. Appealing to exhibitors with a two-page trade paper ad (*Motion Picture Herald*) for *Forbidden Planet*.

In the *Film Bulletin*, for example, a report from the Allied Theatre Owners of Indiana complained about the potential "embarrassment" to those exhibitors who had not agreed to be part of this offer if they were to turn down a family trying to redeem a coupon, and also about the sense of "proprietorship" that MGM, as well as Quaker Oats, seemed to be exercising in giving away not a "few" theater seats but potentially millions, noting that "they get the advertising and you [theater owners] get the privilege of admitting youngsters free."[29] Despite efforts by MGM, including a "personal appearance" by Robby the Robot at the Cleveland convention of the National Association of Film Service Organizations and at another exhibitor meeting in Chicago, similar complaints came from the Independent Theatre Owners of Ohio, who claimed that any exhibitor who "may not wish to go along, is practically compelled to do so . . . because he is put on the spot with the public."[30] Perhaps more telling for perceptions of the sf product was the ironic tone of a comment posed by an official of another exhibitors' group who wondered "how the prestige of great movies must be enhanced by making them cheap premiums in a 20c box of breakfast cereal."[31]

Of course, the main thrust of these and other complaints was not just the giveaway tie-in with Quaker Oats, but also the exhibitors' relationship with MGM (and other major film studios). The advertising connection did, after all, promise to capitalize on the efforts of the cereal company's considerable and long-proven marketing unit. However, there was clearly an undercurrent of resentment over how big studios like MGM had historically treated independent theater owners and the smaller theatrical circuits, as a representative of the Independent Theatre Owners of Ohio suggested in complaining that "the film company is usurping yet another right from the theatre."[32] Despite MGM's claims, most of those theater owners apparently had not been consulted about the marketing arrangement, and many felt that, given current distribution policies, they would never see the real benefit of the initial saturation campaign, even though they would still be pressured to honor the free ticket giveaway. In a pointed complaint about the long-standing pattern of film distribution that gave preferential treatment to studio-owned theaters and the larger theater chains, allowing them to get top films first, the head of Allied Theatre Owners of New Jersey explained, "under the present clearance and runs situation," a film such as *Forbidden Planet* "would not be available to suburban theatres for at least 10 weeks following first-run exhibition in the state."[33] By that point, the touted publicity efforts would have long since run their course. The campaign thus caused some strained relations and long-standing resentments to surface that were increasingly troubling the American film industry, while also, by association, dampening the enthusiasm with which some exhibitors greeted this "different" sort of sf film.

But besides these exhibitor protests, MGM had a more fundamental problem with promoting *Forbidden Planet* and, more generally, sf. One industry commentary noted the obvious: that the aim of the campaign was to leverage "the pressure of children" to draw audiences to the film.[34] In fact, that point could hardly be missed in light of the rhetoric that was used in the various marketing pieces. Numerous trade press reports repeatedly referred to the film's intended audience as "kids," "moppets," and "junior," while the basic version of the tie-in ad that was to be placed in newspapers, magazines, and supermarkets almost seemed to shout to its intended audience with the headline:

"Kids! See Top MGM Movies Free!" And even apart from the promotional materials involving the Quaker Oats link, the official studio pressbook underscored this juvenile thrust, as it suggested various additional promotions in this vein that theater owners might employ. One recommendation was to invite children to create their own, hand-drawn ads for *Forbidden Planet*; it read, "Kids! 'Draw an Ad' Contest. Try it!"[35] Exhibitors were also encouraged to hold a special "Screening for Newsboys," noting that "while MGM's first science-fiction film is outstanding adult entertainment, it is the type of picture that will thrill the youngsters. Pictures of the boys at the special showing should get a break" in local papers and news outlets,[36] which would help build word-of-mouth among other children. Yet another idea was to plug a toy tie-in aimed at children, suggesting that theater owners "Promote Ideal Toy's 'Robby the Robot,'" a licensed version of the film's central attraction.[37] But as I have already noted, such "promos and surrounding textuality . . . form the substance of first impressions" about a film, effectively telling us how to think about the text.[38] And in this case, much of the early ballyhoo surrounding *Forbidden Planet*, certainly much of that "surrounding textuality," conveyed the impression that the film was primarily aimed at a children's audience—one that paid less to see a film—as if it were staking a claim on the same viewership as those previously popular television space operas. However, that claim would prove problematic for a number of reasons. Probably the most obvious one was the film's sexual subtext. Throughout the narrative the young female lead, Altaira (Anne Francis), is seen in skimpy costumes, she has a nude bathing scene in which she invites the male lead (Leslie Nielsen) to join her, and she repeatedly expresses her sexual curiosity toward the male astronauts she encounters. Her character's presentation alone would pose some complications for that "moppet" audience.

The other primary focus of advance publicity also skewed heavily to this youngster appeal. Robby the Robot, the film's centerpiece technological attraction, was quickly identified, as Jack Eden of *Motion Picture Daily* noted, as something that "should appeal to children,"[39] and in making a similar point about the film's appeal to "kiddies," the *Variety* reviewer observed that Robby was "best of all the gadgets" in the film.[40] Indeed, Robby's image was prominently featured in eight-foot cardboard lobby

Vern Huntsinger, manager of the Gopher theatre, Minneapolis, and John Eshelman, manager of the Strand theatre, St. Paul, with the cooperation of Bob Stone, MGM field press representative, built this robot as walking street ballyhoo for "Forbidden Planet"— powered by one boy inside, which served the purposes of science fiction.

4.4. "Street ballyhoo": a cardboard model of *Forbidden Planet*'s Robby (mistakenly named "Roby") the Robot, as reported in the *Motion Picture Herald*.

figures, in the supermarket displays advertising the free children's tickets, and in the Ideal toy robot promotion. He would also become the object of much "street ballyhoo," as it was termed, with cardboard versions of the robot being created and paraded in front of theaters to draw children to the movie.[41] Following another studio suggestion, exhibitors held coloring contests of Robby the Robot, using line drawings provided in the MGM pressbook,[42] with the winners, it was suggested, receiving miniature robot toys. Further targeting that audience, the MGM robot would eventually make a number of grade school appearances, underscoring the impression that, as one publicity group announced, he was actually "the star attraction" of the film and should be most heavily targeted for promotion to the school-age audience.[43]

Despite this emphasis, Robby was also framed as much more than a toy. In fact, advance publicity initially moved in a somewhat different direction, emphasizing the technical complexity of the figure. Created at a cost of approximately $100,000 by Arnold Gillespie of MGM's prop department and Robert Kinoshita of the studio's art department, Robby was actually one of the first "effects" created for the film and was "the most complex of the mechanical props required."[44] John Brosnan describes Robby as "one of the most elaborate robots ever built for a film production," over seven feet tall, requiring more than "2,600 feet of electrical wiring" to operate "all his flashing lights, spinning antennae and the complicated gadgets that can be seen moving inside his transparent dome-shaped head,"[45] as well as an actor inside the robot—veteran actor Frankie Darro in most scenes—to manipulate his appendages. So impressive was he that Robby was sent on a publicity tour with Anne Francis, appearing at industry meetings; doing television, radio, and newspaper interviews in Chicago, Boston, and various other large cities; and guest starring on a number of popular television shows, among them *Queen for a Day*, *Today* with Dave Garroway, and *The Perry Como Show*.[46] But rather than emphasizing Robby's complex technical nature, these appearances typically presented him as more of a comic prop. On *Today*, for example, he plugged the movie while exchanging quips with host Garroway, and on *The Perry Como Show*, he, along with Anne Francis, appeared in two comedy skits, one in which he introduces himself as "president of the Robots for Como fan club" and another in which he portrays a cowboy wearing a ten-gallon hat perched atop his glass-domed head. Both seemed to forecast that Robby, unlike most prior cinematic robots, would essentially play a comic supporting role in *Forbidden Planet*.

Some of that light treatment would be retained in Robby's other major publicity appearances on two episodes of the studio's own prime-time television series *MGM Parade* (1955–1956). The show typically featured clips from older MGM films, along with trailers for its latest releases, hosted originally by the longtime studio star George Murphy, but for these and subsequent episodes he was replaced by Walter Pidgeon, who plays the scientist Doctor Morbius in the film. For both of these appearances (March 14 and March 21, 1956), Pidgeon dons his Morbius costume—and assumes the character—as he describes scenes from the film and introduces Robby, whom he characterizes ambiguously as "the robot of the Forbidden Planet." He also describes how Robby functions in the film, terming him "a housewife's dream" for his ability to cook, clean, and take care of Morbius's house, but as he then steps out of character, Pidgeon offers an aside to the audience, hinting that perhaps Robby is something more. He notes that "I sometimes wonder when we finish work . . . and Robby's here alone and the technicians have all gone home and the machinery is all shut off, is he really off? Or does this machine which we have built, this complicated metal being, does it really have a brain?" Accompanying his comments, a camera slowly tracks in on Robby, seen alone in a dark corner of the studio, where he suddenly lights up, comes to life, and offers an almost fiendish laugh. It is, of course, just another bit of stagecraft on a show that was always highly self-conscious, as Pidgeon's shifting in and out of his *Forbidden Planet* costuming and persona underscores. But this juxtaposition of Robby as cook, cleaner, and bantering guest with a potentially darker, even threatening side underscores the difficult situation that MGM's moppet/toy emphasis in its marketing for the film had created. For Robby was indeed an attractive creation, one that would "appeal to children," as Eden had noted, and he would have a long afterlife in other films and television programs, most often filling comic roles, as he would in shows such as *The Many Loves of Doby Gillis*, *The Addams Family*, and *Mork and Mindy*. But the figure also had other, more serious potential uses that, given the film's foreboding title as well as its sf appeal, might also need to be played up if *Forbidden Planet* was to attract an adult audience and capitalize on Dore Schary's feeling about its "different slant"—or measure up to MGM's boast, proudly announced on the film pressbook's front page, "Nothing Like It Ever!"

And indeed, on closer examination, *Forbidden Planet* proves to be more than another juvenile space opera, or even, as the *Variety* reviewer would qualify it, "*Space Patrol* for adults."[47] In fact, its narrative about a starcruiser's trip to the planet Altair IV to "rescue" survivors of the previous mission headed by Morbius quickly turns into a story that is very much in the classical sf tradition of the utopian/dystopian tale—a complex formal strategy that many see as fundamental to the best sf, a natural embodiment of its basic "what if" thrust. Working in that tradition, *Forbidden Planet* strikes a number of utopian themes, as the rescue party discovers the monumentally scaled, advanced, yet long-extinct civilization

94 —— SELLING SCIENCE FICTION CINEMA

4.5. In costume as Morbius, Walter Pidgeon introduces Robby the Robot on MGM's television series *MGM Parade*.

of the Krell, Altair's previous inhabitants; uncovers the almost limitless power sources available and still functioning thanks to the subsurface "Krell furnaces"; encounters machines that can serve any human need and satisfy any desire, as we see when Morbius's daughter, Altaira, asks for a gown covered with star sapphires or when the ship's cook (Earl Holliman) induces Robby to produce sixty gallons of "genuine Ancient Rocket bourbon"; and learns of devices that can expand the human mind, allowing for, as one character offers, "creation by mere thought" and control "without instrumentality." Qualifying these many utopian imaginings, though, are a number of timely warnings: about the potential for destruction when advanced civilizations (like our own) acquire great powers, about the necessity for limiting rather than giving free rein to our desires, and about the dark possibilities lodged in the human psyche, especially as Morbius unwittingly unleashes from within his own mind a destructive "monster from the Id" that kills the other Earth explorers and later precipitates his own death and the destruction of the entire planet. These are all important—and definitively adult—concerns that suggest a more sophisticated sense of sf and its aims, especially its ability to use utopian themes to comment on contemporary culture and its trajectory, and that further speak to Schary's hopeful instincts about this film and its difference from so many other 1950s sf efforts.

However, communicating—and selling—these ambitious concerns to a potential audience would require a far different marketing strategy than MGM had largely mapped out and so heavily publicized with its kid-directed Quaker Oats tie-in and its robot-led promotions, street ballyhoo, and comic public appearances. And while some of the conventional advertising for the film—its posters, lobby cards, and ad images—does suggest an effort to pivot the campaign, tap into some of the film's serious potential, and address other audience segments,[48] this shift would also miss the mark, especially that utopian dimension, as MGM, prior to *Forbidden Planet*'s release, turned with much of its print advertising to a prevailing pattern of sensationalistic and sexualized iconography of a sort with which movie audiences were already overly familiar. The nine *Forbidden Planet* posters and lobby cards offered to exhibitors in the official pressbook not only provided little variety but also promoted a different tone for the film and invariably misrepresented the narrative. Each advertising piece shows Robby the Robot holding the seemingly unconscious and scantily clad Altaira in his powerful arms, with his domed head and speech box now darkly modeled in a way that suggests a malevolent scowl and decidedly bad intentions. Several others include an image of the male lead, Commander Adams (Leslie Nielsen), responding to this mechanical menace, as he grimaces while firing his laser blaster at Robby. The pressbook also offered exhibitors a "Powerful Full Color Standee," that is, a full-sized cardboard version of this menacing Robby holding Altaira, to be used as a lobby or theater-front attraction. These elements of what I earlier termed "surrounding textuality" seem to prime the audience for a fairly familiar sensationalistic story of this period, one about a robot run amok, perhaps perversely "desiring" a human mate in some atomic-age variation on *Frankenstein*'s image of the monster, who had been similarly depicted carrying off Dr. Frankenstein's wife in the 1931 film. But of course, it is a scene that, like many other such publicity images, is simply a mash-up of various visual elements of the film framed in a darker context. In fact, in the film, Robby essentially functions as Altaira's servant and protector, and he is fully

4.6. A *Forbidden Planet* lobby card typifies the film's imaginative amalgam of sex and violence. MGM Studios.

controlled by his human masters thanks to the film's pioneering introduction of Isaac Asimov's famous "Laws of Robotics." The ad's *suggested* (and suggestive) scene, though, points up the other way in which MGM's marketing campaign would demonstrate its confusion about both the nature of sf and its prospective audience.

Other sf films of this period, and I might particularly note such efforts as *The Day the Earth Stood Still*, *Invaders from Mars* (1953, William Cameron Menzies, dir.), *Robot Monster*, *Tobor the Great* (1954, Lee Sholem, dir.), and the slightly later *Colossus of New York*, were all marketed using versions of this same visual "story." Posters and lobby cards for these films all depict an intensely dramatic yet iconic moment as a large robot or cyborg figure grasps in his/its arms typically a blond-haired and partially dressed woman (usually clad in red) while fighting off surrounding humans. That repeated, consistently detailed scene projects a story about a towering, malevolent technological figure; ongoing conflict and devastation, with destructive rays or weapons being deployed; and a young woman in obvious peril. It is an exciting and complex image, and one that fits well with a larger cultural pattern demonstrated in other period sf films, all of them playing out variations on the technological threat and that "imagination of disaster." It is also, as the details described above suggest, a sexually charged image, underscoring the extent to which, as Dean Conrad observes, "sexual aggression and the objectification of women" seem almost pervasive in the era's films.[49] Moreover, it is a meme that must have left some moviegoers either disappointed or at least puzzled, since this central event that most of the advertising appears to forecast for each of the films cited here simply *does not happen*, and the narratives almost invariably prove different in tone or trajectory from what those marketing materials visually promise.[50]

Of course, film posters, lobby cards, and newspaper or magazine ads often present this kind of imaginative amalgam of alluring or exciting images, snatched from different elements of the film being marketed—as well as from the audience's imaginations. They excite the senses, arouse curiosity, and forge links to other narrative moments (or films) that potential viewers might have previously relished, sometimes playing off of recent cultural events, such as the flying saucer fervor of the period. In effect, they serve as convenient narrative frames and filters to help determine how we see the films. But they also tell us much about how the films, or more precisely, their makers and distributors, have tended to frame *us*. In these repeated instances, the ads present the sf text not as heralding a world of technological potential and human promise, of hopeful change, of the utopian "what if" that commonly primes the pump of sf. Rather, drawing on a sense of widespread audience anxieties, the ads present the text as a sensationalistic cautionary tale, warning about technologically delivered disaster, while they frame the audience as fundamentally insecure, haunted by technological nightmares fueled by Cold War fears of apocalyptic destruction. Such ads also remind us that the audience they envision—or frame—is hardly the one implied in MGM's repeated rhetoric about "kids"; in *Motion Picture Herald*'s speculation about *Forbidden Planet*'s "straight family appeal"; in several trade paper commentaries that, probably without viewing the film, simply labeled it a "family picture"; or even in the pressbook's suggestion that Morbius's home offers homemakers a promising domestic vision, a "Preview of [the] House of Tomorrow."[51] Children would seem to have little to hold their attention here; women are relegated to the status of sexual objects; the family, even in these dramatic images, is clearly imperiled, even broken; and the home is easily destroyed by Morbius's Id monster, whose power springs from the caverns just below that House of Tomorrow—hinting at an inherent instability in both home and family. Such films ultimately seem to speak, as *Variety* surmised, not so much to the family as to the "scare trade" of teenagers and young adults,[52] effectively anticipating the later phenomenon that Thomas Doherty has described as "the progressive 'juvenilization' of the content and the film audience" in American motion pictures of the late 1950s and 1960s.[53] Framed in this way, the utopian possibilities of sf are generally lost, becoming distorted or displaced by dark forebodings of the future.

As I began by noting, the period when *Forbidden Planet* appeared is indeed an important reason for the shifts in viewership—and thus marketing—that the film industry was experiencing. In the mid-1950s, the Hollywood studio system was in the process of being dismantled; television was making significant inroads into the entertainment landscape; and, as Doherty's point about the growing power of the late-teenage/young adult audience underscores, the moviegoing demographic was itself in the midst of a dramatic change, often leaving the studios unsure of their primary viewers. To be successful in this sort of dynamic situation, the film industry would have to be much more attentive to the film marketplace, to identifying and targeting a particular audience, and to providing a clear sense of the nature of the film product that was being offered to that audience—in this case, being more attuned to the primary thrusts of the relatively new sf genre. However, the example of *Forbidden Planet* demonstrates how even a studio like MGM, with enormous resources, talent, a veteran marketing/exploitation department, and even a studio head (Schary) who seemed more aware of the changing marketplace, might miss the mark in many if not all of these areas and, in fact, seem to have very little sense of who the main audience for its film might be. The result was a multidirectional campaign that often seemed at cross-purposes with itself and the film while also having a weak sense of sf and of the genre's appeal.

Certainly, *Forbidden Planet* offered a spectacular alternative to those television space operas that were losing their grip on the public and, in fact, would mostly disappear from home screens by 1956. But its marketing, as some of the exhibitors' derisive comments about presenting movies as "cheap premiums" recognized, seemed to sell the film otherwise. The initial Quaker Oats part of the campaign not only suggested that *Forbidden Planet* was not the sort of quality film that was usually associated with the MGM brand but framed it primarily as a children's product, more comedy than serious sf, and later, with the sensationalistic thrust of the print ads, as more of an exploitation effort than a prestige production. In his study of more recent approaches to film marketing, focused on the development of what has been termed the "high concept" method that would emerge in the later 1960s and 1970s, Justin Wyatt identifies a key problem about most film industry marketing dynamics, that of "breaking continuity in the marketing and public identification with the film."[54] Obviously, MGM fell afoul of this rule of "breaking continuity," as *Forbidden Planet* seemed to oscillate in one marketing direction and then another, charming children, tempering technology with comedy for adult viewers, and then titillating both teens and adults with its intimations of sex and violence. But its uncertain yet high-profile campaign demonstrated another pitfall, as it never quite established an identity for MGM's first modern sf product, something the public could readily identify with and embrace, at least as distinct from a welter of competing sf exploitation films, such as *Earth vs. the Flying Saucers* (Fred F. Sears, dir.), *It Conquered the World* (Roger Corman, dir.), and *World Without End* (Edward Bernds, dir.)—all appearing in the same year (1956) as *Forbidden Planet*, all made for less than $150,000, and all turning a solid profit.[55] The box office only confirmed the problem, with *Variety* reporting the domestic gross for *Forbidden Planet* at just $1,600,000—far below the nearly $2,000,000 spent on this "different" "high-budgeter."[56]

As a final reminder of the confusion that seemed endemic to the film's marketing, we might briefly consider the studio's follow-up to *Forbidden Planet*, *The Invisible Boy* (1957, Herman Hoffman, dir.). Done as an independent production for release through MGM by *Forbidden Planet*'s producer, Nicholas Nayfack, this movie was more nearly a low-budget effort at $400,000, although it managed to look much more expensive by capitalizing

4.7. MGM's tone-deaf marketing for *The Invisible Boy* (1957).

on Robby the Robot and some other holdovers from the previous film.[57] But as Jonathan Gray cautions, "for many viewers and non-viewers alike the title of the film or program will signify the entire package,"[58] and this sequel's title quickly suggested it might have a different and more obvious focus than its predecessor, as if it were embodying the film's intended audience in its nine-year-old protagonist Timmie (Richard Eyer), the son of a renowned computer scientist. A curious and bored child, Timmy amuses himself by putting Robby—who, following a time-travel mishap, has been discovered in a junk bin in a storage room—back into working order, turning him into a kind of large toy or electronic playmate. However, the narrative then takes a dark turn as Robby becomes a surprisingly dangerous toy/playmate when his father's supercomputer runs amok and reprograms Robby to do its bidding, using him as a weapon and Timmy as a hostage in its plot to take over the world.

As with *Forbidden Planet*, the print advertising for *The Invisible Boy* would make a similar pivot to this darker element. Following the earlier film's sensationalistic pattern, the advertising took on a violent and equally sensational character, with the central graphic for all the film's posters showing little Timmie (out of scale) struggling in the clutches of an apparently malevolent and now seemingly gigantic Robby, while flamethrowers, tanks, and missiles fire on the robot. Captioning that violent image, the lead ad provided in the film's pressbook proclaims that "Horror Grips the Earth as Robot Runs Amok!"[59] A two-page industry-oriented spread in *Motion Picture Daily* (September 18, 1957, 4–5) did offer another version of this violent scene when it repurposed the regular advertising image of Robby gripping Timmie with another showing a well-dressed man held by a giant fist, while a headline reworks one of *Forbidden Planet*'s taglines—"Nothing Like It Ever"—to assure potential exhibitors of *The Invisible Boy*, "Nothing Like It Ever to Grip Your Patrons!" It seems a tone-deaf ad, or simply another confused effort, rather neatly summed up in the equally tone-deaf *Variety* review, which labeled the new film as "the type of scifi excitement which will appeal to moppet audiences especially."[60] This linking of sf's "appeal" to a "moppet" audience, while marketing materials emphasized the film's violent content, a violence pointedly directed against children, suggests that MGM was perhaps not that different from the rest of the film industry in this period as it tried out different and often wrongheaded tactics for marketing this still relatively new genre. Facing a host of other challenges—challenges that would also see Dore Schary removed as MGM head at the end of 1956—the film industry would continue to struggle throughout the decade. It would remain largely unsure about the makeup of audiences for this "different" yet (given the 1957 launch of Sputnik and the onset of the space race) seemingly quite timely form or how best to tailor stories so as to reach them.

CHAPTER 5

ANOTHER FORM OF LIFE
Audiences, Markets, and The Blob

As I have demonstrated in the previous chapters, film marketing frames its product, but it also frames the anticipated audience for that product. Consequently, Patrick Vonderau argues that we should think of this marketing process not just as matching "products to already existing markets" but also as a "process of market-making," as an ongoing effort at constructing or framing the film "consumers,"[1] guiding how they approach, consume, and respond to a film, in effect, *making* both audiences and film genres. But though sf in the 1950s had quickly become a large part of the cinematic and televisual landscape, sf films were often marketed in ambiguous or strained ways, as the *Forbidden Planet* discussion suggested. It was as if, despite the genre's growing profile, the industry was always a bit unsure about both the product and the audience at which it was ultimately aimed. Certainly, hard-core sf fans—of the sort that read magazines such as *Astounding* and *Galaxy Science Fiction*—appreciated the emphasis on scientific and technological accuracy that marked a film like *Destination Moon*, but those fans, even when properly targeted by advertising efforts, were never enough to assure box-office success. Moreover, that fixation on "accuracy and trouble with detail," as David Hartwell describes it,[2] often runs afoul of what many see as one of the genre's essential attractions, its ability to consistently lead us beyond the purely scientific and generally known to keep us "still in search of wonder,"[3] as Michele Pierson offers in her study of special effects. Simply put, audiences change, what they seek from a particular type of sf can change, and thus the framing of that viewership also has to change to accommodate these potentials, almost as if there were always another form of life out there needing to be reached or guided in their "wonder." In this chapter, I consider how that audience-focused component of "market-making" functioned in the later 1950s as sf cinema became increasingly reliant on exploitation efforts that sought to chase or frame the genre's current audience. As a case study, I examine one of the period's more notorious yet successful sf films, *The Blob* (1958, Irvin S. Yeaworth Jr., dir.), demonstrating how it navigated these multiple uncertainties and shifting attitudes, and shed some light on the nature of successful sf—and, more broadly—genre "market-making" in this period.

As I have shown, the sf genre rapidly developed and the US audience demonstrated an increasing interest in it, but the film industry initially struggled both with identifying the form—is it horror, adventure, exploitation cinema?—and with effectively marketing it. Through the prewar period, sf was arguably more established in the European cinema, whereas during the 1940s in the United States it had largely been an outlier, the stuff of serials and mad-scientist narratives. And while it quickly gained popularity on television from 1949 to 1956, thanks to cheaply done space operas such as *Captain Video* and *Tom Corbett, Space Cadet*, that new familiarity might only have complicated the film industry's problems, since the movie studios had to not only identify and market their product but also differentiate it from those sf offerings in the new medium and, in many cases, even determine whether its audience was the same as that of the juvenile-oriented space operas. But as the genre gained in popularity, those struggles seemed to dissipate. For example, by 1954, Universal-International, which was far better known for such horror efforts as *Dracula* (1931, Tod Browning, dir.), *Frankenstein*, and *The Wolf Man* (1941, George Waggner, dir.), decided to capitalize on this new status, selling a somewhat traditional monster film, *Creature from the Black Lagoon* (1954, Jack Arnold, dir.), by emphasizing its links to the sf genre. Thus the film's pressbook provided advertising mattes depicting a number of familiar film figures—the Golem, Dracula, the Mummy, and others—which it described in suitably genre-blurring fashion as "Hollywood's Prize Science-Fiction Creatures," while representing the Creature, or Gill-Man, as a continuation of their tradition and the film as a "science fiction adventure."[4] Other ads and radio spots furthered this identification, describing the film as "the strangest science-fiction thriller of them all."[5] While most of the trade commentaries still referred to this story about a prehistoric Gill-Man as a "horror film" (*Motion Picture Herald*), "monster" film (*Motion Picture Daily*), or even a "horror-meller" (*Film Bulletin*), the marketing associations with sf apparently paid off at the box office, as the low-budget film earned an estimated $1.3 million and inspired two quickly made sequels, *Revenge of the Creature* (1955, Jack Arnold, dir.) and *The Creature Walks Among Us* (1956, John Sherwood, dir.).

But the end of the decade would see sf rapidly waning in popularity, with *Variety* remarking in 1958 on the "erratic current market" for the genre, industry executive R. V. Jones opining that "the horror and science fiction type" films had "run their course," a reviewer of *From the Earth to the Moon* (1958, Byron Haskin, dir.) proclaiming that "the science-fiction cycle seems at an end," and the larger studios like MGM (following its problematic experience with *Forbidden Planet* and *The Invisible Boy*) pulling back from sf production and leaving it to the independents and the exploitation market.[6] Even in the shadow of the space race and the cultural enthusiasm it had begun to generate for science and technology, sf cinema in the last years of the decade would thus be largely characterized by cheaply made exploitation films, frequently presented on double bills, increasingly aimed at a juvenile audience, and gaining what Bradley Schauer described as a generally disreputable standing because of their pulp-like character. We might see in that shift some evidence of what John Rieder refers to as the inevitable "pressures of commodification,"[7] as the film industry in the latter half of the 1950s struggled to market the genre while facing internal retrenchment, competition from the upstart television industry, and an inability to sense what exactly constituted a sf film. Was it, after all—and as many of the trade papers seemed to imply—just a temporary inflection on or cycle of more established forms such as horror, mystery, and melodrama? If so, might it be expected, like other film cycles, to run its limited course and be replaced by other popular narrative types, as some were already announcing? While Rieder argues that "the key element of the mass cultural genre system's coherent organizational function," its "binding agent," has always been "the commercial advertisement,"[8] the film industry would, as the decade proceeded, increasingly have difficulty concocting that "binding agent," that is, properly framing an audience for what was, along with the quasi-generic film noir, one of the most important genre developments of the postwar period.

As a test case, we might consider some of that marketing difficulty, as well as the correlative market-making process, that was demonstrated by *The Blob*, a film that appeared in this "erratic" period yet also managed to successfully address some of these problems through its own more careful approach to the exploitation process, one that operated in both its marketing efforts and its narrative. Like a number of other exploitation efforts of this period, it was produced by an independent regional filmmaker, Jack H. Harris, for much less than the cost of a typical Hollywood production, in this case approximately $110,000.[9] Harris shot *The Blob* in several small Pennsylvania towns, employed no big-name actors, and steered away from the space opera formula that had been so popular on television in favor of an amorphous, threatening, and simple-to-create alien presence: a gelatinous, all-consuming blob. Noting the movie's visible cheapness, Bill Warren suggests that it left "a feeling the filmmakers were almost slumming."[10] And yet a major studio also proved willing to participate in that "slumming," as Paramount purchased the film's distribution rights for a reported $300,000. Then, in a telling move, the studio dedicated an additional $300,000 to its marketing campaign, because, as *Variety* observed, in the current market environment, "a sci-fi entry demands a special promotional push" of the sort that the producer, Harris, on his own, would have been "unlikely" to afford.[11] Double-billed with another cheaply made sf film, *I Married a Monster from Outer Space*, and given a saturation marketing campaign in a few select locations—initially over forty theaters in the Los Angeles area—*The Blob* was accompanied by what Paramount's internal magazine, *Paramount World*, touted, in the sort of overstatement that was more than just typical film ballyhoo, as "the greatest exploitation ever given a Paramount feature."[12] Through a series of such select saturation bookings, aided by intense television advertising in major markets, the film proceeded to gross more than $1.5 million in initial domestic rentals, and was rereleased by Harris in 1960 to strong additional profits.[13] In an effort to diagnose what had

ANOTHER FORM OF LIFE — 107

5.1. Paramount gives the industry a measure of its extensive "ad-pub work" for *The Blob* (1958).

made the film so successful, the same *Variety* article concluded that "ad-pub work" had clearly become "almost as important, if not more so, than . . . the 'sell' values of the production itself."[14]

Some reason for this assessment can be seen in the film's

contemporary reviews, for *The Blob* met with the sorts of mixed critical responses that recognized its problematic generic status and its lack of traditional "sell values." The *New York Times* reviewer Howard Thompson, for example, warned off moviegoers, terming it a "horror melodrama" with "pretty phony" special effects and "pretty terrible" acting (including Steve McQueen in his first lead film role), and he pronounced it "woodenly presented on the whole."[15] While suggesting that the film offered several possible "exploitable angles," the *Variety* reviewer had little better opinion of *The Blob*, judging that the story would "tax the imagination of adult patrons" but was "tailored to the teenage set," and noting that what "production values" it sports "are geared to economy."[16] But taking a narrower focus, precisely on how exhibitors might most effectively use "ad-pub work" to counter such problems and reach the most receptive audience, James D. Ivers of *Motion Picture Daily* observed that though the film had an element of "professional polish," the key to selling it was neither its look nor its genre appeal; rather, he says, it was emphasizing "the teen-age angle, an approach pointed up by a chief and sergeant of police [in the film], one of whom has faith in teen-agers and the other who believes them all bad."[17]

To be sure, by the late 1950s, there was nothing especially new about this teen "angle." As Thomas Doherty has chronicled, the middle of the decade saw the film industry beginning to shift from its traditional focus on entertainment fashioned with "the entire family" in mind to a veritable "courtship of the teenage audience," the "one group with the requisite income, leisure, and gregariousness to sustain a theatrical business" in uncertain times.[18] One result of this shift, Doherty suggests, was the development of the "teenpic," a type that generally escaped easy genre classification, while settling—in industry minds—into that vague exploitation category, typically by combining strange or unusual subject matter with equally strange or extravagant approaches to marketing it.[19] By the time *The Blob* appeared, the film industry, especially in its exploitation-type films, was heavily invested in teenpics that favored no specific genre but ranged, in rather scattershot fashion, across a wide variety of film types: high school melodramas such as *High School Confidential* (1958, Jack Arnold, dir.); juvenile delinquency narratives like *Hot Car Girl* (1958, Bernard L. Kowalski, dir.); teen musicals such as *Let's*

Rock (1958, Harry Foster, dir.); teen love stories like *Gidget* (1959, Paul Wendkos, dir.); and of course the Elvis Presley musicals that were sponsored by several of the major studios, including MGM, 20th Century-Fox, and Paramount, and that also framed their musical elements with generic components drawn from a wide variety of forms, including the crime film, the boxing drama, the racing film, and others. Among the more popular of these new mixed types were what Doherty terms "the wierdies," as exemplified by films like *I Was a Teenage Frankenstein* (1957, Herbert L. Strock, dir.) and *Curse of the Faceless Man* (1958, Edward L. Cahn, dir.). These were typically concoctions of "science fiction, fantasy, monster, zombie, or shock" stories that, in their pursuit of the teen audience, he claims, "knew no bounds or shame."[20]

As I have shown, Paramount, especially when dealing with the sf genre, had previously taken a very different tack. In the 1930s, the studio had made a high-profile move into the sf market by purchasing the rights to H. G. Wells's *War of the Worlds* (although it would not produce the film until two decades later). In that same period, it produced several big-budget genre efforts, most notably *Dr. Jekyll and Mr. Hyde* (1931) and *Island of Lost Souls* (1932). While these films would be billed as horror efforts—with *Variety* describing the former as a "time-tested horror tale" and the latter as "a freak picture"[21]—the advertising in both cases emphasized the films' status as prestige productions and adaptations of major literary works. Thus, a full-page insert for *Dr. Jekyll and Mr. Hyde* in *Motion Picture Herald* read, "Paramount announces with pride the coming special production of Robert Louis Stevenson's immortal drama of dual identity" (May 2, 1931). And in the 1950s, as previously noted, Paramount initially returned to sf in a somewhat similar vein, with George Pal's big-budget, technologically sophisticated, and scientifically precise films *When Worlds Collide* (1951), *The War of the Worlds* (1953), and *Conquest of Space* (1955). In the case of these 1950s productions, Paramount had made a singular effort to identify and reach out to a highly specialized and knowledgeable sf audience with the articles it placed in *Astounding Science Fiction*; it crafted traveling science exhibits that toured schools and museums to help publicize several of the films; and it held special screenings for what the studio referred to as "interested groups" in scientific and educational fields.[22] But Pal's high-cost sf efforts "didn't mesh well" with the studio's shift

5.2. An early sf effort: Paramount touts *Dr. Jekyll and Mr. Hyde* (1931) as a "prestige" literary adaptation.

to a strategy of more economic productions, and the studio would handle *The Blob* differently from these earlier efforts,[23] using a variety of marketing approaches demonstrating the film industry's changing perspectives on both the sf genre and its audience.

As the *Variety* column about an "erratic" market might suggest,

Paramount was hardly alone among the large studios in having some difficulty figuring out how to market sf as the 1950s wore on. Despite the genre's success in the first half of the decade, particularly with less-costly productions like the Warner Bros.–distributed *The Beast from 20,000 Fathoms* (1953) and *Them!* (1954), by the later 1950s, as noted in the previous chapter, an industry-wide trend in sf emerged: not eliminating the films but downsizing them, teaming up with independent producers and giving more attention to the process of exploiting those productions. And as I discuss in the following chapter, some studios reacted by pursuing relatively low-cost—and low-risk—purchases of the rights to foreign titles, such as the Japanese *Gojira/Godzilla* (1954) and *Rodan* (1957), dubbing them and undertaking heavy but relatively brief saturation bookings. Taking a different approach, MGM chose to market its one big-budget effort in the genre, *Forbidden Planet*, not by emphasizing its echoes of Shakespeare's *The Tempest* or its pioneering incorporation of Isaac Asimov's "laws of robotics," but rather by framing it at least partly as a children's picture, an approach only underscored by the studio's follow-up, the tellingly titled, and cheaply made, *The Invisible Boy*. As Schauer chronicles, 20th Century-Fox would take a strictly low-budget approach to this market, signing a deal with the independent producer Robert Lippert and his company Regal Films to produce a series of cheaply made films—each done for approximately $100,000—to be shot partly at Fox and distributed by that major firm, typically as parts of double bills.[24] Many of these independent productions were westerns, but two noteworthy but still low-budget sf efforts stood out, *The Fly* (1958, Kurt Neumann, dir.) and *Return of the Fly* (1959, Edward Bernds, dir.). But it is also in this climate that trade papers of the later 1950s often referred to new sf films not by their genre—which, as Bruce A. Austin observes, is, along with plot, one of the two "most important reasons" moviegoers typically give for attending a specific film[25]—but rather more broadly as (per *Variety*) "mellers" or, as Doherty underscores, exploitation films, works that occupied a very fluid formula space, involving a variety of such elements as violence, horror, or titillating sexual content, any of which, industry publications suggested, might easily be promoted for a specifically targeted audience. Thus, even a rather well-received effort, such as the invention-gone-wrong narrative of *The Fly*, would be appreciatively described by

Film Bulletin not with a genre designation but rather vaguely as "not just another exploitation picture," while also noting that the releasing studio (20th Century-Fox) would need to back it "with a great campaign" to get best results.[26]

In his study of movie audiences, Austin also underscores the increasing importance in this period of targeted marketing, describing how "advertising for such a highly perishable product as a film" should be "tailored to audiences who seem most likely to be attracted to it."[27] Industry trade papers would thus suggest a variety of approaches to deal with that erratic market position of sf by more precisely identifying and framing the audience with its marketing, although in retrospect those approaches might themselves seem somewhat "erratic" and often quite questionable. In *Motion Picture Herald*, for example, Curtis Mees, the manager of Atlanta's Paramount Theater and a frequent contributor to the journal's "Method in Management" column, grouped together "science-fiction dramas" and "kid shows" as types that exhibitors should treat similarly, approaching both as "concession pictures," that is, a type of film that will "bring in people who buy more confections than others."[28] With that overt consumer vantage in mind, he suggested that theaters install additional temporary refreshment stands whenever such a "concession picture" was booked and this audience was expected, and that they also arrange contests providing special concession awards to further draw in these snack-conscious viewers.[29] The *Film Bulletin* on a number of occasions described sf films as "gimmick films" that largely appealed to "undemanding addicts"—similar to the audiences for "rock 'n' roll . . . or horror"—and suggested that creating gimmicks of various sorts was the key to attracting that crowd.[30] A feature in *Variety* similarly headlined the importance of identifying possible "gimmicks," especially for sf and horror releases, while also suggesting that most audiences enjoyed the "offbeat excitement" those gimmicks helped generate and that this desire for an excitement that extends beyond the movie itself needed to be cultivated, since in the current moviegoing climate it is what "sells tickets."[31]

As in the case of most other sf films of the period, the new "sell values," whatever they might be—and clearly there was little consensus in the trade publications—would result in a wide variety of ballyhoo efforts for *The Blob* that at times did not seem to have *any* specific audience in mind. One clearly echoed the history of another famed sf production, Orson Welles's 1938 radio adaptation of *The War of the Worlds*. While Paramount had earlier been careful to distance its 1953 film version from the infamous Welles radio event, the panic it evoked, and the widespread criticism that had followed, in the instance of *The Blob*, some radio spots, just as in the Welles broadcast, had an announcer suddenly intrude into a program with a dramatic, news-like message, warning listeners to "Beware of the Blob—It Destroys Everything in Its Path," while not revealing that *The Blob* was simply a movie title.[32] Another such successful effort—and a fairly common form of movie ballyhoo—was described in *Paramount World*: the display of a "mystery case" outside a theater bearing a "Danger" label and the warning "Don't Touch It. This Case Imprisons 'The Blob'" and with apparent bloodstains scattered around the case.[33]

A different sort of ballyhoo—one that apparently aimed to generate the kind of "offbeat excitement" *Variety* noted—appeared in a number of ads that pointedly blurred generic lines by touting the film's frightening capacity and explicitly reaching for a horror audience. One ad (provided as a matte in the Paramount pressbook) emphasized *The Blob*'s horror effect—while seemingly denying its juvenile target audience—by including a warning printed within a red circle that the film was "Suitable Only for Adults." Another, mining a vein similar to that which Paramount would use in *Psycho* (1960, Alfred Hitchcock, dir.), announced in large print that "The Management of this theatre disclaims any responsibility for heart attacks or damage to nerves resulting from the film," and it punctuated this disclaimer with a star and ribbon bearing the curious legend "Certified," as if the announcement bore some sort of official industry seal, perhaps suggesting that it had been authorized by a body such as the MPAA or was part of that organization's Code for Advertising. It is a wrinkle that subtly engaged a kind of reflexive response by inviting the audience's complicity in—and potential enjoyment of—its admittedly fake scare tactics, while at the same time distancing the film experience from the realm of sf, which, as Doherty and others have observed, typically "incites wonder," not "fear."[34]

While these efforts were all the product of Paramount's publicity department, part of its "greatest exploitation" campaign, and seemed curiously disconnected from *The Blob*'s sf connections,

5.3. Part of *The Blob*'s strategy of "offbeat excitement"—"warning" juveniles that the film is only "for Adults." Paramount Pictures.

the producer, Jack Harris, demonstrated a more thoughtful, even complex attitude toward such marketing strategies. In interviews, he readily accepted the "gimmick" label for his film, but he also consistently characterized it as sf, although he would also observe that in the late-1950s climate, even "good science fiction needs" something to attract attention. However, his notion of the gimmick was a fairly conventional one and, like some of that other ballyhoo, largely unrelated to a specific audience. For *The Blob*, it was partly having "a monster you cannot kill," and, taking an obvious swipe at some of the recent Japanese sf imports and their American imitators, he explained that it should not be "a man dressed up in a suit, or a mechanical doll, or a marionette. It is another form of life."[35] Reflecting traditional notions of product differentiation while also following that pattern of blurring generic lines, in this case linking sf with horror, Harris was mainly trying to suggest that the gimmick in his film, his "monster," was unlike that found in any other such films, and that his blob-monster's relentless and amorphous nature was what intrigued audiences and was largely responsible for its box-office success. I suggest that his notion of "another form of life" was not that far off the mark, although the real gimmick of his film may well have been the *many* forms of ballyhoo employed and how they spoke to the potential audience for *The Blob*, as well as various other sf films in this period of erratic market conditions and a fluctuating viewership.

The main "form of life" that *The Blob* would ultimately capitalize on was not its shapeless monster but, as the *Motion Picture Daily* review had hinted, its teenaged subjects, who were framed, both within and outside the narrative proper, *not* in the vein of "juvenilization" that Doherty describes, not as easily construed, passive subjects, but as something more complex and in the midst of change. Within the film, those subjects prove to be both victims of the shapeless thing and heroes, much as they are also presented, somewhat metaphorically, as both the victims and heroes of modern American culture, and thus as attractive avatars for the youth audience that had indeed been targeted, if in an unconventional way. Certainly, that youth demographic was starting to dominate the American film market and provide a model for how many in the film industry were envisioning the main audience for most of their movies. Small production/distribution companies, such as American International Pictures (AIP), were finding a successful niche by addressing this demographic with cheaply made, sensationalistic films, many of them in a sf vein. And that audience was framed precisely within the felt anxieties of the new "space age" in several other low-budget and much less successful sf films clustered around the time of *The Blob*'s release, such as *Teenage Monster* (1957, Jacques R. Marquette, dir.), *The Space Children* (1958), *Monster on the Campus* (1958, Jack Arnold, dir.), and *Teenagers from Outer Space* (1959, Tom Graeff, dir.), with an industry review of *The Space Children* tellingly dismissing it simply as "exploitable merchandise for the juvenile trade."[36] That featured teen image suggested that the US film industry, both large and small studios, recognized an easily targeted and exploitable audience that could be addressed through many different genres or combinations of genres. However, the mixed success of that targeting can be seen in the precipitous drop in sf production as the 1960s began. This drop can be measured in the disappearance of those easily identified "juvenile" sf titles, as if that exploitable audience link had suddenly dissolved,[37] at least for sf if not for other "gentrified" (Doherty's term) teenpics such as the Presley musicals or for newer, emerging cycles.[38]

In fact, over the next decade, such major independent film companies as AIP, New World Pictures, and Crown International—studios that largely marketed exploitation products to a youth demographic—clearly shifted their focus in both subjects and attitude. As Peter Stanfield has observed, after recognizing that it had gotten all the mileage it could from several high-profile film types, such as Edgar Allan Poe–based horror and beach-and-bikini films, AIP began exploring new types and new genre combinations, such as the biker and even the horror-biker and biker-documentary films, while still trying to embody "the teen-agers' viewpoint."[39] But what was becoming clear is how much that "viewpoint" itself was changing, necessitating a more complex framing of films to reach that demographic. AIP thus "toned down the sensationalistic aspects" of both the films and their marketing and instead amplified their social context, including broader audience-identifying elements of social protest and rebellion.[40] But that change was not applied to all types of films. Reflecting this development, AIP, New World, and Crown announced in 1969 that they would collectively be releasing forty-two new titles, films with such generic indicators as "drama," "melodrama," "horror," "comedy," "mystery," and "motorcycle drama"; however, that number included only two sf pictures.[41] The implication is not just that the sf cycle by that time was largely over but that despite the larger cultural emphases on space and science, the flourishing of sf literature, and the emergence of New Wave sf literature in the 1960s, there seemed little interest in finding a strategy for reaching an audience invested in the developments in science and technology or the changes associated with them.

And yet, the popular teen angle had been on the mind of the producer Harris from the start, as he described how, in creating *The Blob*, he hoped to bring a "fresh approach" both to sf and to the late-1950s treatment of that youth demographic. While acknowledging the general industry belief that "science-fiction is fading," he suggested that the public might simply be "fed up" with the way it was being handled, and especially with many of the "extreme" elements that had made their way into popular films of the time, not so much sf-related themes but real-life concerns such as "rape, beatings, stabbings, and general delinquency," and he thought it might be effective to combine a sf narrative with a novel approach: "teen-agers who are good" if also misunderstood or misperceived by their culture.[42] Thus, the core of *The Blob* is not the rather silly-looking red glob that is its "alien invader," its apparent gimmick, and its science fictional foundation, but rather the constant clashes between the film's teenagers and the adults' *impressions* of those teenagers, particularly as embodied in the police, who assume that if teens are riding through the streets at night they must be delinquents, a situation effectively dramatized by the lead couple Steve and Jane (Steve McQueen and Aneta Corsaut).

Recalling the central characters in Paramount's more adult-oriented *War of the Worlds*, Steve and Jane find themselves drawn into a typical sf situation quite by chance when they see what appears to be a nearby meteor crash. Upon investigating, they encounter an old man who pleads for help to remove a throbbing red blob from his arm, and like responsible adults, the young couple try to help by taking the old man to a doctor and reporting the incident to the police. However, they find the police not just skeptical of their story but ready to accuse them of a typical teen hoax, especially as the purported old man, the doctor, and his nurse have all suddenly disappeared. Caught in that atmosphere of doubt and the general climate of "delinquency" to which Harris refers, they then have to take matters into their own hands, convincing other similar "delinquents" to help search for the blob, to warn people in the town about the danger, and eventually to help defeat it by using carbon-dioxide fire extinguishers to freeze the thing. Obviously, the broad outlines of this narrative lend reason to *Variety*'s observation that the film had been "tailored to the teenage set,"[43] but this description avoids the more important issues of how that audience was seen by much of the movie industry or how teenagers were viewed by the dominant and judgmental adult culture within the movie, the very people that they help save.

The film eventually decides the latter question for us by framing Steve, Jane, and their high school friends in a sympathetic and highly mature light, rising to the occasion to deal with this shapeless invader and, like responsible—surrogate—parents, even endangering themselves to save Jane's little brother when he is menaced by the creature. That visualization of the teen demographic as both victimized and heroic is hardly unique, as a film like *Rebel Without a Cause* (1955, Nicholas Ray, dir.) perhaps most obviously suggests, especially with its lead character, Jim Stark (James Dean), who is clearly more adult than his father. But a key scene in the series of encounters with the blob adds another dimension that recalls its "certified" scare tactics and speaks to this film's more distinctive framing of its audience. For the blob conveniently arrives on a night when the local theater is offering a "Midnight Spook Show," featuring *Daughter of Horror* (aka *Dementia* [1955, John Parker, dir.]), a fright film that, Steve notes, has drawn most of the local teenagers. As its title suggests, *Daughter of Horror* is hardly a sf film; rather, it is a psychological horror story that is almost a parody of traditional horror, a cheap, over-the-top "spook show" of the type that many exploitation filmmakers of the period were making, largely with a teen audience in mind.[44] But as repeated shots of the audience illustrate, it is a film that does not so much frighten as amuse those mainly juvenile viewers. The audience's laughter suggests their ability to see through such fare, to find some other entertainment value in it, suggesting in the process that simply framing them for

5.4. The audience of *Daughter of Horror* reacts with laughter at its over-the-top horrific effects. Paramount Pictures.

promotional purposes as "the teenage set" or "juveniles" might have been an inadequate bit of "market-making" for this film.

That the teenagers in the film are not all delinquents, not pranksters, not irresponsible, and certainly not frightened by typical industry "spook shows" begins to suggest that *The Blob* at least has a somewhat more complex sense of audience that might have contributed to its success. It is a sensibility that is perceivable in the conclusion of the theater scene, and one that worked its way into the film's other marketing elements. When the blob makes its way into the theater's projection booth, easily absorbs the inattentive adult projectionist, and then proceeds to ooze through the booth's portals and into the theater proper, it prompts first some consternation when the projector and its lurid if amusing projections suddenly stop, and then a general flight when the audience recognizes the reality of the blob, oozing from the projection booth and into their seats, as a real threat that replaces the laughable cinematic exploitation material. The resulting scene, which has taken on a kind of cult character, with fans periodically reenacting the "run-out" at the annual Phoenixville, Pennsylvania, Blobfest,[45] depicts that audience running from the theater, almost if they were fleeing the film, bailing on what was being shown on the screen, racing from the sorts of ill-conceived pictures and empty generic formulas that much of Hollywood was not only offering to them but in which it was consistently casting them. Typical Hollywood efforts repeatedly framed that audience not as concerned young people, as Police Chief Dave believes is the case with Steve and Jane, but as the delinquents, pleasure-seekers, and dangerous pranksters that Sergeant Bert identifies, or perhaps as the helpless victims of alien invaders, as numerous other sf films of the period had all-too-simply cast them. Instead, *The Blob* finally frames that audience neither as delinquents nor as defenseless victims but as heroes of a certain type. More aware than the adults, they are the first to recognize the threat, the first to respond to it, *and* the first to realize its weakness and fight it off. In effect, the film's teen characters take on the image of responsible adults—but ones who are able to see their world more clearly than the actual adults in the film—and recognize the dangers that this world holds despite any appearance of normalcy.

If this characterization of the teen audience as being not just easily constructed, passive subjects but as more aware, even self-conscious, especially about the way many other sf films had been framing them, seems overly subtle, consider another and certainly quite successful element of *The Blob*'s marketing campaign. As illustrated earlier, at the start of the decade and with the beginning of the new enthusiasm for the sf film, RKO had been quite careful about avoiding the wrong associations for its *Thing from Another World*, even to the extent of describing the film simply as a "mystery." It has also been claimed that the latter part of the film's title—"from Another World"—was appended mainly to avoid associating it with a popular "gimmick" song of the time, Phil Harris's comic "The Thing." But as the decade of sf was nearing its "erratic" end, Paramount chose to exploit *The Blob* from precisely this angle, with the commissioning of an upbeat, comic song, "The Blob," created by Burt Bacharach and Mack David, and sung by a studio group dubbed "The Five Blobs."[46] Described by *Variety*'s Mike Gross as a "cute novelty with a swinging melody,"[47] the song combines a bouncy, cha-cha-like beat with a self-conscious, even campy approach to the film's sf "gimmick," its blob-y monster, as it describes how the blob "creeps and leaps and glides and slides across the floor," like a "splotch or blotch." It is as if the lyrics were portraying some popular dance of the period, but that is precisely the association Paramount desired, as it also commissioned the Fred Astaire dance studio

5.5. Playful paratext—and hit record: *Billboard* ad for *The Blob*'s theme song.

to begin "devising a new dance to be called 'The Blob'" to help market the film, while also selecting a "Miss Blob" who would "tour the deejays in the key markets" to represent the film's fresh teen spirit and, presumably, to demonstrate its signature dance.[48] In any case, "The Blob" was a hit on the pop charts, reaching number 33 on the Billboard Hot 100 records; it was subsequently covered by several other groups and took its place alongside a wave of other, similarly comic and also highly self-conscious pop songs that were released the same year, including "Witch Doctor," "Purple People Eater," and "Western Movies"—all of them assuming a knowing, media-savvy young audience who found pleasure or amusement in these songs' reflexive lyrics.

But more than just another piece of exploitation advertising designed to make audiences aware of the film original, the song in its self-conscious attitude was somewhat removed from *The Blob*, inviting listeners to approach what one of Paramount's original and more conventional publicity releases had described as the "most horrifying of screen monsters" with more than a bit of tongue-in-cheek attitude. That vantage recalls the same sort of double perspective that would, in this period, also come to characterize an emerging cult cinema, perhaps signaled more obviously by such sf films as *Plan 9 from Outer Space* (1959, Ed Wood, dir.) or even *The Blob*'s double-bill mate, *I Married a Monster from Outer Space*.[49] After the fashion of the lyrics for "The Blob" or the histrionics of *Daughter of Horror*, these films practically invite viewers to see *through* their thin texts rather than immerse themselves in them, to become aware of the various and far-from-subtle mechanisms they employ—very much a "creep and leap" effect—to manipulate reactions and exploit viewers, while also taking some pleasure in their awareness of those effects. It is a pleasure that Susan Sontag, in her discussion of an emerging camp sensibility, notes might well be "worn" somewhat proudly, as "a badge of identity" by those viewers.[50] Though they opened pathways for multiple marketing possibilities, such add-on texts, when combined with the treatment of the teens here, suggest the emergence of a new strategy that other accounts of teen and genre marketing have overlooked. It is marketing that invites the possibility for reading and responding in *multiple* ways to films like *The Blob*: seeing it as a typical Hollywood sf text, but also seeing it as aware of and even sensitive to its intended audience, while providing that audience with, as the decade was ending, a more complex and satisfying self-image. Far from accidental, that audience sensibility resulted, as Jack Harris would later explain, from his own efforts to try to understand the ever-changing marketplace by canvassing his intended audience, doing surveys, and letting them "tell you what they like and don't like. And Listen!"[51]

Just a few months before *The Blob*'s release, James Nicholson, the head of American International Pictures, would also allude to this sort of multiple potential as he sought to explain his own studio's phenomenal success in the same period. Responding to charges that AIP's various horror, sf, and other exploitation productions, films such as *I Was a Teenage Frankenstein* or *Invasion of the Saucer Men* (1957, Edward L. Cahn, dir.), were actually dangerous because they had the potential for causing "psychological damage" in naïve teenage audiences, Nicholson flatly rejected the notion, arguing that the industry needed to take a more complex view of that audience. As he explained, AIP pictures typically "strive for unbelievability. Teen-agers who comprise our largest audience recognize this and laugh at the caricatures we represent, rather than shrink in terror," while "adults, more serious-minded perhaps, often miss the point of the joke," much as, he implied, the critics of his studio's films so often did.[52] It is an interesting stance, implying, on the one hand, that the makers and viewers—or at least many of the intended viewers—of these films did not take them very seriously. And on the other, it suggests that the various ways in which they were marketed, with other paratextual "forms of life" that existed both within and around the films, were an important part of the total film experience. The films' caricatured figures, ballyhoo campaigns, exaggerated warnings, saturation advertising, songs, dances, even beauty contests signaled certain attitudes to the youth-dominated audience, providing a different, extratextual richness. In that erratic market period for sf, Nicholson implied, all of these filmic and profilmic elements helped frame the "joke" that was the film—a joke that this audience, if not a "more serious-minded" adult one, clearly got.

Of course, it is hardly an insight to recognize that the film industry made a decided turn to the youth demographic in the mid- to late 1950s, at a time when older generations were retreating from theaters in favor of television's free domestic entertainments. But the nature of that turn and the ways in which the industry framed and reframed an audience, especially for sf, as the decade wore on and filmmakers, along with genres, responded to new economic realities and new cultural concerns, seems especially telling. As Lisa Kernan has observed, even the trailers for this period's sf films often seemed to function unlike those of the past, to have a different and somewhat ambiguous sense of audience—a point especially observed in the trailers crafted for many foreign sf films of the period, as I demonstrate in the next chapter. Thus Kernan notes—as Doherty also implies—that their "rhetoric no longer addressed an implied universal audience"; however, she reads that changed sensibility in a more complex and telling light than does Doherty.[53] Instead of simply accepting that the intended audience was a juvenile one, she finds a distinctive approach at work in those trailers, as they seemed to "enter a realm of the playful that functions . . . differently in terms of audience address" than the trailers that were typical of classical Hollywood films.[54] It is a rather shifty, even somewhat postmodern, characteristic that is clearly noticeable in *The Blob*'s trailer, which markets the movie with both a promise of "scares" and, almost incongruously, images of laughing teens in a movie theater, while a voice-over narrator archly announces that the blob will soon "be oozing into this theater."

The film industry, especially in its exploitation efforts, seemed to be dismissing an earlier sf fascination with technical accuracy and dissolving much of the genre's emphasis on science and technology into a genre-straddling "monster mash" whose primary payoff often seemed to be one of shock or the "offbeat excitement" *Variety* described. However, a targeted youth audience was also obviously wanting something more, as the erratic response *Variety* noted and the dwindling sf box office at decade's end underscored. What *The Blob* especially suggests is that while the traditional ballyhoo "gimmicks" could still prove useful, the ways in which that dominant youth audience was positioned, imaged both within the narrative and outside of it, and addressed not by one type but by a variety of ballyhoo, were also crucial and might provide that something more. Perhaps by allowing youths to find a reassuring position as viewers and as subjects, making them privy to the "joke" of the films, and providing them with a kind of double vision, the film industry—or at least a demonstrably successful work like *The Blob*, with all the elements surrounding it—might suggest that the genre still had something special to offer the youth audience, something that made them seem special.[55]

This point is implicit in John Rieder's reminder that our various "modes of publicity" have the ability to "disrupt and revalue the meaning of any particular generic identity."[56] Clearly, by the end of the decade, sf was in the midst of change, or what Rieder terms "revaluing." A blob-like yet much smaller mass of sf films was still being released, aimed at a general teen audience but typically without the more precise and imaginative targeting that marked the Paramount–Jack Harris effort. Low-budget, decade-ending films like *The Hideous Sun Demon* (1958, Robert Clarke, dir.), *Teenagers from Outer Space* (1959), and *The Cape Canaveral Monsters* (1960, Phil Tucker, dir.), while brandishing such easily identifiable marketing terms as "Outer Space" and "Cape Canaveral," not only offered little of the science fictional but also framed their main audience, as did many other exploitation efforts, simply as undemanding juveniles. Thus, advertisements for the unremarkable *Teenagers from Outer Space* would bill it as a film about "Thrill-Crazed Space Kids Blasting the Flesh Off Humans," that is, as a work about quite literally alien-ated teens that effectively trivialized that audience's very real sense of alienation. Other, more ambitious efforts at revaluing that generic identity would result in films that inflected sf in a variety of ways, not just as typical alien invasion or giant monster stories, but as comedy (*Visit to a Small Planet* [1960, Norman Taurog, dir.]), as social commentary (*On the Beach* [1959, Stanley Kramer, dir.]), and as dark satire (*Dr. Strangelove* [1964, Stanley Kubrick, dir.]), while fragmenting the sf audience and further challenging the film industry's usual modes of publicity. But while *The Blob* could hardly be described as invoking serious science or breaking new ground for sf, its success, as well as that of Jack Harris's follow-up effort, *4D Man* (1959, Irvin Yeaworth, dir.), suggests that sf, even in this erratic period, could still prove an effective vehicle when the movie industry engaged in the proper sort of "market-making" and when it sought to more effectively match the genre with that most significant "other form of life," a sf audience.

CHAPTER 6

SELLING JAPAN
Making, Remaking, and Marketing Japanese SF

Donald Richie, one of the foremost historians of Japanese film, has observed a pattern of assimilation at work in Japanese culture that would become especially prominent in postwar cinema. The Japanese, he argues, have always been particularly adept at adopting elements from other cultures—Korea, China, the United States, among others—and fitting them, sometimes almost unrecognizably, into their own traditions, embracing what seemed valuable and discarding what seemed not. Within the world of the cinema, this process has been marked by an interplay between what Richie identifies as a native "presentational ethos," achieved "through various stylizations, with no assumption that raw reality is being displayed," and, particularly in the postwar period, a Western "representational ethos," which "assumes that 'reality' itself is being shown."[1] As other commentators have contended, the resulting amalgam, or what the Japanese critic and film historian Inuhiko Yomota terms "cultural hybridity," has helped make Japanese films more accessible to a global audience by affording different "layers" or avenues of familiarity and access.[2] For the purposes of this discussion, I want to focus on both the Japanese assimilation of sf in a particularly stylized form, their *kaiju eiga*, or giant monster films, and on US efforts to market these films in the late 1950s, which demonstrates another sort of assimilation as the film industry sought to open up films like *Godzilla, King of the Monsters* (1954, US 1956, Ishiro Honda, dir.), *Gigantis, the Fire Monster* (1955, US 1959,

Motoyoshi Oda, dir.), *Rodan* (1956, US 1957, Ishiro Honda, dir.), *The Mysterians* (1957, US 1959, Ishiro Honda, dir.), and *Mothra* (1961, US 1962, Ishiro Honda) to American audiences.[3] Coming near the end of the decade, when many in the US film industry saw a waning popularity for sf, the successful marketing of these films helped rekindle interest in the genre, broaden our understanding of what constitutes cinematic sf, and, just as significant for an emerging global film market, demonstrate the increasingly important issues involved in marketing international productions to nonnative audiences.

I want to focus specifically on the marketing of Japanese sf films in this chapter for a number of reasons. One is that the postwar Japanese film industry, partly due to the country's occupation by US forces until 1952, underwent a kind of cultural Americanization. Its film industry in particular closely mirrored the US industry, with six large studios dominating production, a roughly similar number of films being produced through much of the decade, and a similar drop-off in movie attendance and production as the decade was ending and television became more readily available and an increasingly important part of the culture.[4] Another is that, in seeking to introduce the postwar Japanese cinema to a global marketplace, the indigenous industry found some models for its aggressive growth, development, and marketing in the US industry, easily the most popular and successful film industry in those immediate postwar years, as well as one that, in its own sort of cultural occupation, had inundated the Japanese marketplace. As a result, Japanese film companies, like those in the United States, became very active in trying to reach out to a worldwide audience rather than just relying on a domestic viewership. A third and perhaps most important reason is that Japan would develop its own highly popular approach to the relatively new regime of sf cinema in this period. Its *kaiju* films and their offshoots, including their own alien invasion narratives, as demonstrated in such near-*kaiju* efforts as *The Mysterians, Battle in Outer Space* (1959, Ishiro Honda, dir.), and *Invasion of the Neptune Men* (1961, Koji Ohta, dir.), would demonstrate a highly successful version of that "cultural hybridity" Yomota describes and, in the process, offer major competition to American sf films of the time. Following the reconstruction and release to Western audiences of its 1954 *Gojira* as *Godzilla, King of the*

Monsters (hereafter simply termed *Godzilla*) in 1956, the Japanese film industry would provide a host of similar films to the American sf community, its products would be marketed successfully in many other countries by both US and Japanese distributors, and it would even open a door in the market for a more "presentational" style of sf cinema that continues in the present-day *kaiju* cinema, as represented by films such as *Pacific Rim* (2013, Guillermo del Toro, dir.), *Kong: Skull Island* (2017, Jordan Vogt-Roberts, dir.), and *Godzilla vs. Kong* (2021, Adam Wingard, dir.).

The specific way I want to explore this issue of "cultural hybridity" is by framing these films in the context of what Matthew Fuller terms a "complex medial system,"[5] that is, as a system of linked, interdependent, and even multimedia practices. As Fuller explains this element of media ecology, texts do not just exist as autonomous narratives; rather, they "make the world and take part in it, and at the same time, synthesize, block, or make possible other worlds. It is one of the powers of art or of invention . . . to cross the planned relations of dimensionality—the modes or dynamics that *properly* form or make sensible an object or a process."[6] In short, the elements—and extratextual dimensions—of those texts are, as he explains, always working to generate "something more than the sum of their parts."[7] And that something more forms an important, even essential, component of the films' marketing.

In the case of the Japanese *kaiju* films, this system involves much more than the original Japanese movies, aimed mainly at an indigenous audience. It also includes their US adaptations or release versions (which often were re-edited and dubbed, included newly shot or acquired file footage, added new characters, and were retitled); the materials involved in their various marketing efforts, such as ads, trailers, and pressbooks; and the production of multiple other related texts, including sequels or series entries that were inspired by that successful marketing. In this way, the Japanese *kaiju* films also presented audiences with a new kind of hybrid: blending elements from Japanese culture with Western sf motifs about alien invasion and atomic paranoia; fusing proven ballyhoo tactics with the emerging practices of the 1950s, especially saturation booking and heavy use of the still-new television medium for advertising; and bridging any "planned relations" or natural narrative similarities with the production of sequels and the use of recurring elements that would help link texts in a series and provide audiences with continuing access, or what Fuller describes as a "thicker relationship"[8] to their narrative worlds, similar to the sort of fan relationship often observed among sf literature and media buffs. In this pattern of development, Japanese and American texts came together; new, combinatory marketing practices were deployed, and successful marketing helped inspire a body of texts that would also contribute substantially to the richness of sf cinema, both in this period and beyond.

The system of media ecology that can be observed in what I collectively refer to as the *kaiju* efforts, particularly those emerging from Japan's Toho Studio, was partly driven by industrial pressures in the postwar period. While the war had left Japan with a still-dynamic film industry, buoyed especially by the presence of such experienced and talented filmmakers as Akira Kurosawa, Yasujiro Ozu, and Kenji Mizoguchi, it was also one that was constrained by the US occupation's censorship, and that, along with the loss of the country's various colonies and occupied territories, took a markedly insular turn. What Yomota describes as the "new idea" films that began appearing reflected an emerging "postwar ideology of Japan as an ethnically homogenous, unified linguistic unit."[9] As a result, its productions, at least through the end of the US occupation in 1952, tended to be aimed largely at an internal audience and focused on particular changes with which the "unified" culture was then struggling: the anxieties about war responsibility, new democratic ideas encouraged by the censors, the shifting roles of women in society, among others.[10] Even though many of these films adopted more of a Western representational approach, such productions were not easily exportable, and they did not allow the Japanese film industry—as the German film industry had managed to do following World War I—to bring in much foreign currency. In fact, in 1954, the year that the first *kaiju* film appeared, Japan imported approximately 200 films (141 of them American-made) that produced revenues of over $30 million, but it earned only a reported $1.5 million from its own film exports, even though that group included such highly lauded works as Teinosuke Kinugasa's *Gate of Hell* (1953) and Kurosawa's *Seven Samurai* (1954).[11] In response to this ongoing situation, the Japanese film industry began to organize international publicity and marketing efforts, such as the 1955 Japanese film fair in Paris and, starting in 1957, annual film weeks at New York's Museum of Modern Art, while also trying to produce films that were more in line with contemporary international concerns and that thus had more potential for being leased or purchased by international distributors for exhibition abroad.

While Japanese films like *Godzilla* and *Rodan* reflect part of that effort to emulate other concerns, especially the rising global interest in sf, they were not a part of this initial industry-organized marketing offensive. Rather, the films that were selected for these cultural promotions were meant to demonstrate the film industry's highest artistic aims, its claims for a modern consciousness, and a technical ability that matched what was seen in other well-received international film movements, such as the highly representational Italian neorealist films. For example, the first Japan Film Week, which was well publicized in American trade papers and newspapers and hosted by key Japanese film industry representatives, screened such works as *The Burmese Harp* (1956, Kon Ichikawa, dir.), *Women in Prison* (1956, Seiji Hisamatsu, dir.), and *Undercurrent* (1956, Kozaburo Yoshimura, dir.)—a war drama and two works about the difficult situation facing women in modern Japanese society; and the following year's Japan Film Week was headlined by *Times of Joy and Sorrow* (1957, Keisuke Kinoshita, dir.) and *Emperor Meiji and the Great Russo-Japanese War* (1957, Kunio Watanabe, dir.)—a domestic melodrama and a historical study. Despite the recent theatrical successes in Japan and the United States of the first *kaiju* efforts, particularly *Godzilla*, no sf films were included in these widely reported promotional showcases.

In fact, some high-placed figures in the Japanese film industry initially saw the surprising success of their first sf efforts as part of the larger problem they faced in marketing a Japanese cinema abroad, at least beyond what was termed the typical "art house" audience. Thus, while on a 1958 publicity and informational tour of the United States, Shiro Kido, president of the Motion Picture Producers Association of Japan and head of Shochiku, the oldest of Japan's major studios, discussed the problematic acceptance of Japanese productions in the American film market. On the one hand, he acknowledged that there had been a general "failure of Japanese films to catch on with American audiences," despite the international accolades that had already been received by works like Akira Kurosawa's *Rashomon* (1950) and *Seven Samurai* (1954), and he attributed this failure to both Japanese filmmakers and the American exhibition system, that is, to the lack "of sufficient promotion on the part of producers" and to similarly weak efforts by American distributors in advertising and attracting viewers.[12] On the other hand, he pointed to the types of films that American production and distribution companies such as DCA, Embassy Pictures, American International, and King Brothers seemed to relish, suggesting that contemporary American tastes were also a large part of the problem. While accepting some blame for the weak economic showing of his country's efforts, Kido said that he "regretted" that the two most successful Japanese films to reach American audiences had been the "monster epics" *Godzilla* and *Rodan*. Although he allowed that any success of Japanese films in the US market was welcome, Kido explained that these successes were not "an honorable experience" because they sent the wrong signals about the broader Japanese film industry and the people in it who "are so positively and artistically inclined."[13]

And yet in the same year and while on a similar tour to stimulate American distribution of his country's products, particularly Toho Studio's latest films, that company's sales manager, Nagamansa Kawakita, offered a very different perspective on the ability of Japanese films to attract American viewers. He suggested that his country's film industry had "made a mistake" in trying to push its more artistic but also culture-bound or insular efforts, especially "classical costume dramas," for the US market.[14] These and many other Japanese productions of this period, as Joan Mellen has observed, were heavily concerned with "the passing of the traditional way of life" and "the fate of traditional Japanese values" in the face of an ongoing and seemingly inevitable Westernization.[15] While such films were largely *representational*, evoking the everyday lives of normal Japanese citizens, in much the same way as the high-profile Italian neorealist works and American social problem films of the 1950s did, they also required audiences to understand and embrace the Japanese reality, the individual and familial conflicts and crises that were depicted in such critically praised works as *Early Summer* (1951, Yasujiro Ozu, dir.), *Ikiru* (1952, Akira Kurosawa, dir.), and *Late Chrysanthemums* (1954, Mikio Naruse, dir.).

6.1. A strained US effort to market *Ikiru* (1952), a critically acclaimed film about the changing Japanese culture. Toho Company.

Moreover, Kawakita specifically contrasted these efforts with the recent success of such Toho films as *Godzilla* and *Rodan*, along with the apparent eagerness of American companies to purchase distribution rights to other Toho sf films, particularly the forthcoming *The Mysterians* and *The H-Man* (1958, US 1959, Ishiro Honda, dir.). In his opinion, the secret to such successful global marketing was not looking to the past, as in the *jidai-geki*, or period dramas, nor to mirroring everyday Japanese concerns about cultural change, but rather focusing on modern audience interests and especially "offering the West what it wants," which is "currently . . . science fiction,"[16] or at least sf done in the Japanese fashion. In naming and staking a claim on the genre at a time when many in the American film industry had become skeptical about its future, Kawakita was, in fact, taking the pulse of both his own and the American audience. Moreover, he predicted a long-term popularity for the genre in both cultures, noting that "all over the world people are talking about outer space and the H-Bomb, and it doesn't look as if those things will stop" in both their appeal and influence.[17] He thus predicted that Western film markets would see many more Japanese films in this vein—films that, in the hybrid way noted earlier, built on demonstrated Japanese strengths in this area while also incorporating plots and themes that were familiar to American and other Western audiences. Kawakita's observations would receive a succinctly economic endorsement several months later when *Variety* (April 15, 1959), in a special issue devoted to the international film industry, clearly picked up on these conflicting assessments by Japanese executives. Offering an overview of the few recent Japanese successes in the US market, while noting the upcoming releases of *Gigantis, the Fire Monster* (a sequel to *Godzilla*) and *The Mysterians*, was an article whose headline concisely made the point: "Japanese Arters Wow Critics, but Horror Films Get Coin."[18]

In the light of Shiro Kido's apologetic comment about Japan's "monster" films and the suggestion that there might be something less than "honorable" about them, it is also significant that Kawakita, speaking for Toho, Japan's foremost purveyor of such films, insisted on a more precise framing for these works. He pointedly identified his studio's efforts not as "horror" or "monster" films—despite their *kaiju* stars—but as sf, affirming a market for the genre in his belief that "science fiction will last quite a while."[19] That affirmation is particularly noteworthy at a time when many American commentators still tended to lump horror, sf, and thrillers into the same generic category (thus the *Variety* reference to "Japanese . . . horror films"); repeatedly suggested that despite some recent successes, the vogue for such films was just a fleeting one;[20] and even framed the audiences for such products in a broadly generic, often even disparaging way—as what *Variety* termed "juvenile trade," as "thrill-fans," as "followers . . . of chill making," or, as Dave Jampel disdainfully described them, "horror addicts."[21] Even after nearly a decade in which, according to Peter Biskind, sf films had repeatedly "recast familiar fifties themes in terms that were peculiarly its own"[22]—that is, in terms of modern technoscientific culture with both its promises and its perils—the genre still seemed a bit "foreign" to some in the US industry, as if they, too, wanted to apologize for the film type or at least for the turn in the US film market from what were seen as more serious or traditional Hollywood films, even if that turn had realized some significant profits in otherwise quite difficult times.

But the Japanese efforts that Kawakita promised were not quite like American sf films of the period, or, more accurately, they were both like and unlike them—assimilations or hybrids. *Godzilla, King of the Monsters*, as it was billed in the United States, can be considered a model for those that would follow. It was partially inspired by the 1953 American effort *The Beast from 20,000 Fathoms*, which was easily one of the most profitable and influential sf movies of the decade. *Beast* earned approximately $2.25 million for an initial cost of just $210,000, and it inspired a host of subsequent similar and mostly profitable efforts, such as *Them!* (1954), *Monster from the Ocean Floor* (1954, Wyott Ordung, dir.), *It Came from Beneath the Sea* (1955), and *Tarantula* (1955, Jack Arnold, dir.). Its story about a giant prehistoric monster awakened by atomic testing and then wreaking havoc on modern society, as represented by the city of New York, would form the general template for the original *Gojira*, once it was paired with a story drawn from recent headlines—that of the Japanese fishing boat *Lucky Dragon 5*, which had accidentally been caught within the fallout area of the first hydrogen bomb test at Bikini Atoll and whose crew developed radiation sickness from the encounter.

The Japanese film would amplify that highly publicized incident by depicting a series of fishing and cargo ships being destroyed or mysteriously disappearing, and it would metaphorize the destructive potential of the hydrogen bomb explosion in its massive, awakened creature, explained by some as a mythic figure or god long worshiped by the inhabitants of Odo Island and by others, such as the paleontologist Dr. Yamane (Takashi Shimura), as simply a hibernating dinosaur. In any case, that mysterious mixture of mythic and historical explanations becomes linked and collectively identified in the film as "Gojira" and labeled by the press in the film as a "child of the H-bomb." The film thus managed to effectively blend an American sf story with the frightening headlines from Japanese newspapers, and mythic elements from Japanese culture with a modern scientific perspective, while fashioning a fantastic visual tapestry out of a multitude of miniatures, a full-size man-in-a-Godzilla-suit (played by Haruo Nakajima and Katsumi Tezuka), and stock footage of the modern Japanese military in action. The result of this mix of representational and presentational elements, accompanied by a stirring score from Akira Ifukube, one of Japan's top classical composers, was hardly typical American sf, but it was something different enough that the historian David Kalat, responding to its many over-the-top elements, effectively describes it in his own hybrid terms as "a monster opera."[23] It was also a film that became the twelfth highest-grossing movie of the year in Japan, which demonstrated the potential marketing appeal of this new blended approach to sf.

While *Gojira* initially drew no export interest, just over a year later—and as its Japanese box office became better known—its rights were purchased by a group of American investors, including Joseph Levine of Embassy Pictures, and a new company, Trans-World Releasing, was formed to distribute the film. The now renamed *Godzilla, King of the Monsters* would also follow the path of many other foreign films in the US market, enduring what Kalat terms "some form of Americanization,"[24] or what can be considered another level of hybridization. The plot was trimmed considerably, the film was dubbed into English, and a number of additional scenes were shot, most of them involving a new character, a visiting American journalist named Steve Martin and played by Raymond Burr. Martin provides a voice-over/flashback framework for the slimmed-down story and injects a kind of documentary or representational flavor that anchors some of the more fantastic elements of the film. He witnesses the monster's attacks, presents them to his listeners/readers, and attests to their reality through his own shocked responses (suggested through numerous close-up reaction shots). In the process, his character provides audiences a kind of hybrid narrative space wherein they can accept the visual excesses of the actor in a monster suit portraying the titular *kaiju*, of models that stand in for a modern civilization and the Japanese military, and of what many American viewers might have seen as histrionic responses by characters—including Burr—facing the horrors of this monster. This Americanization quickly proved a success, returning an initial box office of approximately $1.2 million dollars on a rights purchase of just $25,000 and eventually being successfully released (or rereleased) in Japan with Japanese subtitles as *Monster King Godzilla*.[25] This success, though, might best be measured and understood when seen in the context of the complex medial system that I detail in what follows.

While the film historian David Cook simply attributes the popularity of *Godzilla* and its various *kaiju* offspring to "their imaginative special effects and model work,"[26] this initial success, as well as its later global appeal, was due to much more. Certainly, audiences had by this point come to associate elaborate special effects work with sf cinema, and as noted, a trend of giant, nuclear-born sf monsters had already flickered across American screens well before *Godzilla*'s appearance. Both method and monsters gave sf a distinctly different dimension from the prevailing film and television space operas of the early 1950s and produced different audience expectations. The first Japanese efforts in this new vein were impressive not because of their use of highly expressive actors playing such menaces as Godzilla and Rodan—in place of the stop-action, animated creatures of Ray Harryhausen that populated such films as *The Beast from 20,000 Fathoms* and *It Came from Beneath the Sea*. And their impact was not because of the highly detailed scale models with which the filmmakers surrounded these figures—and which they then impressively destroyed. Certainly, the Toho Studios' special effects work, especially that done by Eiji Tsuburaya, was world class, and these heightened effects, coupled with some documentary-style footage, did allow

138 — SELLING SCIENCE FICTION CINEMA

Wednesday, April 4, 1956 — *VARIETY* — 21

WHEN IT COMES TO BEASTS
!! *We Got 'em* !!
THE KING OF THE MONSTERS
"GODZILLA"
The Mightiest of them all

with

A MONSTER CAMPAIGN THROUGHOUT NEW ENGLAND

to launch this

MIGHTIEST OF THE MIGHTY

400 TOP THEATRES
Extended Playing Time Everywhere!!

150 THEATRES DAY and DATE MAY 2nd (a record)
MIGHTY SATURATION ON TELEVISION AND RADIO

BOSTON • PROVIDENCE • NEW HAVEN • BANGOR • PORTLAND • HARTFORD
MT. MANSFIELD • MT. WASHINGTON • SPRINGFIELD

AND THE FULL YANKEE RADIO NETWORK

COLOR ADS and a BLASTING NEWSPAPER CAMPAIGN

Under the Direction of
TERRY TURNER
Who With His Hollywood Colleague
DON THOMPSON
have handled a hundred pictures, among which were
"KING KONG" (RKO), "BEAST FROM 20,000 FATHOMS" (Warners), "WAR OF THE WORLDS" (Paramount), "THE CONQUEROR" (RKO)

and TERRY says:

Dear Joe—
"I think 'Godzilla' tops any monster picture we have ever handled. Don's TV and radio spots will be the best he has ever made because this baby really breathes fire. Why gents, one short snort from this monster and 'poof' there goes another city."

JOE LEVINE
Embassy Pictures Corp.
19 Winchester St.
Boston, Mass.

6.2. *Variety* announcement about the "Monster Campaign" for *Godzilla* (1956).

audiences to relish what Susan Sontag felt was one of their central appeals: "the aesthetics of destruction," marked by "the peculiar beauties to be found in wreaking havoc,"[27] as Godzilla and other *kaiju* trampled detailed models of modern cities. But I would argue that a major part of their success was because the films went so far beyond the scale of their American sf forebears, including a figure like King Kong, an effect that their US marketing efforts much appreciated and on which they heavily capitalized.

In 1952, the iconic American figure of King Kong had been reintroduced to global audiences with a highly successful rerelease of the original 1933 film, its new profits arguably opening the door for the decade's many other large and more pointedly sf monster efforts, including the Ray Harryhausen films. But Godzilla easily surpassed King Kong in size, with the original US pressbook exaggeratedly describing him as a "Film Terror 400 ft. Tall!" and suggesting as a publicity claim that he "makes King Kong look like a midget."[28] The publicity materials also repeatedly emphasized that, compared to American movie creatures of 1950s sf, the "havoc" Godzilla brought was monumental in scale, thereby evoking the equally monumental issues that this new kind of sf figure seemed to embody. The sheer size of the Japanese *kaiju*, as well as the carnage that Godzilla and his progeny wrought, underscored an element of their quite different presentational ethos, for it established the spectacular nature of their narratives, framed their events in a rather stylized manner that rendered them more "operatic" than representational, and also provided an effective emblem of the films' significant—even gigantic—concerns, issues that were endemic to the new sf cinema, if treated somewhat less metaphorically in most American films. Indeed, the Japanese films' giant monsters, giant robots, and equally giant alien spaceships (depicted most effectively in *The Mysterians*) were presented to the public as more than newly discovered forces of nature, like Kong, or vastly superior alien technologies, as in a work like *The War of the Worlds*. They insistently embodied the very real—and very large—problems that had been spawned by science, technology, and the recent World War, problems that were now facing Japan, America, and indeed all of civilization, such as the possibility of another global war and the inescapable accompanying threat of not just national but global nuclear annihilation. As Inuhiko Yomota explains, this thrust was a significant contributor to their impact on Japanese audiences. Thus, in describing *Godzilla*, Yomota labels it a straightforward "antinuclear film with an ecological perspective," embodied in the confrontation of its spectacular monster with modern society.[29] Moreover, he observes that for the home audience, the depicted violence and destruction were multiply allusive, certainly "unthinkable without considering the air raids by the American forces that scorched the Japanese archipelago just nine years before."[30] And indeed, even many American reviewers recognized this dimension of the films, typically tying their "spectacular pictorial effects" of widespread destruction to growing fears of world war and atomic holocaust.[31]

That linkage is significant because it would become a recurring component of the complex medial system in which these films operated. The Americanized version of *Godzilla* had toned down some of those nuclear fears, while also eliminating some very pointed references to Japanese suffering during the war, but in light of the film's success, the American distributors of both *Rodan* and *Gigantis, the Fire Monster* (aka *Godzilla Raids Again*) tried to establish both visual and thematic ties to *Godzilla* by again inserting new footage—or rather, old file footage—as they introduced stock scenes of missiles firing and atomic explosions, accompanied by stilted narration that framed the respective narratives precisely within that sensitive nuclear context. For example, *Gigantis, the Fire Monster* begins with footage of a hydrogen bomb test as its narrator intones that the bomb "inaugurated a new and frightening era in the history of man," and *Rodan*'s narrator, following the US cut's similar added scenes of nuclear explosions, directs a leading question to the film audience: "What have these tests done to Mother Earth?" Of course, such a question served to lend significance to the monster films, giving their fantastic stories a metaphoric thrust; but it also thematically linked them to their successful predecessor while helping construct a *kaiju* mythos: of monstrous figures that humanity's dangerous fumbling with atomic weapons has disturbed and whose monumental onslaught it has brought upon itself.

However, that linkage also posed some problems, as Sontag's comments that these films are mainly "about destruction" and symptomatic of a new cultural fascination with extreme violence might suggest.[32] Since the film industry was already under fire for various disturbing changes in its pictures' content and, correspondingly, what Thomas Doherty describes as changes "in the moral universe Hollywood had posited for so long,"[33] it would seem that emphasizing those images of violence and carnage for their own sake could have put off many viewers, or at least the traditional audience for the sorts of films produced by the major studios. Underscoring this effect, Jason Barr observes that one of the most unsettling aspects of many of the Japanese efforts is how, "as the credits roll on most *kaiju* films, the viewer is . . . left with images of massive destruction and a heightened sense of anxiety."[34] But that effect might be seen as part of their *presentational* rather than their *representational* character. Thus, Mike Bogue observes that the *kaiju* "were not the rational monsters of the West: They were monster-gods whose motivations often defied logic,"[35] and, he might have added, who were being framed within a larger mythos in which Earth, its monsters, humanity, and its own technological monstrosities were all intimately involved and whose narrative was still being played out. That implicit premise would eventually create other avenues of marketing for these films in later years: producing not only a sympathy for some of these creatures but a possibility for rehabilitation, for depicting them as guardians or protectors of "Mother Earth" and its often-careless human inhabitants.

Besides such narrative recastings, another part of the medial system involving these films was the ballyhoo sent out in advance of their US appearances, conventional efforts that sought to promote them in many of the ways that were used for other exploitation films of the period and that thus framed them for viewers in a more familiar light. That is, all were accompanied by special promotions, gimmicks, and product tie-ins mainly designed, as Mark Thomas McGee explains, to have slight reference to the narratives while working mainly "to attract people's attention."[36] In this context, I might note that three weeks prior to *Godzilla*'s US premiere, Joe Levine of Embassy Pictures and Trans-World Releasing placed a full-page ad in *Variety* fashioned, with various rhetorical flourishes, not so much to attract viewers but to attract the attention of his potential exhibitors by heralding all that his company was doing to draw in prospective viewers. The ad announced a forthcoming "monster campaign" for this "monster picture," indicated that "400 Top Theatres" were already scheduled for the film's rollout, and touted the fact that he had employed two of the era's most noted marketing "handlers," Terry Turner (previously RKO's head of exploitation) and Don Thompson, to design the marketing campaign (April 4, 1956)—in short, Levine was advertising his intended advertising. In a more conventional bit of ballyhoo, DCA, the US distributor for *Rodan*, sought attention by announcing that it was going to issue "shock insurance policies" of $1,000 each for any "patrons who suffer disability or death because of 'shock' induced" by the film.[37] Rather more ambitiously, Columbia Pictures, the US distributor for Toho's *H-Man*, created a "horror show on wheels," a traveling display housed in a thirty-two-foot trailer. Touring thirty-six cities in eight states, it offered a walk-through of "the Home of the H-Man" that included a variety of familiar sf effects, such as "bubbling atomic pools, dripping phosphorescent water, ultra-violet lighting and eerie sound effects."[38] After acquiring the release rights for Toho's *Mysterians*, MGM, in a move that echoed its much-publicized tie-in with Quaker Oats for *Forbidden Planet*, arranged a partnership with Sonny Boy chocolate drink, once again prominently linking sf—in this case, sf about an alien invasion—to a children's promotion and children's audience.[39] And in an effort to capitalize on a recent American space achievement, Ernest Emerling, MGM's vice president of advertising and publicity, announced that he had contacted the Army Ordinance Missile Command at Cape Canaveral in Florida about the possibility of hiring Abel and Baker, the two monkeys who had recently traveled into space aboard a Jupiter rocket, to do promotional appearances for the film.[40] With the possible exception of the *H-Man* trailer, though, this sort of ballyhoo seems largely intended to link these Japanese films to the American audience's typical experience with such exploitation films, rendering them, in various familiar ways, as less "foreign" while also creating an exciting atmosphere for their reception.

Another conventional component of that medial system was the typical publicity materials—and promotional suggestions—common to most sf films of the period, as demonstrated by some of the pressbooks prepared for the release of films such as *Godzilla*, *Gigantis, the Fire Monster*, *Rodan*, and *Mothra*. All provide dramatic "ad slicks," that is, standard designs that could be used for posters, lobby cards, and newspaper advertisements, and most also include brief "general advance stories" intended to be placed in local newspapers to whet the audience's appetite for the forthcoming films. All offer more of the typical exploitation ideas that theater owners were encouraged to pursue on their own. These suggestions included: placing dinosaur models or pictorial exhibits in lobbies to emphasize the kinship to Godzilla and other *kaiju*; stenciling dinosaur "footprints" on the streets leading up to theaters; locating a wrecked car next to the theater, with signs suggesting it had been smashed by a monster; arranging for window-display tie-ins with local toy stores, showing toy versions of military items or spaceships seen in the films; holding costume contests at children's matinees with attendees invited to create outfits seen in the films or even to dress as monsters; having coloring contests based on simple character mattes that would be provided by the theaters; even displaying samples of supposedly radioactive materials along with a Geiger counter to further underscore how films like *Godzilla*, *Rodan*, and *Mothra* were tied to the "atomic age" and the issues it heralded. In fact, by the time of *Mothra*'s release, just after the end of the decade, the pressbook created by its distributor, Columbia Pictures, would provide two full pages of such suggestions for marketing activities, promising exhibitors multiple ideas for what it termed "Showmanship for Every Situation."[41]

While these sorts of exploitation suggestions differ little from those typically found in pressbooks for many Hollywood films of the period, some notable variations remind us of the special character of the Japanese imports and of how they were being assimilated into the US marketing system. For example, while the artwork is invariably dramatic and usually emphasizes the scale of the various monsters or monstrous aliens—measured against images of people fleeing in terror or attacking planes and tanks—it is typically limited to one or two poses depicting the eponymous monster. The artwork for *Rodan*, for example, either shows Rodan diving from on high toward a devastated city while groups of terrified humans flee and tanks and aircraft fire on it, or it depicts the creature rearing skyward above the same destroyed cityscape while the same terrified humans run and the same tanks and aircraft fire back. These ads simply but effectively identify two primary thrusts for the film: the much larger-than-life nature of the monster, depicted in iconic presentation, and

6.3. Raymond Burr, as journalist Steve Martin, offers an eyewitness account of Godzilla's attacks. Toho Company/Trans World Releasing/Embassy Pictures.

the spectacular display of action and destruction to be found in the films. Moreover, both the people depicted and the city in flames more closely resemble those of the United States than they do any place or people in Japan, thereby further masking its foreign nature. In fact, an advance article prepared for one of the pressbooks pointedly outlines this strategy. It suggests that such a blurring of nationality should be encouraged as a natural part of the contemporary film industry's "eye to a wider market potential," while explaining that, after all, the film "is truly an international" story. Thus, though it "was conceived by Japanese and is set largely in Japan . . . the climactic action . . . takes place in a country remarkably like America."[42]

In the light of this designed thrust, the other significant difference in these marketing materials is perhaps predictable but similarly telling: the accompanying commentary lacks almost any of the usual credits, such as the names of actors, directors, producers, and technicians. Certainly, the distributors could assume, at least for the first few *kaiju* films, that the names of the

Japanese artists involved in these films would be largely meaningless to most American audiences, although in the case of the standard *Godzilla* posters, a singular actor credit appears at the very bottom, the name of Raymond Burr, and one of the "general advance" articles in the film's pressbook focuses on his "starring" role in the film. The Canadian American actor had been essentially grafted into the film for the US release, his presence and his flashback narration, as noted, providing US audiences with a frame for properly seeing "every earth-shaking, screen-shattering thrill" that the poster promised. In fact, in place of the usual credits, the *Godzilla* poster underscored the film's visual thrills, offering a bullet list of amazing things that audiences must "SEE!," and several of the *Rodan* posters and ads provided in its pressbook literalized this same thrust, accompanying the identical "SEE!" injunction with three small images of events from the film. While artwork for the later release *Gigantis, the Fire Monster* simply offered head and shoulder images of its two starring *kaiju*, Gigantis (aka Godzilla) and Anguirus, as they engaged in battle, it did consistently include a vaguely sensationalistic credit promising "A Cast of Thousands!" It is not until *Mothra*'s US release in 1962 that even a limited set of Japanese credits appears on the posters and ads included in the film's pressbook—a sign that the marketing had successfully linked these films into a complex medial system, one in which audiences were starting to recognize and be attracted to the work of directors like Ishiro Honda and special effects experts such as Eiji Tsuburaya.

But arguably the most important element of the marketing campaign for Japanese sf in this period was not this sort of conventional ballyhoo but rather something that could most effectively "sell" the spectacular visual elements emphasized in the posters and ads: the television spot. Further extending the medial system in which these films operated, in fact becoming crucial to it, television was rapidly becoming a regular part of most US film advertising by the time of *Godzilla*'s arrival. As Christopher Anderson recounts, Hollywood, despite early fears about television as a competitor, had quickly "recognized television's ability to reach into the household, the privileged site of consumer culture, and was as eager as any manufacturer to place its products in the American home" by exploiting this new medium.[43] And relatively cheap movies—or at least cheaply acquired movies such as *Godzilla*—did leave more money available for investing in their promotion through television. Thus, when Joe Levine introduced the first Japanese sf film to the US market, he immediately sought to tap into this relatively new dimension of the consumer culture, as his full-page *Variety* announcement about *Godzilla* illustrates. The "monster campaign" it promised gave special emphasis to a planned "Mighty Saturation on Television and Radio," with approximately $80,000 spent on promotional spots in the New England area alone (see figure 6.2). Opening the film almost simultaneously in four hundred theaters in that region—a mixture of first-run theaters, neighborhood movie houses, and drive-ins—maximized the results of those media spots and confirmed Levine's profit strategy, as the film earned approximately $1.2 million at the box office.[44] In fact, Levine's advertisement that vaguely boasted of offering audiences "the mightiest of them all" might just as well have been describing his promotional campaign as his new film "star," Godzilla.

The main components of that television marketing campaign were a series of spots drawn from two prepared trailers, one approximately fifty seconds in length and the other just over one hundred seconds (both available online). As Jonathan Gray points out, the purpose of such spots is typically to provide "vivid ideas of what to expect and transport . . . viewers into their storyworlds,"[45] and both US trailers accomplish these purposes simply but effectively. In each, a montage of the monster wrecking a modern city, of jets firing missiles, and of people reacting in terror is accompanied by a narrator repeatedly intoning the title phrase "Godzilla, King of the Monsters" (six times), as if shouting a warning, but also driving home the film's title. A series of titles flash over the images of devastation, describing "Dynamic Violence," "Savage Action," and "Spectacular Thrills," emphasizing both the subject and the tone of the narrative. And while some identifiably Japanese faces can be glimpsed in these scenes, both trailers freeze on a close-up of Raymond Burr, who, as the American reporter Steve Martin, lends his constantly amazed reaction to the film's action. Accompanying his close-up is another voice-over that almost seems to speak Martin's reaction, as it observes, "You may wish to deny it, but your eyes tell you it's true!" While his look assures the audience of an effective placement within the narrative, it especially illustrates the sense of amazement that even Western viewers could expect to experience thanks to the promised "violence," "action," and "thrills."[46]

Employing a similar marketing combination of saturation bookings and heavy television advertising, *Rodan* would find even greater success with its US release. For its opening in the New York metropolitan area, the film had what *Motion Picture Daily* termed a "record weekend," with police reportedly being called out on both Saturday and Sunday "to control lines" at several theaters,[47] and *Film Bulletin* directly attributed that response and a box office of approximately $500,000 during its opening week to distributor DCA's similar blitz of television ads.[48] The seventy-nine-theater saturation engagement in the New York area had again been backed by a reported $80,000 advertising outlay that broadcast approximately seventy television spot announcements in the days immediately leading up to the film's opening. That campaign produced results that Irving Wormser, the DCA sales head, claimed were "better than any recent science fiction picture," and that "equaled or bettered the returns of some recent [non-sf] blockbusters."[49] Moreover, that campaign would prove a model for continued success as the film gradually opened across the country. Noting with some surprise the film's consistent drawing power, *Variety* described *Rodan*'s box office in the Midwest as "one of the most sensational of the winter season," while again suggesting that much of the credit for this "sensational" showing was "due to the heavy backing given the engagement on radio and tv," including approximately fifty television spots scheduled in several major metropolitan areas on the days just prior to the Midwest opening.[50]

As in the case of *Godzilla*, the central focus of *Rodan*'s television marketing campaign was a series of spots drawn from a trailer of just over one hundred seconds. Despite the initial ballyhoo about the film's previously noted "shock" elements, the trailer directly touted the film's sf status. Echoing wording that was provided in the film's pressbook, it described *Rodan* as "the science fiction masterpiece of all time." And recalling the marketing of *Godzilla*, it emphasized the outsized nature of the *kaiju*, describing the resurrected pteranodon as the "monster of monsters," and "big as a skyscraper." As with the *Godzilla* spots, it offered a montage

6.4. Rodan depicted attacking a typical Western metropolis and its inhabitants. Toho Company.

of images of destruction while incorporating file footage of the latest American jets and missiles being used to combat the flying monster, thereby hinting at an allied effort against a global threat. While dubbing the film into English, DCA, unlike Levine's Embassy Pictures, did not reshoot any scenes for *Rodan* or insert an American actor like Raymond Burr to give a Western face and feel to it, so there was no effort to disguise the Japanese locations. However, the narration frames those locations in a presentational manner, as does the film's appended prologue depicting nuclear explosions: as metaphoric of a potentially global calamity. To further emphasize this global thrust, superimposed titles in red letters over images of destruction warn audiences that "This could be your terror" and "This could be your city." In effect, the video presentation encouraged a level of identification while also allowing for any anxieties to be displaced onto the depicted "other" culture.

The success of these promotional strategies would prove lessons learned for subsequent distributors of the Toho products. When Warner Bros. acquired the rights to the *Godzilla* sequel, *Godzilla Raids Again*, retitling it *Gigantis, the Fire Monster*, the company's ballyhoo would add another, synergistic twist to the complex medial system in which these films were, by now, clearly operating. Tellingly, the studio would actually point to its television advertising, as if the life of the film and the life of its visual advertising were linked or at least complementary texts. Posters and ad copy provided in the film's pressbook repeatedly described *Gigantis* as "The picture you've been hearing about on Radio and TV!," while exhibitors were similarly reminded to play up the television connection, to "Let your patrons know—via every exploitation idea at your command—that 'Gigantis' is the Picture They've Been Hearing About on TV and Radio!"[51] When in the same year MGM acquired the rights to another Toho effort, *The Mysterians*, for $250,000—which the studio hyped as "the highest price ever paid for a Japanese picture"[52]—it similarly followed with a highly touted, television-heavy publicity effort. Supporting a one hundred-theater saturation opening, the four-week campaign included some specific audience targeting, such as promotional "spots on numerous children's programs," while the film's pressbook offered instructions on how to "sell this picture to all age groups," including those it identified as part of "the craze for science fiction."[53] Terry Turner, who had previously headed *Godzilla*'s publicity and exploitation campaign, estimated that the full video effort MGM was undertaking would "expose 'The Mysterians' to an estimated 137 million viewers" prior to its opening.[54] A two-page ad in *Motion Picture Daily* (April 15, 1959,

6.5. MGM touts a publicity campaign for *The Mysterians* (1959) that "out-circuses the circus!"

4–5) further pitched the nature of this promotion to exhibitors, touting its "terrific tv trailers" and other elaborate promotional materials that, the ad boasted, "out-circuses the circus."

Those "terrific" trailers also followed the general pattern of previous highly effective *kaiju* promotional pieces, and, as was becoming the case for all the Japanese "monster" films, would pointedly label the film as sf. Echoing the *Godzilla* advertising, a narrator rapidly repeats *The Mysterians* title three times, sounding as much like an incantation as an announcement. Thereafter, the narrator introduces the film's aliens from the planet Mysteroid, using direct address to tell viewers that "you are now inside a flying saucer" while also evoking the now common trope of alien invasion. What follows is a montage of futuristic weaponry and images of destruction, with a main emphasis on the invaders' unleashing of a giant, Godzilla-like robot, Mogera, seen smashing through cities and defying the usual medley of human weapons—jet fighters, guided missiles, and tanks—while the landscape burns. The accumulation of these images leads to the narrator's summation, once again recalling a line in the film's pressbook and repeated on most of its posters—that *The*

Mysterians is "the greatest science-fiction picture man's imagination ever conceived."[55] While hardly that, the campaign would pay off with a box office similar to that of *Rodan*, bringing in more than $500,000 in *The Mysterians'* initial saturation booking, a success that *Motion Picture Daily* directly credited to its elaborate "television campaigns."[56]

By the time of *Mothra*'s release in mid-1962, the sf market seemed to be shrinking, with *Box Office* noting that despite "improved" film production for the year, Columbia was apparently the only US studio that remained invested in the genre.[57] In keeping with the studio's increased reliance on independent productions and acquired properties, it had scooped up this latest Japanese *kaiju* production,[58] entering into a coproduction deal with Toho that involved its investment in *Mothra* prior to the film's completion.[59] However, the finished film presented Columbia with a number of difficulties. It was one of the most expensive Japanese productions to date at a cost of approximately $700,000,[60] and, though it was one of the most successful releases in Japan, it could prove a harder sell in the United States given the extent of its hybridization, which Steve Ryfle and Ed Godsziszewski describe as "a resplendent mix of science fiction and fantasy."[61] Its monster, a giant caterpillar/moth, while also linked to atomic testing, seemed an unusual, even unlikely menace. Furthermore, it featured another element that seemed firmly grounded in Japanese mythology, the *kaiju*'s twin fairy guardians, whose presentational character made for a problematic link to sf. Thus, despite Columbia's involvement, Bill Warren judges that in this case there seemed to have been much less "effort to direct the film at an international audience."[62] Despite the complex medial system that had been developing for the Japanese sf films over the course of six years, and what *Film Bulletin* termed Columbia's "aggressive showmanship" for the film,[63] *Mothra* faced a tough marketing challenge.

The television saturation campaign that was once again planned to precede the film addressed these difficulties in several ways that suggest a developing flexibility in the way that medial system might operate. In what must have seemed a surprising tactic, the two main trailers (a short and a long one) offered hardly a glimpse of this new monster. The short version is composed of black-and-white still drawings, stylized or presentational renderings of the film's events that offered audiences no images of this new monster. In its place, the stylized images are accompanied by a narrator asking, "Who is Mothra? What is Mothra? Why does all the world fear Mothra?"—questions that recall the marketing strategy used for *The Thing* by only underscoring the mystery surrounding the creature's appearance. The longer version offers scenes from the film, but they are almost exclusively ones that emphasize its special effects, showcase its vibrant Eastmancolor photography, and still consistently present Mothra in a veiled or absent manner. At one point, the creature is shown within a cocoon that deflects attacking rockets and rays, while a narrator underscores its invulnerability, describing it as "enveloped in a shell that no human force can penetrate." In other instances, Mothra's presence is indicated solely by its effects, such as the gale-like forces it generates—recalling Rodan's similar destructive power—or the massive waves it creates that, we are told, can wreck ocean liners. And here, too, the narration concludes with a leading question: "What is the secret of Mothra?" Also recalling the relatively recent strategy used for Alfred Hitchcock's *Psycho*, whose prerelease advertising sought to keep its plot secret and to which no one was admitted after the screening had begun, this "policy of secrecy"[64] used the most public of media both to veil the possibly challenging image of the creature and to arouse potential viewers' curiosity about the film.

The television spots would also effectively employ other strategies of absence and substitution. One instance is their treatment of the twin fairies who tend to Mothra's egg on the mysterious Infant Island. In the trailer—and on the posters—these innocent and isolated figures are sexualized, described as "the tiniest, loveliest women in all creation," and as "sacred beauties of a lost tribe," while Mothra itself is described as "ravishing a universe for love!" Moreover, the fairies' call to Mothra is presented as a kind of performance, echoing not only King Kong's presentation in the original *King Kong* but also their extrafilmic role as the popular singing duo The Peanuts (Emi and Yumi Ito). In a further extension of the medial system here, the group was signed to a contract with Columbia Records, a subsidiary of Columbia Pictures, and their first US album was released in concert with the film's debut.[65] Another example is the effort to inject into the film a more outward-facing or global thrust. Thus, few Japanese faces

SELLING JAPAN — 153

6.6. Sexualizing the *kaiju* tale, with Mothra "Ravishing a Universe for Love!" Toho Company/Columbia Pictures.

are shown, and the city we see being devastated by Mothra—one named in the film as New Kirk City—looks very much like New York. This "look," though, was not accidental, but rather another bit of intentional hybridization, part of an effort to give the film more external appeal, as was the naming of the country in which New Kirk City is located, Rolisica—an anglicized combination of Russia and America.[66] The hoped-for effect was that "this god-monster Mothra," as it is termed in the trailers, would come to seem very much like a global threat.

This heavy media reliance, specifically on a television market saturation campaign in the days immediately preceding a film's saturation release, proved key to the success of *Mothra* and many other Japanese sf films in the US market, as well as a sign of promise for future film marketing. In the course of the television industry's rapid development, it had, by the time of *Godzilla*'s appearance, become not so much a rival to the movie industry as a media companion, a key part of the larger medial system, that could form an effective part of the ballyhoo for films and a tool that might be used almost like an electronic usher—as the pressbook for *Gigantis, the Fire Monster* promised exhibitors—to help "move audiences from their living-room chairs to the seats of your theatre."[67] Given television's own advertiser-driven nature, distributors thus found it a willing accomplice in helping them quickly reach a mass audience; in targeting specific groups, such as children or young adults, through selective placement of the advertising spots; and in framing audience expectations by tailoring images to emphasize the appeals of a particular film or even, as noted in the case of *Mothra*, to de-emphasize or veil any of its perceived weaknesses. The result was indeed, as Joe Levine had advertised, a series of "monster campaigns" that promoted these new creatures to the American public[68] while also helping launch a new sf tradition.

But more than just promoting monsters, the marketing campaigns for the various Japanese *kaiju* and alien invader films of the 1950s and early 1960s gave a new thrust to sf at a time when many in the US film industry were looking in other directions to attract audiences. As Thomas Doherty chronicles, the emergence in the late 1950s of a teenage "subculture" armed with a large discretionary income was prompting the domestic industry to directly address this burgeoning audience mainly with films in a rock 'n' roll, horror, or juvenile delinquent vein—all low-budget, featuring distinctly teenaged types, and emphasizing their specific cultural concerns. Despite the crossover appeal to this group that sf's adventurous narratives had, the genre, with its requisite special effects, special sets and props, most often adult figures, and more global concerns, seemed to have lost much of its popularity or, what some saw as a worse fate, to have been trivialized. In fact, at the end of the decade, a dedicated sf periodical such as *Amazing Stories* editorialized about the current film "trend" of "taking good science fiction and making it seem either juvenile, sadistic, or sexually presented"—a trend that the author Norman M. Lobsenz lamented "isn't building good-will or interest in science fiction."[69] At the same time, *Box Office* noted that the domestic film industry was showing only "light" interest in the genre, *Variety* claimed that the "science fiction product" had "lost its potency," and *Film Bulletin* argued that sf was "considered almost taboo by those who persist in . . . harnessing public taste to the chains of the cycle pattern."[70]

And yet the Japanese imports, many of them attractively shot in color and widescreen, offering elaborate special effects, and providing a new level of fantasy, managed to connect with multiple audience segments and even build a following that would prompt the creation of additional films in this vein, a practice demonstrated by *Godzilla*'s hurried sequel, *Gigantis, the Fire Monster*. Thanks to the films' relatively cheap leasing costs—and recall that Levine originally purchased the US rights to *Godzilla* for just $25,000—distributors could afford to market them elaborately in ways that capitalized on their many attractions. And though the various monsters these films featured were often anchored in Japanese traditions or myths—and thus to what I earlier termed a presentational approach—American moviegoers were able to access these fantastic visions through hybrid elements that readily connected a Japanese mythos to the most recent concerns of US sf: their atomic consciousness, their familiar scientist types, their elaborate demonstrations of military pyrotechnics (usually US-branded weaponry), and what Sontag describes as their overall "aesthetics of destruction."[71] These elements proved to be easily exploitable through both conventional movie ballyhoo and the powerful medium of television, and they also helped contribute to the birth of a new—and still-popular—subgenre of sf.

Just as significantly, they were marketed, almost as a badge of pride, *as* sf. While many US sf films from this late 1950s period tended to be grouped together with a wave of cheap horror films—such as *Macabre* (1958, William Castle, dir.), *A Bucket of Blood* (1959, Roger Corman, dir.), and *The Tingler* (1959, William Castle, dir.)—and given disparaging names, as when *Variety* referred to them as "horrorifiers,"[72] this was not the case with the new Japanese fare. From Nagamansa Kawakita's assertion that the Toho films were sf and that sf was something that a global audience demonstrably wanted, to the posters that proudly proclaimed *The Mysterians* to be "the greatest science-fiction picture ever conceived by the mind of man," these films clearly branded themselves as sf. In fact, as an aid in marketing *Mothra*, the film's pressbook pointedly advised exhibitors to seek out "science fiction clubs" in their area, as "these clubs are a natural for 'Mothra'" and could offer valuable "assistance in publicity planning."[73] As science and a global science-mindedness were starting to look ahead to a reinvigorated space race in the 1960s, spurred by President John F. Kennedy's promise to put a man on the moon by the end of that decade, sf cinema, thanks in large part to the creation and successful marketing of these Japanese films, was also staking out new territory that would expand its boundaries and even the definition of the genre. As these Japanese efforts demonstrate, with their contemporary legacy and continuing relevance marked by such films as *Shin Godzilla* (2016, Hideaki Anno and Shinji Higuchi, dirs.), *Godzilla: King of the Monsters* (2019, Michael Dougherty, dir.), and *Godzilla vs. Kong* (2021), there consistently seems to be *more* to sf than any momentary definitions, descriptions, or marketing appeals have ever been able to adequately encompass.

CONCLUSION

At the end of the 1950s, Roger H. Lewis, the head of advertising and exploitation at United Artists, sought to sum up how recent developments in both the film industry and the culture were affecting US marketing practices. While describing film promotion as "a complex and unique form of merchandising," even "a dynamic art rather than a science," he recommended that future film marketing should be guided by two simple yet similarly "dynamic" principles: that audience taste—or "public responsiveness"—is constantly changing and that each picture must be "given a new, unique identity."[1] That sense of continuously shifting components within a changing web of commercial activity posed an obvious challenge to the industry's conventional practice, one wherein films were commonly treated as stable, largely predictable commodities—the standard products of a "movie factory"—and moviegoers as passive, largely predictable subjects. But failure to respond to the new dynamic conditions of the marketplace would, Lewis suggested, lead to more box-office disappointments at an already difficult time for the industry. Moreover, he advised that in the current market, all industry efforts needed "a fresh approach and fresh thinking."[2]

As chronicled in the previous chapters, the burgeoning sf cinema of the 1950s, itself a relatively new and decidedly dynamic phenomenon, afforded the industry many opportunities for putting such "fresh thinking" into practice by employing new marketing tactics. But as the problematic, shifting genre titles that cropped up in the trade papers might suggest, marketing for the sf films that began pouring out of both major and minor US studios in this period often just seemed to evoke the "scarers," fantasies, and "mellers" of earlier years, despite having little in common with those movies. The new sf films were products of the shifting audience tastes Lewis notes, and they reflected different cultural concerns. They would also play out that pattern of dynamic change over the course of the decade as the era's once-popular space operas disappeared and, especially in the second half of the decade, were replaced by a pageant of giant, scientifically awakened, and irradiated monsters roaming across film screens in the United States, Japan, and elsewhere. And yet, the industry only slowly began to recognize that the "product" of sf had never been a constant, or as Rob Latham puts it, a "fixed and coherent" story type[3] like the western, musical, or mystery had seemed to be; rather, it was something evolving, always becoming something "more" than it had seemed—or than had been advertised.

This same industry hesitancy also characterized much of its approach to the audience for this amorphous, or blob-y product, which proved equally hard to identify, pin down, or reach with those advertisements. If what had been identified as sf prior to the 1950s might not be seen or marketed as such by 1960, the ad audience or, more narrowly conceived, the general fandom for sf product would prove equally elusive and difficult to target or "frame." Clearly, given its advertising patterns, the industry did not think it was just those people who purchased the dedicated pulp magazines or the gaudily covered mass-market paperbacks issued by new publishers such as Ace Books and Ballantine Books. And as seen earlier, even when a targeting notion such as "juvenilization" gained traction in the second half of the 1950s, it often seemed to miss the mark, underestimating the attitudes of that sf audience or typecasting them as little more than passive subjects.

Despite these many issues, the sf genre and its audience did manage to find a place in US and world culture by the end of the decade, largely because both were the products of a technoscientific culture that was itself being powerfully born and whose most visible birthmark was one of ongoing change. Like the film industry, this culture required its own "fresh approach" to thinking through the many challenges it faced, with sf—although certainly not just in its cinematic form—providing some useful alternatives. And despite Sontag's assessment that films of this period offered only "an inadequate response" to "the most profound dilemmas of the contemporary situation,"[4] they did, in fact, present audiences with a broad canvas (quite literally so with the industry's adoption of such new widescreen technologies as CinemaScope, VistaVision, Superscope, Toho Scope, etc.) on which the era's most important political and social developments repeatedly found metaphoric shape, affirming their prominent and pressing place in the public consciousness. If often in exaggerated proportions, the film images directly and repeatedly evoked the threat of nuclear apocalypse, as the very titles of such films as *Day the World Ended* (1955, Roger Corman, dir.), *The Night the World Exploded* (1957, Fred F. Sears, dir.), and *The Day the Sky Exploded* (1958, Paulo Heusch and Mario Bava, dirs.) practically shout out; they took up the difficult-to-discuss issue of race relations in works like *The Mole People* (1956, Virgil W. Vogel, dir.) and *The World, the Flesh and the Devil* (1959, Ranald MacDougall, dir.); they foregrounded gender-related tensions and challenged traditional women's roles, as films like *Untamed Women*, *Attack of the 50 Foot Woman* (1958, Nathan Juran, dir.), and *I Married a Monster from Outer Space* illustrate; and they explored the subtler psychological territory of widespread human alienation in such movies as *Invasion of the Body Snatchers* and *The Incredible Shrinking Man* (1957, Jack Arnold, dir.). For a dynamic—and apparently multiply threatened—world and citizenry, the "cognitive estrangement" central to these sf films proved a natural complement, an appropriate frame through which an already cognitively estranged (and not just conventionally "alienated") audience might better see that world of the Cold War, space race, and dizzying technological and cultural change. And though they never provided audiences with satisfying solutions or even the "adequate" responses to these problems Sontag called for, films in themselves rarely do.

The genre's positioning was also supported by another, primarily postwar development that would lend marketing support to this range of concerns. As the economics historian Lizabeth Cohen has chronicled, the postwar period witnessed a "fundamental shift" in marketing practices not only in film but in most industries, a turn "from mass marketing to market segmentation."[5] This veritable "revolution in market segmentation," as she describes it, was largely a response to the era's new economic conditions, as "the meteoric rise of discretionary income in the postwar period" meant that each member of the typical family could have a greater "influence on purchase decisions," as well

160 — SELLING SCIENCE FICTION CINEMA

7.1. Atomic anxieties writ large—in Superscope—with *Day the World Ended* (1956). American International Pictures.

as a measure of independence in buying products.[6] The resulting range of influences would require marketers—in the film industry and elsewhere—to think more about the mixed nature of their audiences, both their interests and their anxieties, and it would especially force them to consider how to identify, differentiate, and target those specific audience segments, rather than broadly aiming their publicity at what had been seen as the typical family or even the "average" viewer.

Of course, class and gender had already been employed in this fashion with, as Cohen notes, "histories that stretched back to the early twentieth century."[7] In fact, sf cinema offers some early examples of this practice, as Paramount in 1932 drew on the former notion when it marketed *Dr. Jekyll and Mr. Hyde* not as sf or even horror, but as a "prestige" production, and, in the same year, Fox aimed for a gender appeal when it promoted *Six Hours to Live* as a romantic melodrama, with posters showing its lead couple in a passionate embrace while a headline suggestively described its protagonist (Warner Baxter) as "A Man Who Had Six Hours to Love." But in the postwar era, other identifiable—and self-identifying—groups, particularly those of age, ethnicity, profession, and other special interests (including science enthusiasts), began to be recognized as "marketing segments that advertisers determined were well worth catering to."[8] While Cohen's primary case studies are popular magazines, such as the teen-oriented *Seventeen*, and consumer products, such as Pepsi with its late-1950s and early-1960s identification of a "Pepsi Generation," her comments apply equally to the movies in this period. Filmmakers, aware that fewer people were going to the movies, constrained by the postwar reshaping of (and constraints on) the film industry, and faced with increasing competition from television, of necessity began to identify targetable audience segments and their primary concerns, as with the case of rock 'n' roll films, "race" pictures, what Thomas Doherty vaguely labels "adult-content films," and, of course, those interested in sf and the new world it seemed to address.[9] As I have shown, even this not completely "fresh approach" had some impact, as it produced clearly targeted efforts by the major US studios that tried to determine whether sf moviegoers were lovers of mystery and horror (*The Thing*), fans of hard science (*Destination Moon*), excitable moppets (*Forbidden Planet*), or just alienated teens (*The Blob*). Targeted marketing, even when it somewhat missed its target, had obviously become integral to the industry's thinking about sf, from reaching appropriate audience segments to addressing their key concerns.

What a truly fresh approach might have recognized—although it was never quite managed by those in the film industry itself—was the extent to which sf, marketing, and the movies all seemed to share certain thrusts and were in a sense natural allies, even kin. We might begin to make out the shape of that commonality in the sf historian Adam Roberts's description of how the genre developed "a consistent *outwardness*" as it came to rely for much of its effectiveness on a "strong visual component."[10] While literary sf is hardly the same sort of "vision machine" that the movies have often been termed, the genre might be considered a kind of rhetorical tool for *producing* images of things that might yet be, its content effectively capitalizing on what Miriam Hansen has described as "the new visuality" of the modern era that saw the nearly simultaneous birth of both sf and film.[11] This highly visual emphasis shows up not only in the many striking images described throughout the genre literature—of massive spaceships, strange creatures, alien worlds, futuristic cities—but also in a marked movie consciousness that ran throughout the pulp literature of the 1920s–1940s. There we can find stories set in the film industry, stories about the development of new cinematic or image-related technologies, and even stories using cinematic terminology and techniques.[12]

Another filmic link can be acknowledged in the visually exciting and sometimes even lurid pulp magazine covers that offered the most extravagant versions of those enticing images. These elaborate covers, as well as the ones found on their paperback progeny of the 1950s, were themselves, first and foremost, effective marketing tools that closely paralleled movie posters and lobby cards in the dynamic, exciting imagery they featured and in their colorful nature. Moreover, both the pulp editors and the artists who produced these cover illustrations were, as the various letters columns in the magazines testify, well aware of the effects of their work, that the art was, as the pulp historian Mike Ashley notes, "a major sales attraction."[13] In fact, as Yaszek and Sharp observe, many of the women artists who contributed such art to the pulps had originally been "trained in commercial art" and thus knew how to best utilize its marketing appeal.[14] Crafted by such artists as Hans Wesso, Frank R. Paul, Margaret Brundage, and Howard V. Brown, these filmic-sf-marketing tools were, Roberts argues, "in many ways more important than the prose" content they introduced or advertised.[15]

Another element of that commonality is found in the economic analysis offered by John Rieder, among many others, when he attributes the genre's emergence to the cultural conditions of modernity. He argues that literary sf was a response "not just to changing social conditions but also to the new commercial opportunities being opened up by . . . mass cultural distribution" and new market conditions.[16] Thus, taking a page from Cohen's analysis, he suggests that marketers sought to exploit the "vein of opportunity" represented by the "increasing importance of science and technology" in daily life by seeking "to target specific groups . . . and turn them into habitual consumers" of stories about such subjects.[17] While that economic context is useful, it also casts sf as a largely commercial development, as if it were a specialized marketing opportunity that prompted writers and publishers to fill a certain product niche. It also recalls similar arguments that have been made by economic historians of film, who have interpreted the movies mainly as financial engines, both in their earliest days when Edison sought to extend the economic power of his phonograph by allying it with an image machine, and later as the movies became almost synonymous with the products of the Hollywood "dream factory." On the one hand, Rieder's contention that the group targeting that resulted centered largely on those who had a "fascination with science"[18] seems to oversimplify the implications of his main point and is little more satisfying as an explanation of sf's origins and attractions than histories that read Hollywood primarily in terms of the box office. But on the other—and more importantly—it underscores the extent to which the identity of sf has, from its start, been intertwined with the rise of modern marketing practices, much as has indeed been the case with film.

Yet one more, and perhaps the most important, component in that relationship is the fact that advertising itself is what I earlier referred to as a "disguised" sf text. With that description I simply meant to underscore the inherently utopian premise that is built into all marketing activities—just as it is into the movies and sf. The desire to visualize and sell us other possibilities, to put forward something more, is certainly an inherent element of the cinematic dream, just as it is part of the very premise of sf, a genre that invites our wonder and speculation about what might be. And while sf would, during that crucial formative period on which I have focused, pose a challenge to a number of traditional Hollywood marketing practices, particularly the work of those marketers who did not know how to draw effectively on sf's sense of wonder, it would also provide a valuable response to some of the economic issues that were then facing the changing film industry, as Warner Bros. quickly appreciated when it capitalized on such low-budget, if effects-heavy films like *The Beast from 20,000 Fathoms* and *Them!*, and which other large US studios—MGM, Columbia, Universal-International—obviously recognized as they jockeyed to buy the distribution rights for Toho's increasingly popular US imports. *Selling* the future, or at least other possibilities for self and culture, was clearly becoming a major enterprise in the period when sf cinema was making such a strong entry into the market and an equally strong impression on audiences.

This commonality, or what might be thought of as a set of shared or intertwined aims, simply seems fundamental to the great success of sf in this period, and it is probably one of the main reasons for the genre's eventual emergence as, arguably, the most popular cinematic type. To further contextualize this sense of common impulses—of wonder, of promotion, and of utopian desire—I want to consider them in the context of André Bazin's famed "myth of total cinema" or what he saw as the ultimate trajectory of the movies. Writing in this same heady postwar period, Bazin argued that the underlying "myth" of cinema involves not just a desire to produce "a perfect illusion of the outside world" but also "the converging" of "various obsessions" we have about reproduction and its appeal, all involving technologies that, in a science fictional turn of his own, he noted, had "not yet been invented"[19] but seemed just off in the future. While the outcome of these related impulses might seem to diverge from the simple aim of the reproduction of reality, the point on which most of Bazin's commentators have converged, the trajectories follow a similar arc, especially when he frames the entire cinematic enterprise in this sort of futuristic, utopian mode, as something whose goal is still "a long way away,"[20] only to be achieved, or more nearly approached, by what a cinema of the future might offer—almost implying that all cinema might hold a science fictional character.[21]

Of course, this frame, which tries to bring sf, marketing, and cinema together by way of suggesting their intertwined impulses, does not provide us with any better sort of definition or identity than that with which other genre commentators have so often wrestled. It roughly describes a kind of nexus of scientific and technological developments, human "obsessions" or "habitual" consumption, and hoped-for satisfactions. Moreover, it reminds us how science and technology—the most powerful driving forces of modern life—have empowered our imaginations, helping produce desirable images while also selling us on the notion that those images (the stuff of the imagination) can become real. But what this framing does offer is a better sense of the complex series of relationships between the sf texts, their creators, their consumers, and their culture, all part of a developing *idea* of what constitutes sf cinema, or what might even be termed a *myth of total sf*—a myth that, by its very nature, must always seem, as Bazin emphasizes, "a long way" from being realized.

While offering only a nod in the direction of the issue of marketing, Garrett Stewart, in his 2020 study on the intersections of film, sf, and digital technology, has undertaken a bit of media anthropology that sheds further light on this element of commonality. He observes how contemporary applications of film technique, particularly as they have become an integral part of the digital regime, increasingly seem to echo and remind us of the technology involved in the process of filmmaking, resulting in, as he nicely puts it, "the momentarily blown cover of the movie's image engineering" as it is "obtruded under narrative stress."[22] As examples of such telling obtrusion, he points especially to several such highly stressful and digitally dependent recent narratives: *Transformers* (2007, Michael Bay, dir.), *Lucy* (2014, Luc Besson, dir.), and *Ex Machina* (2014, Alex Garland, dir.). In these films—sf all—we see how "the science of the image" repeatedly "becomes part of the fiction," as their narratives depicting the emergence of new or other forms of life strain at film's traditional efforts to image the imaginable, and as their fantastic digital images and equally fantastic transformations of those images practically seem to celebrate the "technique behind" the movies.[23] In these and other films of the twenty-first century, technique seems to work in what he terms an "unmanned" fashion,[24] almost as if it had a will of its own, presenting itself simultaneously as part of the films' appeal and part of their story.

Stewart suggests that we think of such obtrusions as accidental "metaphors"[25] that are the natural product—or fallout—of the broad range of today's digitally dependent cinema. But he sees these metaphors surfacing most powerfully in our sf cinema because the tradition of technical "trickery," from the time of Méliès to the present, is so conducive, even increasingly necessary, to achieving the genre's key goal of wonder, to making viewers believe in, among other things, flying saucers, world-destroying death rays, menacing gelatinous blobs, atomically resurrected monsters, even the various sorts of amazing transformations—and Transformers—that feature in the contemporary films noted above. It is a trickery that works to "sell" us on the very business

7.2. With the android Ava (Alicia Vikander), the "science of the image" takes center stage in *Ex Machina* (2014). Universal Pictures.

of sf as it invites us to voyage on the latest examples of what—in its own remarkable and much earlier bit of reflexive obtrusion—the opening of the original *King Kong* (1933, Merian C. Cooper and Ernest B. Schoedsack, dirs.) referred to as "the movie ship." And at this point I would hope that the multiple senses of "selling" I have used here remind us how marketing itself might serve in this same way, as another one of those metaphors, denoting another way in which sf cinema has often seemed to "blow its cover," letting us see how that desire for wonder works, powers our movies, and empowers their narratives in our culture. It is, I believe, a very useful way of thinking about sf in the formative period discussed here, when it most needed to be sold—and when the US film industry sorely needed a product like sf to sell.

Certainly, by the 1950s, the industry needed something, whether gimmicks, new technologies, or just different sorts of stories, that would resonate with those receding postwar audiences—or audience segments—and lure them back into the theaters. And with sf it had a viable candidate for that something, although one that, prior to this period, had not been particularly well understood or effectively explored. Consequently, the film industry as a whole seemed to struggle with this burgeoning form, as if reenacting that early scene from *The Thing* in which soldiers and scientists "spread out," surrounding an indistinct form they can barely see buried in the ice below, and, by spreading their arms, collectively try to trace out its shape—discovering in the process and to their surprise an early icon of cinematic sf, a flying saucer. In this instance, too, we find one of those *accidental* metaphors suddenly surfacing, giving form to the convergence of sf, cinema, and marketing, pointing up their almost inevitable linkage. It reminds us how, throughout this period, both major and minor studios repeatedly tried to take the measure of this new genre form, to determine its shape, its usefulness, and how it might best be sold to different groups of moviegoers. Obviously, they did so at times, as these soldiers and scientists do, hesitantly and quite awkwardly; at others with mixed, even accidental success; and at others enthusiastically and rather effectively, especially as the industry learned to partner with the new technology of television, to better gauge its changing audience, and to embrace other sf visions, such as those coming from Japan, not to mention those starting to emanate from various other global investors in the genre, such as Britain, Italy, the GDR, the Soviet Union, and other countries. But the key was coming to some understanding of sf itself, that shifty or "restless" form that had been given so many names and been so easily confused with other story types.

Of course, the sudden flourishing of sf in this period has been attributed to a great many factors. Among the usual suspects are the science and space consciousness of postwar audiences; the UFO phenomenon of the late 1940s and early 1950s; the shift of sf literature from what was largely a pulp form into the publishing mainstream; changes in the film industry that brought a willingness, even a necessity to explore—and exploit—new film formulas; and the sudden competition of television, which, because of its willingness to explore new possibilities, successfully found a ready audience for its early sf series: the space operas, sf adventures, and sf anthology shows that captured the imaginations of kids as well as many parents. Even the new internationalism of the film marketplace would eventually play a role, boosting the visibility of the form while providing added competition and new areas for development and marketing. However, this explosion of sf cinema was hardly unproblematic. As many commentators have observed, it was accompanied by similarly unprecedented

7.3. An "accidental" metaphor: trying to trace out a science fictional shape in *The Thing* (1951). RKO Pictures.

changes in the American film industry, resulting in a situation wherein, as Bradley Schauer notes, it was not so much stories as issues like "budgets," "exploitation," and especially "marketability" that became both primary considerations governing the making of sf[26] and influential forces affecting how audiences and the film industry thought of the genre.

Besides ushering in the popularity of sf cinema, the marketing developments of the 1950s also paved the way for the larger cultural convergence of sf and consumerism. This convergence has been marked by a wide variety of developments that have enabled versions of what Matthew Fuller has termed a complex medial system, including ever more sophisticated graphic advertisements; an expanded alliance between the film and toy industries, wherein some films seem designed from the outset to create a market for the toys they inspire; a surprising partnership—rather than rivalry—between the television and film industries that has seen even greater success today with the development of new streaming services; the creation of movie-centric (and film industry–owned) theme parks; the flourishing of a video game industry that not only contributes source material for new sf narratives but also produces paratexts for practically every successful sf film; and use of the World Wide Web as a kind of universal access point to film advertisement, film-related games and products, various franchise offshoots, and even film viewing itself. Through the narrowcasting of product ads on subject-specialized blogs, vlogs, Twitter messages, and Facebook announcements, any film can immediately reach many in its most likely market segment via a kind of electronic word-of-mouth that would seem like a sf dream for those movie industry exploiteers of the 1950s. Moreover, this dynamic "system" seems not only intent on but fully capable of marketing itself, in what Stewart cannily describes as "unmanned" fashion, by constellating around any text a host of such paratexts that lend yet another dimension to Bazin's notion of "converging" visions or even what he also seems to have correctly measured as "obsessions."

The "thicker" relationship previously forecast as part of these earlier efforts at sf marketing has, in the process, become ever more densely packed, as if inviting film fans to find a place for more of their lives within these extensive precincts, to identify more with these medial systems, to "cosplay" with and in them, ultimately to become part of their marketing practice. As an example of this development writ large, consider how Disney's opening of its new Galactic Starcruiser hotel in Walt Disney World offers to thicken its guests' relationship to what is already one of the most influential sf film franchises, George Lucas's *Star Wars*. Described as an "all-immersive adventure," the hotel inserts guests into the *Star Wars* universe as they "voyage" in the starcruiser *Halcyon* and participate in the ongoing struggle against the film franchise's repressive First Order government. Once "on board" (or checked in), lodgers are invited to assume roles in a partially scripted narrative; encouraged to purchase and wear costumes (thoughtfully offered for sale in the hotel's gift shop) suited to the characters they imagine themselves to be; and, through in-room screens, hand-held communicators, and the professional actors who make up a part of the *Halcyon*'s crew, constantly prodded to participate in the story or, as the website marketing this film-like experience puts it, to "accept a mission."[27]

And yet that elaborate "adventure" is just one part of a larger and quite powerful medial system. This system includes the special "Star Wars: Galaxy's Edge" land, located in Disney's Hollywood Studios theme park, which voyagers visit as part of their "cruise"; the rides there—and in other Disney parks—that feature their own immersive narratives; the various *Star Wars* television spinoff series, such as *The Mandalorian* (2019–2022), *The*

7.4. Disney's *Halcyon* cruise-goers enter into the world of *Star Wars*. The Walt Disney Company.

Book of Boba Fett (2021–2022), and *Obi-Wan Kenobi* (2022), which appear on the Disney+ streaming service and which play in the "cruise" rooms; and the future feature continuations of George Lucas's original *Star Wars* saga that are already in the offing. Together, these various media extensions reframe the *Star Wars* films and television series not as an adventurous vision of "a long time ago in a galaxy far, far away," but as something quite nearby, inhabitable, and filled with our utopian dreams. Moreover, this elaborate web of sf texts reminds us of the extent to which the sf feature has practically become its own marketing trailer, not only helping sell its home videos and on-demand streaming but constructing a viewership for all of the related sf texts, including those slated to follow it—as well as the ones that imitate it—and that together constitute the film supertext, ensuring its persistence in the cultural imaginary.

In effect, it is as if sf has, following a trajectory traced out from the 1950s, become its own primary marketing device, a generic rhizome that continues to surface in both expected and unexpected places, sprouting throughout contemporary culture, trying in more and more ways to fulfill its promise or feed our Bazinian "obsessions." Thus, in her observations about "the current ubiquity of the promotional message,"[28] Lisa Kernan points specifically to sf cinema and its metaphors, which also seem so ubiquitous and culturally insistent—so "promotional." This multiplicity, this thickness, is certainly more than might have been expected of sf in the postwar period, probably much more than the founding father of the genre, Hugo Gernsback, could ever have anticipated, even in his visions of movie-like adventures that we could dream through the use of his *hypnobioscope* device and of an electrified everywhere. But it might help explain *why*—to return to one of this book's starting points—we have always struggled to define sf, why there has always seemed to be, elusively yet insistently, something more to it.

NOTES

Chapter 1: Marketing and Making Science Fiction

1. The release date and director's name appear at first mention of a film; thereafter, just the title is used or, if pertinent, title and year.
2. Laemmle, "The Business of Motion Pictures," 153.
3. Ibid., 168.
4. Dupont and Augros, "Cinema and Marketing," n.p.
5. Ibid.
6. It has been estimated that in 2019—a useful year to consider since it is prepandemic, an event that influenced both production budgets and marketing costs—the average cost of a major Hollywood (or MPAA member) film was approximately $65 million, with distribution and marketing costs in the neighborhood of $35 million. See Annie Mueller, "Why Movies Cost So Much to Make," *Investopedia*, April 28, 2020, n.p. www.investopedia.com/financial-edge/0611/why-movies-cost-so-much-to-make.aspx.
7. Gray, *Show Sold Separately*, 7.
8. Kernan, *Coming Attractions*, 1.
9. Kreimeier, *The UFA Story*, 117.
10. Chapman and Cull, *Projecting Tomorrow*, 36.
11. "'Things to Come' Gets Class Capital Preview," *Film Daily*, April 6, 1936, 14.
12. "Korda-Wells Film Debated in Legislatures of World," *Motion Picture Daily*, April 7, 1936, 8.
13. "'War of Worlds' Gets CDA Premiere Aid," *Motion Picture Daily*, July 28, 1953, 7.
14. "TV, Radio Campaign on 'War of the Worlds,'" *Motion Picture, Daily* August 7, 1953, 2.
15. "Boxoffice Extra," *Motion Picture Herald*, August 22, 1953, 25.
16. "Most Newspapers Fail to Support Films: Leon Brandt," *Motion Picture Daily*, April 14, 1950, 3.
17. "Eagle-Lion Classics Set to Market an 'A' Film Monthly," *Motion Picture Daily*, June 1, 1950, 4.
18. In 1949–1956, American television screens offered approximately a dozen different space operas, some even having dual lives as both television and radio dramas, while one, *Captain Video* (1949–1955), managed to engage audiences with television, radio, and film incarnations.
19. Patrick Lucanio and Gary Coville, "Shooting for the Stars: Captain Video, the Rocket Rangers, and America's Conquest of Space," in *1950s "Rocketman" TV Series and Their Fans: Cadets, Rangers, and Junior Space Men*,

ed. Cynthia J. Miller and A. Bowdoin Van Riper (Basingstoke, UK: Palgrave Macmillan, 2012), 104.

20. Ibid.

21. Nick D'Alto, "Supermarket Spaceships," *Smithsonian Magazine*, January 22, 2015, n.p., www.smithsonianmag.com/air-space-magazine/supermarket-spaceships-180953861/.

22. Pomerance, "Introduction: Movies and the 1950s," 6.

23. Lucanio, *Them or Us*, 1.

24. Evans, *Celluloid Mushroom Clouds*, 75.

25. Warren, *Keep Watching the Skies!*, 11.

26. Schatz, *Hollywood Genres*, 10.

27. Ibid.

28. Landon, *Science Fiction after 1900*, 32.

29. Latham, "Introduction," 17.

30. Cheng, *Astounding Wonder*, 8.

31. Ibid.

32. Gernsback, "A New Sort of Magazine," 3.

33. Gernsback, "Science Wonder Stories," 5.

34. A December 1955 piece in *Variety*, for example, announced that "Hollywood appears to be embarking on another scientifiction trend." See "Universal Paces New Round of Scientifiction," *Variety*, December 14, 1955, 3.

35. James, *Science Fiction in the Twentieth Century*, 10.

36. Bould and Vint, *The Routledge Concise History of Science Fiction*, 41.

37. Roberts, *The History of Science Fiction*, 112.

38. Quoted in Yaszek and Sharp, *Sisters of Tomorrow*, 3.

39. Suvin, *Metamorphoses of Science Fiction*, 7.

40. See "'The Invisible Man,'" *Film Daily*, November 18, 1933, 4; "'Non-Stop New York,'" *Film Daily*, October 7, 1937, 6; and "As I See Them," *Film Bulletin*, November 6, 1935, 12. Phil M. Daly, in his "Along the Rialto" column, reported that Universal was "puzzled over how to effectively present 'The Invisible Man' in their newspaper ads" (*Film Daily*, August 18, 1933, 4).

41. See "The Invisible Ray," *Motion Picture Herald*, January 25, 1936, 39; "'The Invisible Ray,'" *Film Daily*, January 11, 1936, 3; and "'The Invisible Ray,'" *Motion Picture Daily*, January 11, 1936, 4. It is worth noting that generic categorization—or lack of same—figured prominently in trade advertising for the film, where it was described, whether as promise or warning, as "Not a Horror Picture!"

42. For discussion of this little-chronicled development of sf in the popular cinema, see Telotte, *Animating the Science Fiction Imagination*.

43. Rieder, *Science Fiction and the Mass Cultural Genre System*, 35.

44. Ibid.

45. Ibid., 45.

46. Ibid., 10.

47. Doherty, *Teenagers and Teenpics*, 2.

48. Rieder, *Science Fiction and the Mass Cultural Genre System*, 35.

49. Fuller, *Media Ecologies*, 4.

50. Ibid., 6.
51. Ibid., 4.
52. Ibid., 18.
53. Gray, *Show Sold Separately*, 2.
54. Ibid., 3.
55. Ibid., 4.
56. Ibid., 7.
57. The various intersections of cult/fan activity with the sf text are surveyed in Telotte and Duchovnay, *Science Fiction Double Feature*, especially 143–158.
58. Virilio, *The Art of the Motor*, 6.
59. I conclude on this conditional promise in part because that media profusion or, as Virilio puts it, pervasive "mediatization" (*The Art of the Motor*, 6) tends to make isolation and assessment problematic practices. It is a difficulty also sensed by Lisa Kernan in *Coming Attractions*, where she observes that "neither advertising theory nor narrative film theories adequately address what consequences the current ubiquity of the promotional message might hold for contemporary definitions and understandings of moving-image narrative forms" (p. 2).

Chapter 2: What Is This *Thing*?

1. See, for example, Jackson's review of *The Thing*, "'The Thing' Bloodcurdling Chiller Is Exploitation Natural," *Film Bulletin*, April 9, 1951, 12, which, while noting the film's cast of "unknowns," also commends them as "fine performers."
2. "Top Grossers of 1951," *Variety*, January 2, 1952, 70.
3. "Exhibitors Forum," *Film Bulletin*, January 1, 1951, 15.
4. Lipton, "Advertising and Publicity," 227.
5. RKO was the first major studio to respond to the government's 1948 antitrust decision against the film industry, announcing that it would enter "a consent decree" to "separate completely its production-distribution interests from its exhibition interests," including selling its shares in 241 theaters jointly owned with several independent theatrical firms. See the report "RKO and U.S. Sign Decree," *Motion Picture Herald*, November 6, 1948, 13–14. That decision would put added and almost immediate pressure on the studio's distribution arm, which previously could have relied heavily on company-owned or -affiliated theaters, but which now had to work to secure appropriate venues for its forthcoming releases.
6. Gray, *Show Sold Separately*, 3.
7. Ibid.
8. Ibid., 6.
9. Fuller, *Media Ecologies*, 11, 4.
10. James, *Science Fiction in the Twentieth Century*, 1.
11. Rieder, *Science Fiction and the Mass Cultural Genre System*, 162.
12. Altman, *Film/Genre*, 101.
13. Rieder, *Science Fiction and the Mass Cultural Genre System*, 16, 21.
14. Ibid., 5.
15. "National Pre-Selling," *Motion Picture Daily*, September 18, 1951, 3.

16. While the placement of an article about the making of *Destination Moon* by the noted sf writer Robert Heinlein in *Astounding Science Fiction* might be construed as an "advertisement," the piece was not illustrated with any of the emerging sf icons and focused largely on Heinlein's experience as a technical adviser. See the discussion of Heinlein's "Shooting 'Destination Moon'" in chapter 3.

17. The term "scientifilm" appears in a great many letters to the editors of the pulps, particularly in the 1930s, although it is especially prominent in the correspondence of one of the leading figures of sf fandom in this period, Forrest J. Ackerman. See, as an example, the exchange between Ackerman and the editor of *Wonder Stories* headlined "More Scientifilms" in the October 1933 issue. Here Ackerman shares his information that "there are over twenty-five scientifilms forthcoming" from American studios, with the editor responding that he takes "the announcements of some of these scientifilms with a grain of salt" (p. 286).

18. Sontag, "The Imagination of Disaster," 224.

19. As part of its featuring of the story, *Thrilling Wonder Stories* commissioned a cover painting by the famed pulp illustrator Howard V. Brown that was reproduced from a publicity still for the film, and it offered commentary on the production by Kuttner, who visited the set during filming.

20. "Shooting 'Destination Moon,'" *Astounding Science Fiction* 45, no. 5 (July 1950): 6–18; "Brass Tacks," *Astounding Science Fiction* 47, no. 1 (March 1951): 148–162, Campbell quote on 160.

21. That estimate, as a studio footnote explained, assumed that each publication would be viewed by an average of four readers. A similar number was cited on the cover of the official pressbook for *The Thing*.

22. The original story title, "Who Goes There?," was changed to *The Thing*, and it has often been claimed that the additional phrase "*from Another World*" was added just prior to the release campaign to distance the film from the popular novelty song "The Thing" recorded by Phil Harris in the previous year. See Warren, *Keep Watching the Skies!*, 774.

23. Barn (Barney Stein), "Short Subjects," *Film Bulletin*, April 9, 1951, 14.

24. Hedda Hopper, "My Predictions for 1951," *Modern Screen*, January 1951, 68.

25. The extent of Hawks's involvement with the film has been the subject of much debate. Hawks bought the rights to Campbell's story "Who Goes There?" in late 1948 or 1949, probably at the urging of his friend and collaborator, the noted sf writer Leigh Brackett. He then "hired two good screenwriters" (Charles Lederer and Ben Hecht, neither with any prior background in sf) to turn the story into a preliminary script based on what he estimated as four pages of the original tale, and he worked with those writers to fashion a final script. Officially, Hawks served as producer for his own company, while Christian Nyby, who had previously edited several of Hawks's films, was billed as the director. However, it was widely known in the film industry that Hawks was involved on an almost daily basis in the shooting process. His own explanation is that although he did not actually direct the film, he "was on the set for all the important scenes"

(see Sarris, "Howard Hawks," 235). Certainly, the finished film contains many of the typical trademarks of Hawks's films: fast dialogue, a group focus, mixed tone, professional figures, and the presence of a strong—or "Hawksian"—woman.

26. "RKO Will Have Mellers," *Film Bulletin*, March 26, 1951, 26.

27. "RKO to Stress Three Exploitation Films," *Motion Picture Daily*, March 20, 1951, 4. As a measure of such exploitation activity, I note that another of RKO's trio of exploitation releases, *Jungle Headhunters*, also employed a midnight release. And at its Chicago premiere, "two animated models, one of a native girl doing a barbaric dance, and the other of a warrior shrinking a human head over fire," were placed in front of the theater, while newspaper ads proclaimed that "Some Lucky (?) Person Will Win a Shrunken Head." See "May Work, or Else Scare 'Em to Death," *Motion Picture Daily*, June 12, 1951, 6.

28. "'The Thing' Bloodcurdling Chiller Is Exploitation Natural," *Film Bulletin*, April 9, 1951, 12.

29. Quoted in John Kobler's interview of William Castle, "Master of Movie Horror," *Saturday Evening Post*, March 19, 1960, 97.

30. Schauer, *Escape Velocity*, 7.

31. Quoted in Irving Rubine, "Boys Meet Ghouls, Make Money," *New York Times*, March 16, 1958, x7.

32. Schauer, *Escape Velocity*, 7.

33. "Trade Press Writers on RKO Promotion," *Motion Picture Daily*, June 1, 1951, 4.

34. *The Thing from Another World*: Campaign Book, author's collection.

35. "'Head Hunters' Scare 'Em into Theatre," *Motion Picture Daily*, June 15, 1951, 2.

36. The "run-zone-clearance" system was long a part of the American film distribution and exhibition practice. "Clearance" was a period following a run when no other theater within a specific zone or city could play a particular film. That "delaying mechanism," as John Izod terms it, was designed to provide a measure of exclusivity that would "enhance the profitability of the first-run houses," most often those owned by the major film studios. See Izod, *Hollywood and the Box Office, 1895–1986*, 41.

37. "What the Picture Did for Me," *Motion Picture Herald*, December 15, 1951, 45.

38. Quoted in Westfahl, *The Mechanics of Wonder*, 181.

39. Altman, *Film/Genre*, 54, 57.

40. Rivette, "The Genius of Howard Hawks," 71.

41. Sontag, "The Imagination of Disaster," 228.

Chapter 3: Pondering the "Pulp Paradox"

1. Schauer, *Escape Velocity*, 7.
2. Ibid.
3. Rieder, *Science Fiction and the Mass Cultural Genre System*, 44.
4. Yaszek and Sharp, *Sisters of Tomorrow*, 340.
5. "The Vizigraph," *Planet Stories* 2, no. 7 (February 1944): 123.

6. "The Reader's Forum," *Amazing Stories* 25, no. 1 (January 1951): 147.
7. James, *Science Fiction in the Twentieth Century*, 47.
8. Carter, *The Creation of Tomorrow*, 176.
9. See "The Motion Picture Production Code," *Censorship in Film*, https://censorshipinfilm.wordpress.com/resources/production-code-1934/.
10. "Par Experiments with 'Cyclops,'" *Variety*, January 24, 1940, 20.
11. These descriptions are all taken from the "Critics' Quotes" column in the movie trade paper *Motion Picture Daily*, April 22, 1940, 8. This column regularly excerpted critics' comments from around the country during a film's first weeks of release and, in so doing, provided a thumbnail sketch of the way recently released films were being received.
12. Henry Kuttner, "The Story Behind the Story," *Thrilling Wonder Stories* 16, no. 3 (June 1940): 126.
13. "Par's Outside Publicity Man," *Variety*, October 9, 1940, 8.
14. "Inside Stuff-Pictures," *Variety*, May 24, 1950, 30.
15. "High Costs Preclude Shorts Payoff—Pal," *Variety*, May 24, 1950, 18.
16. William J. Heineman, "Since Pix More Than Ever Today Compete with Home Entertainment, Real Selling Is a Must," *Variety*, January 3, 1951, 13.
17. Heinlein, "Shooting 'Destination Moon,'" 7.
18. Ibid., 6, 8, 7.
19. Ibid., 12.
20. Ibid., 17.
21. Ibid., 18, 7.
22. Ibid., 7.
23. Ibid., 17.
24. Brog, "Destination Moon," *Variety*, June 28, 1950, 6.
25. See the report "This Week in Pictures," *Motion Picture Herald*, October 13, 1951, 11.
26. Winthrop Sargeant, "Through the Interstellar Looking Glass," *Life*, May 21, 1951, 130.
27. "'When Worlds Collide' Special Exploitation," *Motion Picture Herald*, November 17, 1951, 49.
28. "Para. Releases Boosted to 15," *Motion Picture Daily*, April 30, 1951, 4.
29. Richardson, "Making Worlds Collide," 84.
30. Ibid., 90.
31. Ibid., 84.
32. Partly because of such pronouncements, Pal received "The Invisible Man" award at the 1951 San Francisco convention of science fiction writers and editors, honored as "the man who contributed the most toward science-fiction in the past year." See "National Pre-Selling," *Motion Picture Daily*, July 3, 1951, 3.
33. According to Bill Warren, while *When Worlds Collide* was originally conceived as a big-budget special effects film, the studio's rush to release the film resulted in a number of effects shots being canceled. As a result, the film was actually brought in for under $1 million and managed to earn approximately $1.6 million at the box office. See Warren, *Keep Watching the Skies!*, 897.

34. Keith Williams notes that Paramount had purchased the rights to *War of the Worlds* in 1925 as a possible project for Cecil B. De Mille, and he recounts the studio's preparation in 1930 of a script that was offered to the Soviet director Sergei Eisenstein. Other efforts in the 1930s and late 1940s attest to Paramount's continued interest in turning the Wells novel into a marketable film. For background on these various efforts, see Williams, *H. G. Wells, Modernity and the Movies*, 138–139.

35. Largely a photographic essay, "Hollywood Builds Flying Saucers," *Popular Science* 161, no. 5 (1952), 132–134, focuses on George Pal's dedication to scientific plausibility, even when he was dealing with "a make-believe flying saucer," as he "wanted to set the style for space vehicles of the future" (132).

36. "Pal, Dr. Rose Study Audience Reactions for B.O. Analysis," *Motion Picture Daily*, August 4, 1953, 7.

37. Paramount had been a partner in the DuMont television network since 1939, and in 1949, at approximately the same time that the government forced the major US film studios to divest themselves of their theater chains, the studio launched its own Paramount Television Network as a potential alternative to traditional theatrical distribution.

38. "Inside Stuff-Pictures," *Variety*, August 19, 1953, 15. While only *Astounding* of the sf pulps would be involved in the publicity campaign for *The War of the Worlds*, *Thrilling Wonder Stories* reviewed the film and featured several publicity stills as illustrations. But even as it praised the latest Pal effort as "the most outstanding science fiction film made to date," the review also noted the more horrific tone of this effort, describing it as "more impressive than Orson Welles' panic-provoking radio version." See Pat Jones, "Worlds at War in Technicolor," *Thrilling Wonder Stories* 42, no. 3 (August 1953): 92–93.

39. "Filming 'War of the Worlds,'" *Astounding Science Fiction* 52, no. 2 (October 1953): 100.

40. Ibid.

41. Ibid., 107.

42. Ibid.

43. Ibid., 110.

44. A. H. Weiler, "The Screen in Review: New Martian Invasion Is Seen in 'War of the Worlds,'" *New York Times*, August 14, 1953, 10.

45. Williams, *H. G. Wells, Modernity and the Movies*, 153.

46. Samuel D. Berns, "Hollywood," *Motion Picture Daily*, January 3, 1955, 6.

47. There was no Rotterdam International Exposition in 1955, although there was a local fair, Expo E55, the theme of which was "the National Energy Manifestation." While this description may simply have been a misconstruction or mistaking of events on Pal's part, it also suggests a deliberate publicity effort to link the film to the world of legitimate science.

48. See *Conquest of Space*, Paramount pressbook, 3, 8. *Zombo's Closet*, https://www.zomboscloset.com/zombos_closet_of_horror_b/2015/12/pressbook-conquest-of-space-1955.html.

49. "Selling Approach," *Motion Picture Herald*, May 7, 1955, 51.

50. "The National Spotlight," *Motion Picture Herald*, March 12, 1955, 25.

51. "Space Promoter," *Film Bulletin*, March 7, 1955, 22.

52. "Legion Approves Eight of 15 New Productions," *Motion Picture Herald*, March 12, 1955, 34. Most probably responsible for the Legion of Decency rating is a scene in which the character Rosie McCann (actress Joan Shawlee), via videolink, adopts various suggestive poses while telling her astronaut boyfriend how much she misses him—even as she is obviously preparing to two-time him with someone just off-camera.

53. "Conquest of Space," *Astounding Science Fiction* 55, no. 3 (May 1955): 95.

54. Ibid., 94.

55. Ibid., 96.

56. While estimates on the grosses of *Conquest of Space* vary somewhat, *Variety*'s annual assessment places its earnings at approximately $1 million, making it the least successful of any of the Paramount-Pal sf efforts.

57. These final Paramount films, all released in 1958, were *The Colossus of New York*, *The Space Children*, *The Blob*, and *I Married a Monster from Outer Space*. The first two were produced by William Alland Productions for Paramount distribution, and *The Blob* was done independently by Tonylyn Productions. While *I Married a Monster from Outer Space* was actually done at Paramount by the producer/director Gene Fowler, it hardly received the lavish treatment of other studio features. Intended as a low-budget quickie, it was shot in just eight days, for only $175,000, and was also released as part of a double bill. See Bill Warren's account in *Keep Watching the Skies!*, 385.

58. Warren, *Keep Watching the Skies!*, 158.

59. Ibid.

Chapter 4: Moppets and Robots

1. "Universal Paces New Round of Scientifiction," *Variety*, December 14, 1955, 3.

2. Schauer, *Escape Velocity*, 67.

3. "Universal Paces," 3.

4. Schatz, *The Genius of the System*, 452, 447.

5. Ibid., 452.

6. Clarke and Rubin, "Making *Forbidden Planet*," 25.

7. *Forbidden Planet: MGM Pressbook*, 7, Zombo's Closet, www.zomboscloset.com/zombos_closet_of_horror_b/2019/10/forbidden-planet-pressbook.html.

8. Schary, *Heyday: An Autobiography*, 290–291.

9. Gray, *Show Sold Separately*, 3, 21.

10. Clarke and Rubin, "Making *Forbidden Planet*," 16.

11. Arthur Lonergan quoted in ibid., 29.

12. Ibid., 20.

13. Ibid., 29.

14. Dore Schary quoted in ibid.

15. I draw most of the budgetary figures and commentary on the production history of *Forbidden Planet* from the extensively researched article by

Clarke and Rubin, "Making *Forbidden Planet*." For this piece, the authors interviewed many of those associated with the production, including the art director, Arthur Lonergan; the special effects artist, Joe Alves; and the MGM executive, Dore Schary.

16. The special effects artist, Joe Alves, notes that "Disney was very expensive to contract out," and using Disney's effects animation people, including Josh Meador and much of his staff, made the post-production process both protracted and costly (quoted in Clarke and Rubin, "Making *Forbidden Planet*, 38).

17. Grace Fischler, "Studio Size-Ups: Inside Story of Production," *Film Bulletin*, March 21, 1955, 14.

18. Doherty, *Teenagers and Teenpics*, 118.

19. Schauer, *Escape Velocity*, 67.

20. Marquette, *Brands, Trademarks and Good Will*, 51.

21. Mirroring the land deed publicity scheme used for *Sergeant Preston*, Ernie Emerling, the advertising and publicity director of Loew's Theatres, sent numerous trade press editors and reporters "a general quitclaim deed to one acre of land on the moon" in a bid to publicize *Forbidden Planet*. See the report "Deed to a Moon Acre Received with Thanks," *Motion Picture Daily*, March 30, 1956, 4.

22. Marquette, *Brands, Trademarks and Good Will*, 16–17.

23. Walter Brooks, "MGM Provides a New Promotion Plan for 1956," *Motion Picture Herald*, December 24, 1955, 35.

24. Ibid.

25. Ibid.

26. McGee, *Beyond Ballyhoo*, 157.

27. "Metro-Cereal Co-Op to Lure Families with Free Kid Tickets," *Film Bulletin*, December 26, 1955, 30.

28. "On the Horizon," *Motion Picture Herald*, December 31, 1955, 9.

29. "Exhibitors Forum," *Film Bulletin*, February 20, 1956, 18.

30. "Allied May Object to Business Booster," *Motion Picture Daily*, February 16, 1956, 7.

31. "Exhibitors Forum," 18.

32. "Allied May Object to Business Booster," 7.

33. "N.J. Allied Protests 'Oscar' Nominations on Saturday Nights," *Motion Picture Daily*, February 17, 1956, 6.

34. "MGM Provides a New Promotion Plan for 1956," *Motion Picture Herald*, December 24, 1955, 35.

35. *Forbidden Planet: MGM Pressbook*, 14.

36. Ibid., 10.

37. Ibid., 16. Robby would be extensively exploited as a children's toy throughout the 1950s and beyond. MGM licensed the image of Robby to the Ideal Toy Company, but that same image would quickly and repeatedly be copied by a number of other companies, especially in Japan, where, as Ron Tanner notes, "toy robots accounted for as much as one-sixth of the catalogue of toy exports" from Japan to the United States. Among this group, the Nomura Toy Company produced both a walking,

battery-powered version and a wire-controlled, multifunction version, both of which, with little regard for copyright, were simply dubbed "Robby." See Tanner, "Mr. Atomic, Mr. Mercury, and Chime Trooper," 80.

38. Gray, *Show Sold Separately*, 3.

39. Jack Eden, "Review: *Forbidden Planet*," *Motion Picture Daily*, March 15, 1956, 6.

40. See Brog's "Review: *Forbidden Planet*," *Variety*, March 14, 1956, 6.

41. "Showmen in Action," *Motion Picture Herald*, June 16, 1956, 37.

42. *Forbidden Planet: MGM Pressbook*, 14.

43. "Col. Box Cox and Friends, with 'Robby,'" *Motion Picture Herald*, May 19, 1956, 55.

44. Clarke and Rubin, "Making *Forbidden Planet*," 20.

45. Brosnan, *Movie Magic*, 199.

46. "What the Showmen Are Doing," *Film Bulletin*, March 5, 1956, 22.

47. "Review: *Forbidden Planet*," *Variety*, March 14, 1956, 6.

48. Multiple publicity photos and suggestions in the MGM Pressbook also indicate that MGM hoped to attract women to the film by playing up the character of *Forbidden Planet* as a "2200 A.D. Fashion Picture." See *Forbidden Planet: MGM Pressbook*, 10.

49. Conrad, *Space Sirens, Scientists and Princesses*, 75.

50. For a detailed discussion of these films and their marketing materials, see Telotte, "Sex and Machines," 317–386.

51. *Forbidden Planet: MGM Pressbook*, 2.

52. "Zombie Pix University Pressbeat & Durable," *Variety*, May 9, 1956, 11.

53. Doherty, *Teenagers and Teenpics*, 2.

54. The high-concept approach, as Wyatt describes it, seeks to merge "economics and aesthetics" (8) by relying on a single narrative line that carries the film's central theme while also suggesting its primary marketing thrust to audiences. Ideally, its plot and themes could typically "be explained in a sentence or two" (10), which might, in turn, be matched by a simple marketing concept, perhaps through the use of an iconic movie star, a "timely or fashionable subject" (12), or an evocative image (16). For further discussion, see Wyatt, *High Concept*.

55. See Irving Rubine's assessment of this market in "Boys Meet Ghouls, Make Money," *New York Times*, March 16, 1958, x7.

56. "Top Film Grossers of 1956," *Variety*, January 2, 1957, 1, 4.

57. Clarke and Rubin, "Making *Forbidden Planet*," 65.

58. Gray, *Show Sold Separately*, 2–3.

59. *The Invisible Boy: MGM Pressbook*, 1, *Zombo's Closet*, www.zomboscloset.com/zombos_closet_of_horror_b/2020/07/the-invisible-boy-1957-us-pressbook.html.

60. See Whit, "The Invisible Boy," *Variety*, October 16, 1957, 6.

Chapter 5: Another Form of Life

1. Vonderau, "Introduction," 6.

2. Hartwell, *Age of Wonders*, 66.

3. Pierson, *Special Effects*, 1.

4. See *Showman's Manual: Creature from the Black Lagoon*, 5, 2, *Zombo's Closet*, www.zomboscloset.com/zombos_closet_of_horror_b/2012/10/creature-from-the-black-lagoon-pressbook.html.

5. Quoted in Altman, *Film/Genre*, 79.

6. "Economy-Size Trio Emerges from Par," *Variety*, June 11, 1958, 5; R. V. Jones, "Blockbusters, Profits, and Goldwyn," *Film Bulletin*, July 21, 1958, 10; "'From the Earth to the Moon,'" *Film Bulletin*, December 22, 1958, 23.

7. Rieder, *Science Fiction and the Mass Cultural Genre System*, 41.

8. Ibid., 44.

9. The true cost of the film remains a subject of debate. Bill Warren, relying on comments by the film's associate producer Russ Doughten, pegs the cost at $110,000; see *Keep Watching the Skies!*, 117. Suzanne Murdico's popular account cites a final production cost of $130,000; see Murdico, *Meet "The Blob,"* 20. And although the initial *Variety* review listed a $240,000 production budget, a later *Variety* piece discussing the film's publicity campaign cites a much lower initial expense, $150,000. For the former estimate, see Gilb, *"The Blob," Variety*, September 10, 1958, 6, and for the latter, see "Par's 'Blob' No Slob," *Variety*, October 15, 1958, 3. All accounts list the Paramount purchase price as $300,000.

10. Warren, *Keep Watching the Skies!*, 116.

11. "Par's 'Blob' No Slob," *Variety*, October 15, 1958, 3.

12. Howard Woolfan, "More News from the North American Branches," *Paramount World* 4, no. 11 (1958): 38.

13. In late 1960, the producer, Harris, estimated that *The Blob* had earned him approximately $2,000,000 on his original investment of less than $200,000; see John G. Houser, "Harris' How-to-Do-It," *Variety*, September 21, 1960, 21. While both cost and earnings figures vary from account to account, it is clear from the amount of industry attention paid to Harris and his film that it was an unusually profitable effort in that late-1950s market.

14. "Par's 'Blob' No Slob," 3.

15. "'The Blob' Slithers into Mayfair," *New York Times*, November 7, 1958, n.p.

16. Gilb, *"The Blob,"* 6.

17. James D. Ivers, "Review: *The Blob*," *Motion Picture Daily*, September 10, 1958, 6.

18. Doherty, *Teenagers and Teenpics*, 2.

19. Ibid.

20. Ibid., 119.

21. See Rush, "Jekyll and Hyde," *Variety*, January 5, 1932, 19; and Waly, "Island of Lost Souls," *Variety*, January 17, 1933, 15.

22. "'When Worlds Collide' Special Exploitation," *Motion Picture Herald*, November 17, 1951, 49.

23. See the report "Economy-Size Trio Emerges from Par," *Variety*, June 11, 1958, 5.

24. Schauer, *Escape Velocity*, 89.

25. Austin, *Immediate Seating*, 74.

26. "Analysis of the Summer, 1958 Product," *Film Bulletin*, June 23, 1958, 24.

27. Austin, *Immediate Seating*, 67.

28. Curtis Mees, "Method in Management: In the Good Old Summertime," *Motion Picture Herald*, July 7, 1956, 35.

29. Ibid.

30. See Arthur Mayer, "Hollywood: Save the Flowers," *Film Bulletin*, April 14, 1958, 14; and R. V. Jones, "Blockbusters, Profits, and Goldwyn," *Film Bulletin*, July 21, 1958, 10.

31. "Gimmicks Did Well in 1957," *Variety*, November 6, 1957, 16.

32. "Latin American Film Events," *Paramount World* 5, no. 12 (1959): 29.

33. "Latin American Showmanship Continues to Be Exciting," *Paramount World* 6, no. 10 (1960): 19.

34. Doherty, *Teenagers and Teenpics*, 117.

35. See Floyd Stone, "'Blob' Maker Brings Fresh Approach," *Motion Picture Daily*, September 19, 1958, 3.

36. "The Space Children," *Variety*, June 18, 1958, 6.

37. In 1958, there were approximately twenty-six English-language (i.e., US and UK productions) sf films and twenty-one the following year, both ranking among the higher numbers of sf films produced in the decade. In contrast, just ten English-language genre efforts were released in 1960.

38. Doherty, *Teenagers and Teenpics*, 189.

39. Stanfield, *Hoodlum Movies*, 44.

40. Ibid., 29.

41. Ibid., 165.

42. Quoted in Stone, "'Blob' Maker," 3.

43. Gilb, "*The Blob*," 6.

44. In what he terms his "apparatus reading" of this sequence, Garrett Stewart describes the theater's "spook show" bill as an instance of the film's reflecting on "the derivations of sci-fi and its own mixed bloodlines," that is, its deep relationship to the traditions of horror cinema. But this sort of filmic self-awareness is not simply autogenerated, as a sort of inevitable reflexive feature of the medium, but specifically aimed, directed toward an audience that has grown up with the showy—perhaps even self-showy—nature of both sf and horror and that appreciates such awareness as part of the larger show. See Stewart, *Cinemachines*, 118.

45. The film was shot in Phoenixville and several nearby towns, and as part of an annual festival, Blobfest, the city offers a reenactment of the creature's attack at the Colonial Theater, involving festivalgoers dressed in 1950s-style clothes running from the theater.

46. For background, see Murdico, *Meet "The Blob*," 6.

47. Mike Gross, "Jocks, Jukes and Disks," *Variety*, September 24, 1958, 46.

48. "Col Teams with Par on Bally for 'Blobs,'" *Variety*, September 10, 1958, 135.

49. For discussion of the double nature of the cult film, especially in its sf

manifestations, see Telotte and Duchovnay, *Science Fiction Double Feature*, especially the introduction, 1–20.

50. Sontag, "Notes on 'Camp,'" 277.

51. See John G. Houser, "Harris' How-to-Do-It," *Variety*, September 21, 1960, 21.

52. Quoted in Irving Rubine, "Boys Meet Ghouls, Make Money," *New York Times*, March 16, 1958, x7.

53. Kernan, *Coming Attractions*, 121.

54. Ibid.

55. Early pulp sf was often charged with targeting a teenaged audience and in a sensationalized fashion, but it frequently strove for something more as well, larding magazines such as *Amazing Stories*, *Astounding Stories*, *Wonder Stories*, and *Thrilling Wonder Stories* with columns on serious science, with stories that the editors described as "thought experiments," and with readers columns that invited informed discussion—joined in by writers, editors, and readers alike—about the scientific accuracy and implications of their stories. In short, the magazines succeeded partly by framing their audience in what were essentially more adult and serious ways, even while providing that audience with images (such as the often-titillating pulp covers) and exciting stories that furnished more fundamental attractions.

56. Rieder, *Science Fiction and the Mass Cultural Genre System*, 169.

Chapter 6: Selling Japan

1. Richie, *A Hundred Years of Japanese Film*, 11.

2. Yomota, *What Is Japanese Cinema?*, 16.

3. For purposes of this discussion, I use the titles appended to the US release versions of the films, while giving the dates of both the original Japanese releases and the American versions or rereleases of those titles.

4. In his history of Japanese cinema, Yomota notes that the peak of Japanese attendance occurred in 1958 with 1.1 billion tickets sold that year, and that by 1963 it had dropped to less than half of that number. He sees this decline as parallel to what occurred somewhat earlier in the United States; he attributes the decline in both cases largely to "the rapid spread of television." See Yomota, *What Is Japanese Cinema?*, 127.

5. Fuller, *Media Ecologies*, 6.

6. Ibid., 2.

7. Ibid., 6.

8. Ibid., 18.

9. Yomota, *What Is Japanese Cinema?*, 98.

10. Ibid., 104–106.

11. "Active Film Year Reported by Japanese MPA," *Motion Picture Daily*, February 3, 1955, 2.

12. See Warren G. Harris, "Kido Is a Man with Two Missions," *Motion Picture Daily*, January 23, 1958, 3.

13. Ibid.

14. See Floyd Stone, "'H-Man' Producer Sees Science Fiction as Key," *Motion Picture Daily*, September 23, 1958, 1.

15. Mellen, *The Waves at Genji's Door*, 216.
16. Stone, "H-Man Producer," 1.
17. Ibid., 8.
18. Dave Jampel, "Japanese Arters Wow Critics, but Horror Films Get Coin," *Variety*, April 15, 1959, 46.
19. Stone, "H-Man Producer," 8.
20. Exemplifying that contrary opinion, the review of *The Mysterians* in *Film Bulletin* warned exhibitors that "the market for science fiction fare has dipped" ("The Mysterians," *Film Bulletin*, May 25, 1959, 16), and its piece on the *Godzilla* sequel, *Gigantis, the Fire Monster*, similarly observed that "its box-office prospects are limited to those theatres that still have an audience for hackneyed monster fiction" ("Gigantis the Fire Monster," *Film Bulletin*, June 8, 1959, 14), while a 1957 piece in *Variety* had already described the sf market as "glutted" ("Science Fiction Market Glutted?" *Variety*, May 1, 1957, 14).
21. These comments appear, respectively, in "The H-Man," *Film Bulletin*, June 8, 1959, 15; Warren G. Harris, "Review: *The H-Man*," *Motion Picture Daily*, June 3, 1959, 3; and Jampel, "Japanese Arters," 46.
22. Biskind, *Seeing Is Believing*, 103.
23. Kalat, *A Critical History and Filmography of Toho's Godzilla Series*, 22.
24. Ibid., 25.
25. Ibid., 25, 29.
26. Cook, *A History of Narrative Film*, 501.
27. Sontag, "The Imagination of Disaster," 216.
28. *Godzilla, King of the Monsters*: TransWorld Pressbook, 1, *The Sphinx*, March 19, 22, 2021, www.snakeandboris.blogspot.com.
29. Yomota, *What Is Japanese Cinema?*, 117.
30. Ibid.
31. "The Mysterians," *Film Bulletin*, May 25, 1959, 16.
32. Sontag, "The Imagination of Disaster," 216.
33. Doherty, *Teenagers and Teenpics*, 25.
34. Barr, *The Kaiju Film*, 9.
35. Bogue, *Apocalypse Then*, 180.
36. McGee, *Beyond Ballyhoo*, 2.
37. "Wrap 'Rodan' in Shock Insurance," *Variety*, November 13, 1957, 20.
38. "Touring Horror Show Will Promote 'H-Man,'" *Motion Picture Daily*, May 22, 1959, 7.
39. "'Mysterians' Campaign Outlined by Loew's," *Motion Picture Daily*, June 3, 1959, 2.
40. "Want Able and Baker for 'Mysterians' Promotion," *Motion Picture Daily*, June 2, 1959, 2.
41. *Mothra*: Columbia Pressbook, n.p., *Zombo's Closet*, www.zomboscloset.com/zombos_closet_of_horror_b2012/10/mothra-pressbook.html.
42. Ibid.
43. Anderson, *Hollywood TV*, 20.
44. See Bill Doll, "Boston's Joe Levine: A Profile," *Variety*, April 1, 1959, 18.
45. Gray, *Show Sold Separately*, 52.

46. Significantly, the original Japanese trailer (available online) is much longer and has a very different, more humanly centered emphasis. While it does show the monster and some of his destruction, it also introduces the main characters and emphasizes their reactions to the creature, especially their conflicted efforts to both study Godzilla and find a way to destroy him.

47. "'Rodan' Hits Jackpot," *Motion Picture Daily*, March 19, 1958, 2.

48. "Television Spots Hypo 'Rodan' to Record Box Office," *Film Bulletin*, April 14, 1958, 24.

49. "Jap 'Rodan,' Wilcox's 'Battle Hell' Backed by $80,000 DCA Budget," *Variety*, March 19, 1958, 19.

50. "Japanese 'Rodan' Big (with Plugs) in K. C. Houses," *Variety*, January 29, 1958, 14.

51. *Gigantis, the Fire Monster*: Warner Bros. Pressbook, 3, 10, *Zombo's Closet*, www.zomboscloset.com/zombos_closet_of_horror_b/2018/02/gigantis-godzilla-raids-again-pressbook.html.

52. Jampel, "Japanese Arters," 46. The rights to this film were acquired after RKO's distribution arm went out of business. Originally, *The Mysterians* was to be an RKO release.

53. *The Mysterians*: MGM Pressbook, n.p., author's collection.

54. "MGM Sets 4-Week Campaign to Push 'Mysterians,'" *Film Bulletin*, June 8, 1959, 18.

55. The similar tag phrase appearing in the MGM-issued pressbook for *The Mysterians* is "greatest science-fiction picture ever conceived!"

56. "'Mysterians' Proving Top Box Office Draw," *Motion Picture Daily*, July 17, 1959, 8.

57. See Nathan Cohen, "Improved Trend in Production for 1962," *Box Office*, March 26, 1962, 18.

58. Bernard F. Dick describes this shift in "From the Brothers Cohn to Sony Corp.—And Beyond," 14.

59. Warren, *Keep Watching the Skies!*, 608.

60. Ibid.

61. Ryfle and Godsziszewski, *Ishiro Honda: A Life in Film*, 173.

62. Warren, *Keep Watching the Skies!*, 610.

63. "'Mothra,'" *Film Bulletin*, July 9, 1962, 16.

64. McGee, *Beyond Ballyhoo*, 149.

65. Kalat, *A Critical History*, 53.

66. Ibid.

67. *Gigantis, the Fire Monster*: Warner Bros. Pressbook, 9.

68. As a result of Joe Levine's series of such elaborate marketing campaigns, *Variety* would eventually dub him "million-dollar-campaign Levine." See "Letdowns of 1960 at U.S. Pay-Box," *Variety*, January 4, 1961, 5; McKenna, *Showman of the Screen*.

69. Norman M. Lobsenz, "The Trend of S-F Movies," *Amazing Stories* 33, no. 1 (January 1959): 5.

70. These industry assessments are from Cohen, "Improved Trend," 18; "Cheap 'n' Quick No Longer Goes in Horrorifiers," *Variety*, May 20, 1959, 4; and "Viewpoints," *Film Bulletin*, January 18, 1960, 5.

71. Sontag, "The Imagination of Disaster," 216.

72. "Cheap 'n' Quick," 4.
73. *Mothra*: Columbia Pressbook, n.p.

Conclusion

1. Quoted in "Fresh Approach for Each New Film," *Motion Picture Daily*, May 4, 1959, 7.
2. Ibid., 1.
3. Latham, "Introduction," 17.
4. Sontag, "The Imagination of Disaster," 224.
5. Cohen, *A Consumer's Republic*, 331.
6. Ibid., 318.
7. Ibid.
8. Ibid.
9. Doherty, *Teenagers and Teenpics*, 25.
10. Roberts, *The History of Science Fiction*, 158, 265.
11. Hansen, "The Mass Production of the Senses," 72.
12. In Telotte, *Movies, Modernism, and the Science Fiction Pulps*, I trace the many ways in which that visual sensibility and a movie consciousness surface in early twentieth-century sf, especially in the precincts of the major sf pulp magazines.
13. Ashley, *The Time Machines*, 49.
14. Yaszek and Sharp, *Sisters of Tomorrow*, 331.
15. Roberts, *History of Science Fiction*, 184.
16. Rieder, *Science Fiction and the Mass Cultural Genre System*, 163.
17. Ibid.
18. Ibid., 164.
19. Bazin, *What Is Cinema?*, 20, 22, 21. While Bazin was writing about the various "myths" or "dreams" that inspired the movies, and especially the desire to create "a complete illusion of life," he consistently noted that the much-lauded "realistic" cinema of the 1950s was not the culmination of this myth of total cinema, which was rather something that, tantalizingly, always seemed "a long way away" (20). When we read his emphasis on technological development through a sf lens, his acknowledgment of the strong pull of "illusion" (11), and the way he cast accomplishment always into the future, Bazin's writings about the prospects of film take on a character different from any that those who have seen his work as dedicated to the properties of film realism have ever acknowledged.
20. Ibid., 20.
21. In *History of Science Fiction*, Adam Roberts points in this same direction, as he notes how the success of sf cinema had, at least by the 1980s, "moved the genre's center of gravity from prose to visual texts," such that previous debates—by fans, critics, and writers themselves—"about the proper form of prose SF" had somehow become "much less important" (196).
22. Stewart, *Cinemachines*, 113.
23. Ibid., 152.
24. Ibid., 114.

25. Ibid., 112.
26. Schauer, *Escape Velocity*, 51.
27. "*Star Wars: Galactic Starcruiser* Adventure," https://disneyworld.disney.go.com/star-wars-galactic-starcruiser/overview/.
28. Kernan, *Coming Attractions*, 2.

SELECT FILMOGRAPHY

The following filmography offers primary information on the science fiction films that receive extended discussion here and whose marketing campaigns seem especially noteworthy.

The Blob (1958). Dir.: Irvin S. Yeaworth Jr. Prod.: Jack H. Harris. Script: Kate Phillips, Theodore Simonson. Cast: Steven McQueen, Aneta Corsaut, Earl Rowe, Olin Howland. Fairview Productions/Paramount Pictures.

Conquest of Space (1955). Dir.: Byron Haskin. Prod.: George Pal. Script: Philip Yordan, Barré Lyndon. Cast: Walter Brooke, Eric Fleming, Phil Foster, Mickey Shaughnessy. Paramount Pictures.

Destination Moon (1950). Dir.: Irving Pichel. Prod.: George Pal. Script: James O'Hanlon, Robert A. Heinlein. Cast: John Archer, Warner Anderson, Tom Powers, Dick Wesson. Eagle-Lion.

Dr. Cyclops (1940). Dir.: Ernest B. Schoedsack. Prod.: Dale Van Every and Merian C. Cooper. Script: Tom Kilpatrick. Cast: Thomas Coley, Albert Dekker, Janice Logan, Victor Kilian. Paramount Pictures.

Forbidden Planet (1956). Dir.: Fred McLeod Wilcox. Prod.: Nicholas Nayfack. Script: Cyril Hume. Cast: Walter Pidgeon, Leslie Nielsen, Anne Francis, Warren Stevens. MGM.

Frau im Mond (aka *Woman in the Moon*, 1929). Dir.: Fritz Lang. Prod.: Fritz Lang. Script: Thea von Harbou, Fritz Lang. Cast: Gerda Maurus, Willy Fritsch, Fritz Rasp. UFA.

Godzilla Raids Again/Gigantis, the Fire Monster (1955, US 1959). Dir.: Motoyoshi Oda. Prod.: Tomoyuki Tanaka. Script: Takeo Murata, Shigeaki Hidaka. Cast: Hiroshi Koizumi, Minoru Chiaki, Setsuko Wakayama, Takashi Shimura. Toho Studios/Warner Bros.

Gojira/Godzilla, King of the Monsters (1954, US 1956). Dir.: Ishiro Honda. Prod.: Tomoyuki Tanaka. Script: Shigeru Kayama, Takeo Murata, Ishiro Honda. Cast: Akira Takarada, Momoko Kochi, Takashi Shimura, Akihiko Hirata (Raymond Burr, American version). Toho Studios/TransWorld Releasing/Embassy Pictures.

The Invisible Boy (1957). Dir.: Herman Hoffman. Prod.: Nicholas Nayfack. Script: Cyril Hume, Edmund Cooper. Cast: Richard Eyer, Philip Abbott, Diane Brewster, Harold J. Stone. MGM.

Mothra (1961, US 1962). Dir.: Ishiro Honda. Prod.: Tomoyuki Tanaka. Script: Shinichi Sekizawa. Cast: Franky Sakai, Hiroshi Koizumi, Ken Uehara, Kyôko Kagawa, Takashi Shimura. Toho Studios/Columbia Pictures.

SELECT FILMOGRAPHY

The Mysterians (1957, US 1959). Dir.: Ishiro Honda. Prod.: Tomoyuki Tanaka. Script: Takeshi Kimura. Cast: Kenji Sahara, Yumi Shirakawa, Takashi Shimura. Toho Studios/MGM.

Rocketship X-M (1950). Dir. Kurt Neumann. Prod. Kurt Neumann, Robert L. Lippert. Script: Kurt Neumann, Orville H. Hampton, Dalton Trumbo. Cast: Lloyd Bridges, Osa Massen, John Emery, Noah Beery Jr., Hugh O'Brien. LippertPictures.

Rodan (1956, US 1957). Dir.: Ishiro Honda. Prod.: Tomoyuki Tanaka. Script: Ken Kuronuma, Takeshi Kimura, Takeo Murata. Cast: Kenji Sahara, Yumi Shirakawa. Toho Studios/King Brothers.

The Thing from Another World (1951). Dir.: Christian Nyby. Prod.: Howard Hawks. Script: Charles Lederer. Cast: Kenneth Tobey, Margaret Sheridan, Robert Cornthwaite, James Arness. Winchester Productions/RKO Pictures.

Things to Come (1936). Dir.: William Cameron Menzies. Prod.: Alexander Korda. Script: H. G. Wells. Cast: Raymond Massey, Ralph Richardson, Sophie Stewart, Cedric Hardwicke. London Film/United Artists.

The War of the Worlds (1953). Dir.: Byron Haskin. Prod.: George Pal. Script: Barré Lyndon. Cast: Gene Barry, Ann Robinson, Les Tremayne. Paramount Pictures.

SELECT BIBLIOGRAPHY

The following select bibliography for the study of science fiction and the cinema focuses largely on academic criticism and commentary. It omits reports from film industry sources, film reviews, or citations of publicity materials. For ease of reference, these other sources have been included in the notes to each chapter.

Altman, Rick. *Film/Genre*. London: British Film Institute, 1999.
Anderson, Christopher. *Hollywood TV: The Studio System in the Fifties*. Austin: University of Texas Press, 1994.
Ashley, Mike. *The Time Machines: The Story of the Science Fiction Pulp Magazines from the Beginnings to 1950*. Liverpool: Liverpool University Press, 2000.
Austin, Bruce A. *Immediate Seating: A Look at Movie Audiences*. Belmont, CA: Wadsworth, 1989.
Barr, Jason. *The Kaiju Film: A Critical Study of Cinema's Biggest Monsters*. Jefferson, NC: McFarland, 2016.
Bazin, André. *What Is Cinema?* Translated by Hugh Gray. Vol. 1. Berkeley: University of California Press, 1971.
Biskind, Peter. *Seeing Is Believing: How Hollywood Taught Us to Stop Worrying and Love the Fifties*. New York: Pantheon, 1983.
Boddy, William. *New Media and Popular Imagination: Launching Radio, Television, and Digital Media in the United States*. Oxford: Oxford University Press, 2004.
Bogue, Mike. *Apocalypse Then: American and Japanese Atomic Cinema, 1951–1967*. Jefferson, NC: McFarland, 2017.
Bordwell, David, Janet Staiger, and Kristin Thompson. *The Classical Hollywood Cinema; Film Style and Mode of Production to 1960*. New York: Columbia University Press, 1985.
Bould, Mark, and Sherryl Vint. *The Routledge Concise History of Science Fiction*. London: Routledge, 2011.
———. "There Is No Such Thing as Science Fiction." In *Reading Science Fiction*, edited by James Gunn, Marleen S. Barr, and Matthew Candelaria, 43–51. Basingstoke, UK: Palgrave Macmillan, 2009.
Brosnan, John. *Movie Magic: The Story of Special Effects in the Cinema*. New York: New American Library, 1976.
Carter, Paul A. *The Creation of Tomorrow: Fifty Years of Magazine Science Fiction*. New York: Columbia University Press, 1977.
Casetti, Francesco. *Eye of the Century: Film, Experience, Modernity*.

Translated by Erin Larkin with Jennifer Pranolo. New York: Columbia University Press, 2005.
Chapman, James, and Nicholas J. Cull. *Projecting Tomorrow: Science Fiction and Popular Cinema*. London: I. B. Tauris, 2013.
Cheng, John. *Astounding Wonder: Imagining Science and Science Fiction in Interwar America*. College Park: University of Pennsylvania Press, 2012.
Clarens, Carlos. *An Illustrated History of the Horror Film*. New York: Capricorn, 1967.
Clarke, Frederick S., and Steve Rubin. "Making *Forbidden Planet*." *Cinefantastique* 8, nos. 2–3 (1979): 4–66.
Cohen, Lizabeth. *A Consumer's Republic: The Politics of Mass Consumption in Postwar America*. New York: Knopf, 2003.
Conrad, Dean. *Space Sirens, Scientists and Princesses: The Portrayal of Women in Science Fiction Cinema*. Jefferson, NC: McFarland, 2018.
Cook, David A. *A History of Narrative Film*. 3rd ed. New York: Norton, 1996.
Corn, Joseph J., and Brian Horrigan. *Yesterday's Tomorrows: Past Visions of the American Future*. Baltimore, MD: Johns Hopkins University Press, 1996.
Custen, George F. *Twentieth Century's Fox: Darryl F. Zanuck and the Culture of Hollywood*. New York: Basic Books, 1997.
Dick, Bernard F. "From the Brothers Cohn to Sony Corp.—And Beyond." In *Columbia Pictures: Portrait of a Studio*, edited by Bernard F. Dick, 2–64. Lexington: University Press of Kentucky, 1992.
Doherty, Thomas. *Teenagers and Teenpics: The Juvenilization of American Movies in the 1950s*. Rev. ed. Philadelphia: Temple University Press, 2002.
Dupont, Nathalie, and Joël Augros. "Cinema and Marketing: When Cultural Demands Meet Industrial Practices." *InMedia: The French Journal of Media Studies* 3 (2013): n.p.
Evans, Joyce A. *Celluloid Mushroom Clouds: Hollywood and the Atomic Bomb*. Boulder, CO: Westview, 1998.
Friedberg, Anne. *Window Shopping: Cinema and the Postmodern*. Berkeley: University of California Press, 1994.
Fuller, Matthew. *Media Ecologies: Materialist Energies in Art and Technoculture*. Cambridge, MA: MIT Press, 2005.
Geraghty, Lincoln. *American Science Fiction Film and Television*. New York: Berg, 2009.
Gernsback, Hugo. "A New Sort of Magazine." *Amazing Stories* 1, no. 1 (April 1926): 3.
———. "Science Wonder Stories." *Science Wonder Stories* 1, no. 1 (June 1929): 5.
Goulart, Ron. *Cheap Thrills: The Amazing! Thrilling! Astonishing! History of Pulp Fiction*. Neshannock, PA: Hermes Press, 2007.
Gray, Jonathan. *Show Sold Separately: Promos, Spoilers, and Other Media Paratexts*. New York: NYU Press, 2010.
Gunning, Tom. "The Cinema of Attraction: Early Film, Its Spectator and the Avant-Garde." *Wide Angle* 8, nos. 3–4 (1986): 63–70.

Hansen, Miriam. "The Mass Production of the Senses: Classical Cinema as Vernacular Modernism." *Modernism/Modernity* 6, no. 2 (1999): 59–77.
Hartwell, David G. *Age of Wonders: Exploring the World of Science Fiction*. New York: McGraw-Hill, 1984.
Heinlein, Robert A. "Shooting 'Destination Moon.'" *Astounding Science Fiction* 45, no. 5 (July 1950): 6–18.
Izod, John. *Hollywood and the Box Office, 1895–1986*. New York: Columbia University Press, 1988.
James, Edward. *Science Fiction in the Twentieth Century*. Oxford: Oxford University Press, 1994.
Jones, Pat. "Worlds at War in Technicolor." *Thrilling Wonder Stories* 42, no. 3 (August 1953): 92–93.
Kalat, David. *A Critical History and Filmography of Toho's Godzilla Series*. 2nd ed. Jefferson, NC: McFarland, 2010.
Kernan, Lisa. *Coming Attractions: Reading American Movie Trailers*. Austin: University of Texas Press, 2004.
Kreimeier, Klaus. *The UFA Story: A History of Germany's Greatest Film Company, 1918–1945*. New York: Hill and Wang, 1996.
Laemmle, Carl. "The Business of Motion Pictures." In *The American Film Industry*, edited by Tino Balio, 153–168. Madison: University of Wisconsin Press, 1976.
Landon, Brooks. *Science Fiction after 1900: From the Steam Man to the Stars*. London: Routledge, 2002.
Latham, Rob. "Introduction." In *The Oxford Handbook of Science Fiction*, edited by Rob Latham, 1–19. Oxford: Oxford University Press, 2014.
Lawrence, Mary Wells. *A Big Life in Advertising*. New York: Simon and Schuster, 2002.
Lipton, David A. "Advertising and Publicity." In *The Movie Business: American Film Industry Practice*, edited by A. William Bluem and Jason E. Squire, 227–233. New York: Hastings House, 1972.
Lucanio, Patrick. *Them or Us: Archetypal Interpretations of Fifties Alien Invasion Films*. Bloomington: Indiana University Press, 1987.
Marquette, Arthur F. *Brands, Trademarks and Good Will: The Story of the Quaker Oats Company*. New York: McGraw-Hill, 1967.
McGee, Mark Thomas. *Beyond Ballyhoo: Motion Picture Promotion and Gimmicks*. Jefferson, NC: McFarland, 2001.
McKenna, Anthony T. *Showman of the Screen: Joseph E. Levine and His Revolutions in Film Promotion*. Lexington: University Press of Kentucky, 2016.
Mellen, Joan. *The Waves at Genji's Door: Japan through Its Cinema*. New York: Pantheon, 1976.
Miller, Cynthia J., and A. Bowdoin Van Riper, eds. *1950s "Rocketman" TV Series and Their Fans: Cadets, Rangers, and Junior Space Men*. Basingstoke, UK: Palgrave Macmillan, 2012.
Murdico, Suzanne J. *Meet "The Blob."* New York: Rosen, 2005.
Neale, Steve. *Genre and Hollywood*. London: Routledge, 2000.
Pal, George. "Filming 'War of the Worlds.'" *Astounding Science Fiction* 52, no. 2 (October 1953): 100–111.

Pierson, Michele. *Special Effects: Still in Search of Wonder*. New York: Columbia University Press, 2002.
Pomerance, Murray. "Introduction: Movies and the 1950s." In *American Cinema of the 1950s: Themes and Variations*, edited by Murray Pomerance, 1–20. Oxford: Berg, 2005.
Richardson, R. S. "Making Worlds Collide." *Astounding Science Fiction* 48, no. 3 (November 1951): 83–97.
Richie, Donald. *A Hundred Years of Japanese Film: A Concise History*. Rev. ed. New York: Kodansha USA, 2012.
Rieder, John. *Science Fiction and the Mass Cultural Genre System*. Middletown, CT: Wesleyan University Press, 2017.
Rivette, Jacques. "The Genius of Howard Hawks." In *Focus on Howard Hawks*, edited by Joseph McBride, 70–77. Englewood Cliffs, NJ: Prentice-Hall, 1972.
Roberts, Adam. *The History of Science Fiction*. Basingstoke, UK: Palgrave Macmillan, 2005.
Ryfle, Steve, and Ed Godsziszewski. *Ishiro Honda: A Life in Film, from Godzilla to Kurosawa*. Middletown, CT: Wesleyan University Press, 2017.
Sarris, Andrew. "Howard Hawks." In *Interviews with Film Directors*, edited by Andrew Sarris, 228–240. New York: Avon, 1967.
Schary, Dore. *Heyday: An Autobiography*. Boston: Little, Brown, 1979.
Schatz, Thomas. *The Genius of the System: Hollywood Filmmaking in the Studio Era*. New York: Pantheon, 1988.
———. *Hollywood Genres: Formulas, Filmmaking, and the Studio System*. New York: Random House, 1981.
Schauer, Bradley. *Escape Velocity: American Science Fiction Film, 1950–1982*. Middletown, CT: Wesleyan University Press, 2017.
Sconce, Jeffrey. *Haunted Media: Electronic Presence from Telegraphy to Television*. Durham, NC: Duke University Press, 2000.
Skal, David J. *Screams of Reason: Mad Science and Modern Culture*. New York: Norton, 1998.
Sobchack, Vivian. "Images of Wonder: The Look of Science Fiction." In *Liquid Metal: The Science Fiction Film Reader*, edited by Sean Redmond, 4–10. London: Wallflower Press, 2004.
Sontag, Susan. "The Imagination of Disaster." In *Against Interpretation*, 212–228. New York: Dell, 1966.
———. "Notes on 'Camp.'" In *Against Interpretation*, 277–293. New York: Dell, 1966.
Stanfield, Peter. *Hoodlum Movies: Seriality and the Outlaw Biker Film Cycle, 1966–1972*. New Brunswick, NJ: Rutgers University Press, 2018.
Stewart, Garrett. *Cinemachines: An Essay on Media and Method*. Chicago: University of Chicago Press, 2020.
Suvin, Darko. *Metamorphoses of Science Fiction: On the Poetics and History of a Literary Genre*. New Haven, CT: Yale University Press, 1979.
Tanner, Ron. "Mr. Atomic, Mr. Mercury, and Chime Trooper: Japan's Answer to the American Dream." In *Asian Popular Culture*, edited by John A. Lent, 79–102. Boulder, CO: Westview, 1995.

Telotte, J. P. *Animating the Science Fiction Imagination*. Oxford: Oxford University Press, 2017.
———. *Movies, Modernism, and the Science Fiction Pulps*. Oxford: Oxford University Press, 2019.
———. "Sex and Machines: The 'Buzz' of 1950s Science Fiction Film." *Science Fiction Film and Television* 8, no. 3 (2015): 317–386.
Telotte, J. P., and Gerald Duchovnay, eds. *Science Fiction Double Feature: The Science Fiction Film as Cult Text*. Liverpool: Liverpool University Press, 2015.
Virilio, Paul. *The Art of the Motor*. Translated by Julie Rose. Minneapolis: University of Minnesota Press, 1995.
Vonderau, Patrick. "Introduction: On Advertising's Relation to Motion Pictures." In *Films That Sell: Moving Pictures and Advertising*, edited by Bo Florin, Nico de Klerk, and Patrick Vonderau, 1–18. London: British Film Institute, 2016.
Warren, Bill. *Keep Watching the Skies! American Science Fiction Movies of the Fifties*. 21st Century ed. Jefferson, NC: McFarland, 2010.
Westfahl, Gary. *Hugo Gernsback and the Century of Science Fiction*. Jefferson, NC: McFarland, 2007.
———. *The Mechanics of Wonder: The Creation of the Idea of Science Fiction*. Liverpool: Liverpool University Press, 1998.
Whissel, Kristen. *Picturing American Modernity: Traffic, Technology, and the Silent Cinema*. Durham, NC: Duke University Press, 2008.
Williams, Keith. *H. G. Wells, Modernity and the Movies*. Liverpool: Liverpool University Press, 2007.
Wyatt, Justin. *High Concept: Movies and Marketing in Hollywood*. Austin: University of Texas Press, 1994.
Yaszek, Lisa, and Patrick B. Sharp, eds. *Sisters of Tomorrow: The First Women of Science Fiction*. Middletown, CT: Wesleyan University Press, 2016.
Yomota, Inuhiko. *What Is Japanese Cinema? A History*. Translated by Philip Kaffen. New York: Columbia University Press, 2014.

INDEX

Note: Page numbers in *italics* indicate figures

Abbott and Costello Go to Mars (film), 67
Abbott and Costello Meet the Invisible Man (film), 33
Academy Award, 69
Ace Books, 158
Ackerman, Forrest, 176n17
Allied Theatre Owners, 88, 89
Altman, Rick, 30, 51
Alves, Joe, 180–181n15
Amazing Stories (magazine), 12, 154, 185n55; advertising in, 28; cover art, 36, 185n; letters column, 58
American International Pictures, 42, 116, 123, 132
Anderson, Christopher, 145
animation, 16, 80, 82, 174n42, 181n16
Anno, Hideaki, 156
Arkoff, Samuel Z., 42
Arnaz, Desi, 85
Arness, James, 49
Arnold, Jack, 73, 104, 105, 108, 116, 135, 159
Ashley, Mike, 162
Asimov, Isaac, 96; laws of robotics, 111
Astounding Science Fiction (magazine), 77, 76, 103, 185n55; advertising in, 28, 65; *The Conquest of Space* feature, 72–74; cover art, *61*, 72, 185n5; *Destination Moon* feature, 38–39, 60, 61–63, 176n16; letters column, 60; and George Pal, 56, 109; *The War of the Worlds* feature, 67–68, 70, 179n38; *When Worlds Collide* feature, 64, 66
Attack of the 50 Foot Woman (film), 159
audiences: characteristics of, 111, 112, 117, 157–158; children in, 8, 67, 83–85, 87–88, 90–91, 93, 98–99, 101, 111, 142, 143, 149, 181n37; family focus, 87–88, 97, 98, 108, 160; segmentation, 111, 112, 124, 154, 166; targeting, 159–163; teenage focus, 51, 82, 98, 105, 108–109, 113, *114*, 116, 118–119, 124–125, 135, 154–155, 158

Augros, Joël, 2
Austin, Bruce A., 111, 112

Bacharach, Burt, 120
Ball, Lucille, 85
Ballantine Books, 158
ballyhoo, 27, 34, 45, 69, 90, 106, 115, 123, 142; defined, 5–6, 42; and film exhibitors, 87, 91, 95; and the film experience, 17, 25, 112–113, 124, 141, 147; in the pulps, 60, 62, 72; television use of, 75, 84, 129, 145, 149, 154–155
Barr, Jason, 141
Barron, Louis and Bebe, 82
Barrymore, John, 31
Battle in Outer Space (film), 128
Bava, Mario, 159
Baxter, Warner, 16, 160
Bay, Michael, 165
Bazin, André, 164–165, 169, 170, 188n19
Beast from 20,000 Fathoms, The (film), 84, 111, 135, 137, 163
Beebe, Ford, 9, 33
Bennett, Spencer G., 9
Bergey, Earle K., 56
Bernds, Edward, 99, 111
Besson, Luc, 165
B-films, 67, 81, 82
Big Wheel, The (film), 38
Biskind, Peter, 135
Blackboard Jungle (film), 80
Blade Runner (film), 2
Blob, The (film), 23, 104, 122, 180n57; audience for, 108, 116–120, 161; ballyhoo for, 113–115, 120–121, 124; Blobfest, 119, 184n45; box office, 106, 115, 183n13; budget, 106, 183n9; Paramount purchase of, 106; self-conscious nature, 118, 120, 122–123, 184n44; theme song, 120, *121*, 122; trailer for, 124
Blood on the Moon (film), 38

198

Bogue, Mike, 141
Bonestell, Chesley, Jr., 62, 66, 68, 70, 72, 73, 74. *See also* Ley, Willy
Book of Boba Fett, The (television series), 169–170
Booth, Walter R., 9
Bould, Mark, 12–13
Box Office (magazine), 48, 151, 154
Boys' Life (magazine), 87
Brackett, Leigh, 176n25
Bradbury, Ray, 12
Brain Eaters, The (film), 42
Brendel, El, 15–16
Brick Bradford (film), 9, 35
Brooks, Richard, 80
Brosnan, John, 92
Brown, Howard V., 56, 162, 176n19. *See also* pulp magazines
Browning, Tod, 104
Bruce, Virginia, 31
Brundage, Margaret, 56, 58, 162. *See also* pulp magazines
Bucket of Blood, A (film), 155
Buck Rogers (film), 9
Burmese Harp, The (film), 131
Burr, Raymond, 136–137, *144*, 145, 146, 149
Butler, David, 15

Cahn, Edward L., 109, 123
Campbell, John W., Jr., 51, 64; as *Astounding* editor, 38, 58, 72; "Who Goes There?," 29, 176n25
Cape Canaveral, 125, 142
Cape Canaveral Monsters, The (film), 125
Captain Video: Master of the Stratosphere (film), 34
Captain Video and His Video Rangers (television series), 34, 49, 55, 104, 173n18
Carr, Thomas, 9
Carter, Paul A., 58
Castle, William, 42, 155
Cat-Women of the Moon (film), 67
censorship, 58, 72, 180n52; in Japan, 130; Legion of Decency, 72, 180n52
Chamber of Deputies (France), 5
Chapman, James, 5
Cheng, John, 11
CinemaScope, 82, 159
Clarke, Frederick S., 81
Clarke, Robert, 125
Cohen, Lizabeth, 159–161, 162

Cohn, Joseph, 82
Cold War, 6, 17, 52, 53, 69, 97, 139, 159
Collier's (magazine), 39, 52
Colossus of New York, The (film), 73, 96, 180n57
Columbia Pictures, 34, 37, 79, 84, 142, 143, 151–153, 163, 186, 188, 191
Columbia Records, 152
Connell, W. Merle, 11
Conquest of Space (book; Willy Ley), 70, 72
Conquest of Space (film), 60; box office, 73, 180n56; television marketing, 70–72, 74
Conrad, Dean, 97
Cook, David A., 137
Cooper, Merian C., 166
Corman, Roger, 99, 154, 159
Corsaut, Aneta, 117
Creature from the Black Lagoon (film), 104; box office, 105; sequels to, 105
Creature Walks Among Us, The (film), 105
Crown International Pictures, 116
Cull, Nicholas, J. 5
cult film, 119, 122, 175n57, 184–185n49
Curse of the Faceless Man (film), 109

Dark City (film), *24*, 25
Darro, Frankie, 92
Daughter of Horror, aka *Dementia* (film), 118, 122
David, Mack, 120
Dawn, Norman, 11
Day the Earth Stood Still, The (film), 34, 67, 96
Day the Sky Exploded, The (film), 159
Day the World Ended (film), 159, *160*
Dean, James, 118
del Toro, Guillermo, 129
De Mille, Cecil B., 179n34
Destination Moon (film), 6, 35, 43, 67, 69, 70, 161; and Robert Heinlein, 38–39, 60, 176n16; marketing of, 6–7, 21; and George Pal, 59–60, 62–63; reviews of, 60; scientific accuracy in, 60, 63, 103
Dick, Bernard F., 187n58
Dieterle, William, 16
Dietz, Howard, 84
Disney, Walt, 16
Distributors Corporation of America (DCA), 132, 142, 147, 148

D.O.A. (film), 28
Doherty, Thomas, 19, 83, 98, 108–109, 111, 113, 115, 116, 124, 141, 154, 161
Dougherty, Michael, 156
Douglas, Gordon, 84
Dracula (film), 104
Dr. Cyclops (film): marketing of, 59; novelization, 36, 59; reviews of, 59, 178n11
Dr. Jekyll and Mr. Hyde (film), 38, 59, 79, 109, *110*, 160
Dr. Strangelove (film), 125
Duchovnay, Gerald, 175n57, 184–185n49
Duel in the Sun (film), 38
DuMont Television Network, 75, 179n37
Dupont, Nathalie, 2

Eagle-Lion Films, 6, 60
Early Summer (film) 132
Earth vs. the Flying Saucers (film), 99
Eastmancolor, 82, 152
Eden, Jack, 90, 93
Edison, Thomas, 9, 162
Eisenstein, Sergei, 179n34
El Paso (film), 38
Elvey, Maurice, 14
Embassy Pictures, 132, 136, 141, 148
Emerling, Ernest, 142, 181n21
Emperor Meiji and the Great Russo-Japanese War (film), 131
End of the World (film), 9
Evans, Joyce A., 10, 11
Exciting Western Stories (magazine), 45
Ex Machina (film), 165, *166*
exploitation, 17, 42, 48, 52, 75, 99, 103, 105, 106, 108, 116, 118, 119, 124, 143, 149, 177n27
Eyer, Richard, 100

Facebook, 169
fans, 1, 12, 23, 51, 63, 66, 161, 188n21; advertising to, 7; cosplay, 24, 119, 169; and cult activity, 175n57; and science fiction, 35, 38, 103
Fenton, Leslie, 38
Film Bulletin (magazine), 14, 28, 39, 41, 42, 45, 82, 87, 88, 105, 112, 147, 154–155
Film Daily, 5, 14, 15, 49
film noir, 26, 106
Flash Gordon (film), 9

Fleischer, Max, 59; and Fleischer Studios, 16
Fleischer, Richard, 84
Fleming, Victor, 38
Fly, The (film), 111–112
Flying Disc Man from Mars (film), 35
flying saucers, 27, 34, 49, 51, 67, 97, 150, 165, 167, *168*, 179n35
Forbidden Planet (film), 79–80, 103, 105, 111, 142, 161; budget, 81–82, *83*, 99, 180n15; comic elements, 92, 99; marketing campaign, 84–93, 95–98, 181n21; and Robby the Robot, 80, 82, 85, 88, 90–96, 100–101, 181–182n37; sexual themes in, 95–98, 99; utopian themes in, 93, 95, 98
Forever, Darling (film), 85
Foster, Harry, 109
Foster, Lewis R., 38
4D Man (film), 125
Fowler, Gene, Jr., 77, 180n57
Francis, Anne, 92
Frankenstein (film), 14, 16, 30, 46, 95, 104
Frau im Mond (film), 3–4, 9
Freud, Sigmund, 14
Freund, Karl, 14
From the Earth to the Moon (film), 105
Fuller, Matthew: on media ecology, 20, 22, 23, 129, 168; on memetic buzz, 30; on thick relationships, 130, 169

Galaxy Science Fiction (magazine), 74, 103
Gance, Abel, 9
Garland, Alex, 165
Garroway, Dave, 92
Gate of Hell (film), 130
Gernsback, Hugo: and hypnobioscope, 171; as science fiction editor, 13, 16; and science fiction naming, 12
Gibbons, Cedric, 81
Gidget (film), 109
Gigantis, the Fire Monster, aka *Godzilla Raids Again* (film), 127, 134, 140, 142, 145, 149, 154, 155, 186n20
Gillespie, Arnold, 81, 92
Godsziszewski, Ed, 151
Godzilla, aka *Gojira* (film), 22, 111, 127, 128–129, 131, 132, 134, 149, 153, 155; box office, 136–137; as ecology narrative, 140–141; as hybrid film, 135; marketing, *138*, 139–140, 142–143, 146–147, 150; re-editing, 140–141, 145; trailer, 187n46

Godzilla: King of the Monsters (film), 156
Godzilla vs. Kong (film), 129, 156
Good Housekeeping (magazine), 87
Gordon, Robert, 84
Graeff, Tom, 116
Gray, Jonathan: on paratexts, 29; on textual framing, 3, 22–23, 81, 100; on theatrical trailers, 146
Grinde, Nick, 46
Gross, Mike, 120
Gulliver's Travels (film), 59

Hall, Alexander, 85
Hall, Jon, 33
Hamilton, Edmond, 12
Hansen, Miriam, 161
Hardwicke, Cedric, 33
Harrigan, William, 31
Harris, Jack H., 106, 115, 117, 122, 125, 183n13. See also *The Blob*
Harris, Phil, 120, 176n22
Harryhausen, Ray, 137, 139
Hartwell, David G., 103
Haskin, Byron, 6, 60, 72, 73, 105
Hawks, Howard, 27, 40–41, 176–177n25
Hayden Planetarium, 7, 60
Hecht, Ben, 176n25
Heinlein, Robert A., 60, 64, 66, 73, 74; and *Destination Moon*, 38–39, 62–63, 176n16
Here's Hollywood (radio series), 86
Heusch, Paulo, 159
Hideous Sun Demon, The (film), 125
high concept, 99, 182n54
High School Confidential (film), 108
Higuchi, Shinji, 156
Hillyer, Lambert, 15
Hilton, Arthur, 67
Hisamatsu, Seiji, 131
Hitchcock, Alfred, 113, 152
H-Man, The (film), 134, 142
Hoffman, Herman, 99
Holliman, Earl, 94
Homolka, Oskar, 31
Honda, Ishiro, 22, 127, 128, 145
Hopper, Hedda, 41
Hot Car Girl (film), 108
Howard, John, 31
Hubbard, Lucian, 9
Hughes, Howard, 42

Ichikawa, Kon, 131
Ideal Toy Company, 90, 91, 181n37

Ikiru (film), 132, *133*
I Married a Monster from Outer Space (film), 76, 77, 106, 122, 159, 180n57
Incredible Shrinking Man, The (film), 159
independent film production, 27, 29, 42, 42, 59–60, 76, 77, 99, 105–106, 111, 115–116, 151, 180n57
Independent Theatre Owners, 89
Invaders from Mars (film), 96
Invasion of the Body Snatchers (film), 11, 52, 159
Invasion of the Neptune Men (film), 128
Invasion of the Saucer Men (film), 123
Invisible Agent, The (film), 31, 33
Invisible Boy, The (film), 99–101, 105, 111
Invisible Man, The (film), 14, 38; advertising of, 31–33, 46, 174n40; as series, 31–33
Invisible Man Returns, The (film), 33
Invisible Man's Revenge, The (film), 33
Invisible Ray, The (film), 9, 15, 16, 20, 38, 174n41
Invisible Woman, The (film), 31
Island of Lost Souls (film), 59, 109
It Came from Beneath the Sea (film), 84, 135, 137
It Conquered the World (film), 99
Ivers, James D., 108
I Was a Teenage Frankenstein (film), 109, 123
Izod, John, 177n36

James, Edward, 22; defining science fiction, 1–3, 10, 18, 26; on naming science fiction, 12; on space opera, 58; on varied perceptions of science fiction, 30; on wonder in science fiction, 34
Jampel, Dave, 135
Japanese cinema: American influence on, 128, 130; censorship of, 130; hybridity in, 127, 128, 129, 135, 136, 137, 151, 155; industry revenues, 130, 185n4; Japan Film Week, 131; *jidai-geki* films, 134; *kaiju* films, 127, 128, 129, 130, 131, 134, 137, 139–140, 143, 144–145, 150, 151, *153*, 154; and mythology, 136, 140, 141, 151, 155; popularity in the West, 131–132, 134, 149, 155, 156; presentational style, 129, 136, 141; representational character, 127, 130, 132, 136, 141
Jones, R. V., 105

Jordan, Miriam, 16
Jungle Headhunters (film), 42, 177n27
Juran, Nathan, 159
Just Imagine (film), 15–16, 30, 38

Kalat, David, 136
Kane, Joseph, 37
Karloff, Boris, 16
Kawakita, Nagamansa, 132, 134–135, 155
Kennedy, John F., 156
Kenton, Erle C., 59
Kernan, Lisa, 3, 123–124, 170–171, 175n59
Kido, Shiro, 131–132, 134
King Brothers, 132
King Kong (film), 139, 152, 166
King of the Rocket Men (film), 35
Kinoshita, Keisuke, 131
Kinoshita, Robert, 92
Kinugasa, Teinosuke, 130
Knowles, Bernard, 38
Kong: Skull Island (film), 129
Korda, Alexander, 173, 192
Kowalski, Bernard L., 42, 108
Kramer, Stanley, 125
Kreimeier, Klaus, 3
Kubrick, Stanley, 125
Kurosawa, Akira, 130; *Ikiru*, 132, *133*; *Rashomon*, 132; *Seven Samurai*, 130, 132
Kuttner, Henry, 12; novelization of *Dr. Cyclops*, 36, 59, 176n19; on technical emphasis in science fiction, 62; weird stories, 12

Laemmle, Carl, 2
Lamont, Charles, 33, 67
Landon, Brooks, 11
Lang, Fritz, 2, 3; *Frau im Mond* (film), 3–4, 10; *Metropolis* (film), 2, 10
Late Chrysanthemums (film), 132
Latham, Rob, 11, 158
Lederer, Charles, 176n25
Legion of Decency, 72, 180n52. *See also* censorship
Lesser, Julian, 42
Let's Rock (film), 108–109
Levine, Joseph E., 136, 141–142, 146, 148, 154, 155, 187n68
Lewis, Roger H., 157, 158
Ley, Willy, 70, 72, 73, 74. *See also* Bonestell, Chesley, Jr.

Life (magazine), 60
Lippert, Robert, 111
Lipton, David, 28
Lobsenz, Norman M., 154
Lonergan, Arthur, 81, 180–181n15
Lorre, Peter, 33
Lourié, Eugène, 73, 84
Lucanio, Patrick, 10, 11, 14
Lucas, George, 169, 170
Lucy (film), 165
Lugosi, Bela, 16

Macabre (film), 155
MacDougall, Ranald, 159
Mad Love (film), 14
Mamoulian, Rouben, 59
Mandalorian, The (television series), 169
Man-Made Monster (film), 38
Man They Could Not Hang, The (film), 46
Man Who Could Work Miracles, The (film), 14
Marin, Edwin L., 28
Marquette, Arthur F., 84
Marquette, Jacques R., 116
Marvel Universe, 20
Massey, Ilona, 33
Maté, Rudolph, 28, 60, 66
Matrix, The (film), 25
May, Joe, 33
McCall's (magazine), 87. *See also* slick magazines
McGee, Mark Thomas, 87, 141
McGowan, Dorrell and Stuart, 42
McQueen, Steve, 108, 117
Meador, Josh, 82, 181n16
Mees, Curtis, 112
Méliès, Georges, 9, 165; *A Trip to the Moon* (film), 9
Mellen, Joan, 132
Mendes, Lothar, 14
Menzies, William Cameron, 2, 96
Metropolis (film), 2, 30
MGM Parade (television series), 92–93, *94*
MGM Studios, 79–82, 99, 109, 111, 142, 149, 181n37; exhibitor relations, 85, 87–90; industry position, 81, 101; and Quaker Oats Company, 84–90, 95, 142; and science fiction, 80, 89, 95, 98, 101, 105
Mizoguchi, Kenji, 130
Modern Screen (magazine), 52
Mole People, The (film), 159

Monster and the Ape, The (film), 38
Monster from the Ocean Floor (film), 135
Monster on the Campus (film), 116
Mothra (film), 22, 128, 142, 145; and the atomic age, 143; and Columbia Pictures, 151; hybrid character in, 151; marketing of, 152–153, *153*, 154–155
Motion Picture Association of America, 3, 113, 173n6
Motion Picture Daily, 5, 15, 34, 39, 42, 45, 48, 49, 64, 90, 101, 105, 108, 115, 147, 149, *150*, 151
Motion Picture Herald, 5, 14, 15, 69–70, 72, 84–85, 87, *88*, 97, 105, 109, 112
Motion Picture Producers Association of Japan, 131
Motion Picture Production Code, 58. *See also* censorship
Murdico, Suzanne J., 183n9
Murphy, George, 92
Museum of Modern Art, 131
Mysterians, The (film), 22, 128, 134, 155; box office, 151; and cultural concerns, 139; marketing of, 150–151; MGM's acquisition of, 142, 149; reviews of, 186n20; trailers, 149–150
Mysterious Island, The (film), 9

Nakajima, Haruo, 136
Naruse, Mikio, 132
National Association of Film Service Organizations, 88
Nayfack, Nicholas, 99
neorealist film, 131, 132
Neumann, Kurt, 38, 111
New Love (magazine), 45, 52
Newman, Joseph M., 84
News-Week (magazine), 5
New World Pictures, 116
New York Times, 108
New York Times Magazine, 60
Nicholson, James, 122–123
Night of the Blood Beast (film), 42
Night the World Exploded, The (film), 159
Nocturne (film), 28
Non-Stop New York (film), 14
Nyby, Christian, 27, 176n25

Obi-Wan Kenobi (television series), 170
Oda, Motoyoshi, 128
Ohta, Koji, 128
On the Beach (film), 125

On the Threshold of Space (film), 83
Ordung, Wyott, 135
O'Sullivan, Maureen, 16
Out There (television series), 55
Ozu, Yasujiro, 130, 132

Pacific Rim (film), 129
Pal, George, 56, 74, 75, 79, 81, 109, 178n32, 179n35; *Conquest of Space*, 70 74, 109, 180n56; *Destination Moon*, 59–60, 62–63; and Puppetoons, 60; science fiction award, 178n32; scientific accuracy, 60, 63, 66, 68, 179n35; *War of the Worlds, The*, 66–70, 109; *When Worlds Collide*, 63, 66, 109
Parade (magazine), 60
Paramount Pictures, 38, 56, 74, 77, 81, 109, 111, 180n57; and *Astounding Stories*, 60, 67–68, 76, 109; *Blob, The*, 106, *107*, 113, *114*, 120–122, 125; *Conquest of Space*, 60, 70–73, 83, 109; *Dr. Cyclops*, 36, *37*, 59; *Dr. Jekyll and Mr. Hyde*, 38, 59, 79, 109, *110*, 160; and DuMont television network, 179n37; exploitation, 64, 109, 120; *Gulliver's Travels*, 59; *Island of Lost Souls*, 109; Paramount decision (*United States v. Paramount*), 18, 27, 55, 80, 179n37; *Psycho*, 113; and science fiction, 58–61, 72, 73, 79; and television, 67, 75; *War of the Worlds, The*, 60, 67–70, 83, 109, 113, 117, 179n38; *When Worlds Collide*, 60, 63–65, 109
Paramount World (magazine), 106, 113
paratexts, 22–23, *29*, 30, 35, 55, 56, *121*, 123, 168, 169
Parents' Magazine, 87
Parker, John, 118
Parliament, British, 5
Paul, Frank R., 56, 162. *See also* pulp magazines
Peanuts, The (musical group), 152
Perfect Woman, The (film), 38
Perry Como Show, The (television series), 92
Phantom from Space (film), 67
Pichel, Irving, 6
Pidgeon, Walter, 82, 92–93, *94*,
Pierson, Michele, 103
Plainsman and the Lady (film), 37
Planet Stories (magazine), 58

Plan 9 from Outer Space (film), 122
Poe, Edgar Allan, 116
Pollard, Harry, A. 9
Pomerance, Murray, 9
Popular Detective (magazine), 28
Popular Mechanics (magazine), *21*, 60
Popular Science (magazine), 60, 64, 67
Presley, Elvis, 109, 116
Proyas, Alex, 25
Psycho (film), 113, 152. *See also* Hitchcock, Alfred
pulp magazines, 12–13, 28, 77, 158; advertising in, 29, 35–39, 42–43; cover art, 36, 43, 49, 56, *57*, 58, 162, 185n55; film consciousness in, 162, 188n12; letters columns, 35, 38, 58; readership, 35–36, 45, 52, 53, 56, 83, 185n55; sensationalism, 55, 58, 75
Purple Monster Strikes, The (film), 38

Quaker Oats Company, 84–90, 95, 99. *See also* MGM
Queen for a Day (television series), 92

radio marketing, 105, 113
Ralston-Purina, 8
Rashomon (film), 132
Ray, Nicholas, 118
Reader's Guide to Periodical Literature, 12
Reagan, Charles, 84
Rebel Without a Cause (film), 118
Redbook (magazine), 39, 45, 64, 87
Regal Films, 111
Renegades (film), 37
Republic Pictures, 37
Return of the Fly (film), 111
Revenge of the Creature (film), 105
Richardson, R. S., 64, 66, 73, 74
Richie, Donald, 127
Rieder, John, 18–20, 22, 30–31, 33, 105, 124; on audience targeting, 162–163; commercial advertisement, 18, 19, 56, 106; modernity, 162
Rivette, Jacques, 52–53
RKO Pictures, 27–29, 38; distribution arm of, 175n5, 187n52; exploitation group, 41–42, 44, 48, 142, 177n27; financial problems, 29, 42, 51; and *The Thing*, 41–45, 48, 120
Roberts, Adam: on culture and science fiction, 13; on pulp covers, 162; on visual character of science fiction, 161, 188n21

Robot Monster (film), 67, 96
Rocketship X-M (film), 38, 43
Rocky Jones, Space Ranger (television series), 8
Rodan (film), 22, 111, 128, 131, 132, 134, 140, 142–144; box office, 147, 150; marketing, 147–149; prologue for, 149
Romance (magazine), 28
Ross, Gary, 28
Rotterdam International Exposition, 70
Rubin, Steve, 81
Ruggles, Charles, 31
Ryfle, Steve, 151

saturation advertising, 6, 7, 23; for *The Blob*, 106; for *Forbidden Planet*, 87, 89; for *kaiju* films, 111, 129, 146, 147, 149, 151; for *The Thing*, 39–41; for *The War of the Worlds*, 70
Schary, Dore, 79–82, 93, 95, 98, 101, 180–181n15
Schatz, Thomas, 10–11, 13
Schauer, Bradley, 79, 111; on exploitation films, 43; pulp paradox, 55–56, 58, 75, 105; on science fiction audiences, 83, 168
Schoedsack, Ernest B., 36, 166
Scientific Detective Monthly (magazine), 13
Scott, Ridley, 2
Sears, Fred F., 99, 159
Selznick, David O., 38
Sergeant Preston of the Yukon (television series), 84, 85, 181n21
serials, 9, 34, 35, 38, 49, 55
Seven Samurai (film), 130
Seventeen Magazine, 28, 87, 161
Shape of Things to Come, The (novel, Wells), 4
Sharp, Patrick B., 162
Shawlee, Joan, 70, *71*, 72, 75, 180n52
Sheridan, Margaret, 27, 49
Sherman, George, 37
Sherwood, John, 105
Shimura, Takashi, 136
Shin Godzilla (film), 156
Sholem, Lee, 96
Siegel, Don, 11
Silvercup Bread, 8
Six Hours to Live (film), 16, 30, 160
slick magazines, 44, 45, 52, 64, 67, 87
social media, 24

Sontag, Susan, 35, 53, 75, 139, 140, 155, 158–159; on camp sensibility, 122
Space Children, The (film), 73, 116, 180n57
space opera, 49, 55, 58, 75, 99, 106, 137, 173n18; action focus, 35; audience for, 27, 83, 90, 93, 104, 158, 167; as hybrid form, 136; publicity for, 8
Space Patrol (television series), 7–8, 49, 55, 93
special effects, 68, 72, 82, 103, 154, 181n16; appeal of, 24, 73–74, 137, 145, 155; cost of, 69, 81, 178n33; film emphasis on, 75, 152; quality of, 108
Stanfield, Peter, 116
Startling Stories (magazine), 36, 39, 45, 51
Star Wars (film), 11, 20, 169–170
Stephanie, Frederick, 9
Stevenson, Robert, 14
Stevenson, Robert Louis, 109
Stewart, Garrett, 165–166, 169, 184n44
Strange Tales (magazine), 12
streaming services, 168, 170
Strock, Herbert L., 109
Stuart, Don A. *See* Campbell, John W., Jr.
Stuart, Gloria, 31
Super Science Stories (magazine), 57
SuperScope, 159, *160*
Sutherland, A. Edward, 31
Suvin, Darko, 13–14

Tales of Tomorrow (television series), 55
Tarantula (film), 135
Taurog, Norman, 125
Technicolor, 59
Teenage Monster (film), 116
Teenagers from Outer Space (film), 116, 125
television, 5, 18, 80, 98, 105, 123, 128, 154, 161, 167, 168; advertising on, 3, 6, 7–8, 20, 23–24, 67, 69–70, 75, 129, 145–147, 149, 151–153, 155; audiences, 67, 168; *MGM Parade* (television series), 92–93, *94*; networks, 75, 179n37; and science fiction, 27, 34, 49, 55, 59, 82–83, 90, 99, 104, 106, 169, 173n18; series, 25, 84, 92, 93, 170
Telotte, J. P., 174n42, 175n57, 184–185n49
Tempest, The (play, Shakespeare), 82, 111
Tezuka, Katsumi, 136
Them! (film), 84, 111, 135, 163
theme parks, 168, 169–170
"Thing, The" (song), 120, 176n22
Thing from Another World, The (film), 27, 34, 120; acting in, 27, 49, 175n1; exploitation dimension, 45, 51; Howard Hawks's influence; 27, 42, 176–177n25; marketing of, 28–29, 39–52, 152, 161, 176n; metaphoric character, 166–167, *168*; reception of, 67; teaser campaign, 44–46
Things to Come (film), 2, 9, 38; marketing of, 5–6, 18, 20. *See also* Wells, H. G.
This Island Earth (film), 84
Thompson, Don, 142
Thompson, Howard, 108
3-D films, 8
Thrilling Wonder Stories: advertising in, 28, 36–38, 39, 45, 51; cover art, 36, 176n19, 185n55; *Dr. Cyclops* feature, 36, 59, 176n19; letters column, 35; *War of the Worlds* review, 179n38
Time (magazine), 5
Times of Joy and Sorrow (film), 131
Tingler, The (film), 155
Tobey, Kenneth, 27, 49
Tobor the Great (film), 96
Today (television series), 92
Toho Company, 22, 130, 132, 134, 137, 142, 149, 151, 155, 163
Toho Scope, 159
Tokyo File 212 (film), 42
Tom Corbett, Space Cadet (television series), 49, 104
Tom Fizdale Agency, 59. *See also* Paramount Pictures
Transatlantic Tunnel (film), 14
Transformers (film), 20, 165
Trans-World Releasing, 136, 141
Travers, Henry, 31
True Story (magazine), 87
Tsuburaya, Eiji, 137, 145
Tucker, Phil, 67, 125
Turner, Terry, 42, 44, 142, 149–150
TV Guide (magazine), 87
20th Century-Fox, 34, 67, 83, 109, 111, 112, 160
20,000 Leagues Under the Sea (film), 84
Two Lost Worlds (film), 11

Undercurrent (film), 131
United Artists, 5, 79, 157

Universal-International, 163
Universal Pictures, 2; genre focus of, 79, 104; and *The Invisible Man*, 31–33, 174n40; and Japanese film, 163; profitability of, 84
Untamed Women (film), 11, 159
utopia, 30, 93, 95, 170; and advertising, 18, 97, 98, 163–164

Van Beuren Studios, 16
Variety, 12, 14, 39, 48, 59, 60, 63, 67, 69, 90, 93, 98, 107, 108, 109, 118, 141, 146, 147; on gimmick films, 112, 113, 155; on international markets, 134, 135; on science fiction popularity, 79, 81, 83, 101, 105, 106, 110, 124, 154, 174n34
VeSota, Bruno, 42
Vidor, King, 38
Vikander, Alicia, *166*
Vint, Sherryl, 12–13
Virilio, Paul, 25
Visit to a Small Planet (film), 125
VistaVision, 159
Vogel, Virgil W., 159
Vogt-Roberts, Jordan, 129
von Braun, Wernher, 70
Vonderau, Patrick, 103

Wachowski siblings, 25
Waggner, George, 38, 104
Walt Disney Studio, 80, 82, 84, 169–170, 181n16
Warner Bros. Pictures, 16, 37, 84, 111, 149, 163
War of the Worlds, The (film), 6, 60, 73, 117, 139; advertising for, 67, 69–70, 179n38; and Paramount, 66–70, 113; sensationalism of, 69. *See also* Pal, George
Warren, Bill, 10, 11, 14, 73–74, 106, 151
Watanabe, Kunio, 131
Webb, Robert D., 83
weirdie films, 109
Weird Stories (magazine), 12, 13
Welles, Orson, 6, 68, 113, 179n38
Wellman, William A., 80

Wells, H. G.: critical reputation of, 4; *Invisible Man, The* (novel), 14, 31; *Man Who Could Work Miracles, The* (film), 14; as scriptwriter, 14; *Shape of Things to Come, The* (novel), 4; *Things to Come* (film), 4–5; *War of the Worlds, The* (novel), 66–67, 109, 179n34
Wendkos, Paul, 109
Wesso, Hans, 56, 162. *See also* pulp magazines
Westinghouse, 34
Westward the Women (film), 80
Westworld (television series), 25
Whale, James, 14
When Worlds Collide (film), 60, 69, 70; advertising for, 63–65; *Astounding* feature, 64–66; budget for, 178n33; scientific accuracy in, 66
Whispering Smith (film), 38
Wilcox, Fred M., 80
Wilder, W. Lee, 67
Williams, Keith, 69
Williamson, Jack ,12
Winchester Films, 27
Wingard, Adam, 129
Wise, Robert, 34, 38
Wolf Man, The (film), 104
Woman's Home Companion (magazine), 87
Women in Prison (film), 131
Wonder Stories, 176n19; cover art, 185n55; film petition in, 35; readership, 185n55
Wood, Ed, 122
World, the Flesh and the Devil, The (film), 159
World's Fairs, 16, 34, 179n47
World Without End (film), 99
Wormser, Irving, 147
Wyatt, Justin, 99

Yaszek, Lisa, 162
Yeaworth, Irvin S., 23, 104, 125
Yomota, Inuhiko, 127–128, 130, 139–140, 185n4
Yoshimura, Kozaburo, 131

Zombies of the Stratosphere (film), 35